Prescription *for* Your Soul™

365 MICRODOSES OF HEALING FOR THE MIDLIFE WOMAN

DR. JENNIFER RADEMAKER, PHD

PRESCRIPTION FOR YOUR SOUL™

Dr. Jennifer Rademaker, PhD

Published by Bluebridge Press
Miami, Florida, USA
DrJenniferRademaker.com
info@DrJenniferRademaker.com

ISBN (Paperback): 979-8-218-85675-5
ISBN (Hardcover): 979-8-218-87957-0
First Edition
Printed in the United States of America
Manufactured by print-on-demand.

Created by a midlife woman—with love—as medicine for the midlife woman's soul.

Dedication

For my father — your unconditional love has been the greatest gift of my life.

For my mother in heaven — your loving presence is felt on every page.

For my husband — for the steady patience and space you gave me to write.

For my darling son — the radiant rise of my heart. Thank you for believing in me, and for blessing your mom's dreams with your good wishes.

And to my three Maine Coons — with heads resting and paws stretched across my keyboard — Thank you for keeping me company as this book came to life.

Contents

RELEASE — FALL

RESET — WINTER

RISE— SPRING

RADIATE — SUMMER

Prayer at the Threshold. Part One –

Dear God,

I come before you with my pen trembling and my heart wide open. I have carried this longing for so long—to write, to share, to place my name on pages that will outlive me. Yet fear has bound me: fear of not being enough, fear of being too late, fear of being overshadowed by others who seemed to arrive first.

I release now the sting of comparison. I release the heaviness of competition. I release the ache that tells me I should have been there already.

Reset me, God. Reset my mind, my heart, my spirit to the truth: that my book is not just a project—it is soul medicine.

That its timing is holy.
That the words I have carried are alive in me because you placed them there.

Rise with me, God, into courage. Rise me into discipline, into flow, into joy. May each sentence I write become a doorway of healing for the women who will one day hold this book in their hands. May my words remind them that they are not alone, that they are loved, that wholeness is possible—even in midlife and beyond.

I trust that you are breathing through me. I trust that what I write will be enough. I trust that my story, my wisdom, my truth—are worthy.

Here I am, Lord. I am ready.

And so it is, Amen.

Prayer at the Threshold. Part Two –

My Why

Dear God,

I write because midlife women are aching for a voice that says: *You are not too late. You are not too much. You are not forgotten.*
I write because I have lived in the cracks, the heaviness, the belly of sorrow—and I have found medicine there.
I write because silence has kept too many of us small, and my words will be a doorway back to wholeness.

God, I don't write to be clever. I don't write to impress. I write because there are women right now sitting in their bedrooms, holding their own shame, whispering their own regrets—and they need a soul sister's hand reaching through the page to say: *You are loved. You are whole. You can rise.*

This book is my offering to you and to them—a **Prescription for the Soul**—not born of theory, but of tears and truth.
I write so that the next woman who picks it up can exhale… and finally remember who she is.

Already perfect and whole.

This is **my why**. And because of this, I will not abandon these pages. I will not betray this calling.
I will write, and I will finish, and I will place my name on this offering.

With love, I release, reset, and rise.

And so it is, Amen.

A Tender Welcome

The words you hold in your hands aren't instructions. They're prayers. Quiet poems. Each one a truth-drop meant to settle into the still place inside you that already knows: you are whole.

This book doesn't march in a straight line. It moves as nature moves — circling, softening — because healing is a rhythm, not a checklist. Just as the earth turns from fall to winter, spring to summer, your inner world turns too. Some days you'll feel like leaves letting go; some days like fresh green beginnings; some days like full sunlight and open sky.

This is where your journey begins. This is where you step into the rhythm of Release, Reset, Rise—and beyond.

- **Release (Fall):** loosening what no longer serves, forgiving, letting go.
- **Reset (Winter):** rest, breath, stillness, subconscious renewal — roots gathering strength beneath the surface.
- **Rise (Spring):** courage, new growth, the heart opening to possibility.
- **Radiate (Summer):** joy, freedom, and shining your light into the world without apology.

These seasons mirror your own cycles and remind you that each stage has its medicine. You're never "behind" or "too late."

This isn't a self-help manual. It's a soul-companion — an invitation to walk with the rhythm of the year and of your own becoming.

One sacred truth-drop at a time.

Science + Soul — Why This Works

Have you ever tried to change and still felt stuck?

You're not broken. Your nervous system and subconscious are simply running old instructions. **Mystics call this the hidden flow of your soul; neuroscience calls it your subconscious and nervous system.** Quietly, it filters what you notice, expect, and allow.

From your earliest years your body absorbed stories about what is safe, possible, and allowed. A parent's worry may have planted "abundance is rare." A painful rejection may have whispered "I'm not lovable." Repetition and emotion turned these impressions into "just the way life is." Without awareness, old programming runs the show; with it, you begin to choose. And somewhere between the roles you've played and the dreams you've set aside, a whisper rose up: **"There must be more than this."** That whisper is the beginning of alchemy. This alchemy is not locked in ancient laboratories. It lives inside you. It is the gentle, luminous art of turning heaviness into light. Each time you choose a softer thought instead of a harsh one, bless yourself with a kind word, or breathe and let go, you are practicing alchemy.

You are transforming lead into gold—in your nervous system, your mind, your own heart.

Midlife is not your diminishment; it is your sacred turning point. Here, you become your own alchemist—healing shadows, embodying your light, rising into the freedom you were made for.

This is where the practices in this book matter. When you breathe slowly, place a hand on your heart, or try one of the rituals here, you're sending a new signal: *"I'm here. I'm open, I'm safe."* Over time these gentle practices calm your fight-or-flight response and teach your whole system a new default. Neuroscience calls this neuroplasticity. Somatic psychology calls it regulation. Mystics have always called it transformation — the soul remembering its true nature.

Each entry in *Prescription for Your Soul* is a microdose of soul medicine — a prayer, reflection, breath, or ritual designed to soothe your system, re-pattern your inner stories, and open you to receive. With gentle repetition, old grooves fade, and new ones take root, like fresh trails through a forest. **One step at a time, your inner world shifts — and your outer life begins to reflect it.**

Throughout these pages you'll find not only breath practices, but also other gentle invitations designed to stimulate the vagus nerve— your body's pathway into its natural 'rest-and-restore'. They're simply different paths leading you into the same inner sanctuary. All of them serve the same healing purpose, bringing love back into your cells, calming your nervous system, and opening the space for Spirit to reach you.

You'll also notice gentle notes at the bottom of certain pages— *Soul Companion: "The Bridge" — Truth Drop Card No. 22.*
These quiet signposts connect you with the companion deck, **Prescription for Your Soul — 50 Microdoses of Healing Soul Medicine for the Midlife Woman—**
a sanctuary in your hands, echoing the same truth drops you'll discover within these pages.

Now that you have crossed the threshold, here's how to walk this book with ease...

Walking the 12-Cycle Pathway

How to Use This Book

This devotional isn't a program to master or a book to rush through; it's a gentle rhythm to receive.
Think of it as a soul-sister leaving you a small poem, a love note, one truth-drop at a time —your daily microdose of soul medicine.

Inside these 365 entries, you'll move through twelve soul rotations — reflections, prayers, breath resets, and Soul Movement prompts. You'll sip tea with your heart in Sacred Sips, laugh freely through Laugh-Lift practices (a joyful, *surgery-free soul lift through laughter*), and even receive wisdom straight from the cat herself in Whiskers of the Soul.

Along the way, you'll meet truth drops, gentle whispers, and other micro-rituals of healing.
Together, they create a rhythm for your whole self — mind, body, and spirit —
a cycle of remembering, and renewal for the midlife woman ready to reclaim her calm, her joy, and come home to her wholeness again.

Using the Practices-

You'll notice that I often use the word "fear" in these pages. When I say fear, I don't just mean terror or panic. Fear wears many masks—worry, self-doubt, control, striving, loneliness, resentment, overwhelm. Sometimes it shows up as guilt or shame or hides inside comparison and perfectionism. At other times it slips out as judgment or defensiveness. But underneath every mask, your soul is love. It's where you came from. It's who you are. And each time you lay down a mask, you return a little closer to that truth—the Source of love that heals and makes you whole.

Throughout these pages, you'll find gentle invitations, small, embodied cues to help you feel safe, grounded, and present in your body as you read. Each one is an act of kindness toward your nervous system, a way of reminding yourself: *I'm here. I'm safe. I'm open.*

There's no wrong way to do this. Read one entry a day, open to any page on a sleepless night, or linger with your practice for a few days, if you feel called. What matters is kindness and consistency, not perfection. Let each page be a cue to pause, breathe, and place a hand on your heart. Over time these microdoses calm your system, shift your inner stories, and help you live from a steadier, freer place.

Breathe in with me now.
Exhale slowly and feel the softness in your shoulders relaxing.
You are already on the path.
You are already enough.

Welcome to your microdose *Prescription for Your Soul.*

Timeless truth.
Gentle medicine.
Reaches deep.
Lasts a lifetime.

Letter to You, My Soul Sister
I Have Not Yet Met

To the woman holding this book,

I don't know your story in detail — but I know your soul.
I know what it feels like to carry more than anyone sees.
I know the ache of midlife, the weight of responsibilities, the whispers of regret, the longing for freedom you can't quite name.

If this book found its way into your hands, it's not by accident.
It's a soul appointment — a truth drop you've been waiting for.

These pages are not written to fix you — because you were never broken.
They are written to remind you of who you already are:
Whole. Worthy. Loved.

As you read, you may feel tears rise. Let them.
You may feel resistance. Breathe through it.
You may feel your chest open, your heart soften, your spirit stand taller. Receive it.

From my soul to yours — I love you.

Dr. Jennifer

Release — Fall

You begin here—in the Season of Release.

My beautiful soul…

This is where every journey toward wholeness begins:
loosening, softening, letting go.
Like trees surrendering their leaves, trusting the wind
to carry them where they need to go,
you too are invited to trust the rhythm of your becoming.

Midlife often reveals what can no longer travel with us—old beliefs, worn-out roles, patterns of striving. These pages are your pathway invitation to lay them gently down.

As you step into this section of the book, give yourself permission to pause.
Breathe in slowly through your nose. Place your hand over your heart.
Exhale as if a weight is sliding from your shoulders.
Whisper softly, *"I release with grace."*

Here, you will find poetic soul reflections, prayers, and rituals that help you unclench your fists and create sacred space for the next chapter of your life.
You are not emptying yourself out—you are opening yourself up.

Even now, the ground beneath you is becoming fertile for what's next.
Trust the rhythm. Trust the timing.
Trust your own readiness.

I release with grace and make room for my becoming.

Day 1 – Soul Reflection

The Crack in the Pavement

Life has a way of breaking us open in places we never expected. A sudden loss, a quiet disappointment, a word that lingers too long on the edge of memory — and there it is: a fracture in what felt whole. You stand over it, looking down, and for a moment it seems as though something inside you has shattered beyond repair.

But look more closely. The crack isn't the end; it's the beginning. Just as a flower pushes its green stem through cold concrete, your soul knows how to rise in the very place you thought you had collapsed. The breaking open is not a punishment but an invitation — an opening through which new light can reach you. *Where in your life have you mistaken a crack for a collapse — when it was actually the start of your becoming?*

Breathe for a moment. Imagine kneeling beside that crack and touching it with tender hands. Feel the coolness of the earth beneath the pavement, the hidden roots, the quiet hum of life pressing upward. Don't curse the crack. Bless it. It's proof you are still becoming. You are not finished. You are unfolding.

REFLECT:
Every season of my life has prepared me for this one. I am not broken. I am breaking open into light.
(Whisper it softly until you feel the warmth behind the words.)

Day 2 – Affirmation + Reflection

Somewhere in the middle of life you may have been told your path was set, your script unchangeable, that your best years were behind you. But that is not the truth. The ink of your life has never dried. Each morning you wake is a fresh sheet of parchment placed gently before you. The pen rests in your hand, warm and waiting, whispering: *Write again.*

Each exhale releases an old line you no longer need; each inhale draws in a new word, a new choice, a new way of being. You are not bound to yesterday's storyline. You are the narrator, the editor, and the artist of your life. *If today were a blank page, what one sentence of truth would you write across it right here, right now?*

Today, pause for a moment with me. Place your hand on your heart and feel the pulse of your own authorship. Imagine a soft golden page unfolding in front of you, the edges shimmering with opportunity. What will you inscribe there? What truth, what freedom, what dream longs to be written by your own courageous hand? Reinvention is not betrayal. Its alignment.

Affirmation:
I hold the pen of my own life, and I write the story that sets me free.
(Repeat it softly until you feel it rise inside you.)

Day 3 – Dear God Letter

Dear God,

Lift from me the weight of every belief that says I am too late, too much, or not enough.
Release the fear that whispers I should have done more by now.

Reset my mind, my breath, my body into your truth:
that I am right on time.
That the path unfolding beneath my feet is sacred.
That nothing has been wasted — not one heartbreak, not one delay.

Let me rise today with courage to take one step forward, trusting that it is enough.

And so it is. Amen.

Day 4 – Breath Practice / Ritual Reset

Sacred Pause

Before you rush into the next thing, linger here with me. Feel your body where it rests. Notice how your chest rises and falls — or is it your belly? We so often live on automatic — breathing shallow, moving fast, holding our breath — forgetting that each inhale and exhale is a quiet miracle.

Today you're invited to hold your breath just long enough to feel it.

Breathe in slowly through your nose; let your belly soften. When you reach the top of the inhale, pause — just a heartbeat. Sense the fullness. Let that pause be a soft gathering of everything you need. Then exhale gently, like a sigh of relief, emptying what no longer belongs. Do this three times. With each pause at the top, imagine God's truth filling you. With each exhale, imagine the old fears sliding out of you like mist.

This is not about forcing or perfect technique. It's about remembering. Every pause, every breath, is a doorway back to yourself — a release and reset your nervous system already knows. You don't have to earn it. You only have to choose and claim it.

PRESCRIPTION FOR YOUR SOUL WHISPER:
With each sacred pause, I release and reset my body, my mind, and my soul.

Day 5 – Chakra Soul Movement: Heart Opener

When the heart feels heavy, the body curls inward. Shoulders round, chest tightens, breath shortens. It's the body's way of guarding — but it also blocks the light. My darling, today you're invited to gently teach your body a new story: *I am safe to open again.* Create a soft space for this practice. If you can, put on a piece of music that feels like balm to your chest — something slow, melodic, and expansive, like a gentle instrumental with flowing strings, soft drums, or nature sounds. Let the rhythm become a heartbeat within you.

Like this:

- Stand tall, feet grounded, toes spreading slightly for balance.
- Place both palms gently over your heart. Feel the warmth of your own hands.
- Inhale slowly as you lift your chest, letting your shoulders roll back. Pause for a heartbeat at the top of the breath, sensing the openness.
- Exhale as you imagine a soft green light — the color of the heart chakra — expanding through your ribs and back.
- Repeat for five breaths; let your body sway gently in place, like a beautiful green tree opening its branches to sunlight. Allow the music to guide your soul with movement. This isn't about choreography; it's about allowing your heart to move open to the rhythm of life. Feel the space you've just created inside your chest. Notice the subtle shift in your mood, your breath, your energy. This is your body's way of remembering safety and trust.

Mantra:
My heart is open. I am safe to love and be loved.

Day 6 – Soul Whisker

Have you ever noticed the cat doesn't apologize for stretching into the sunbeam?
He doesn't shrink or wonder if he deserves it.
He simply lays his body down and receives the light.

What if you lived that way?
No apology. No shrinking. Just presence.
You were made for the light, too.

Soul Whisker:
I am allowed to take up space and bask in my own light.
This is your meow-ment of grace — take it.

Day 7 – Sacred Sips Moment

Your daily microdose of stillness — a tea ceremony for your soul.

Imagine holding a warm cup of tea between your palms. The steam rises in delicate spirals, carrying with it the scent of calm. As you breathe it in, your shoulders drop, your jaw softens, and your chest begins to expand. This isn't just tea; it's a tiny ceremony. Each sip moment becomes a pause — a sacred permission slip to slow down and return to yourself.

So much in life tells you to hurry up, to push, to keep pouring out until you're empty. But here, with this cup in your hands, you remember a higher truth: slowing down is not a weakness. It is a way of listening. It is a way of remembering who you are. In this pause you are not falling behind; you are filling up. You are making room for God's timing and for your own soul's rhythm.

Let this sip be more than tea — it's truth. My beautiful soul sister you can begin again at any age. The calendar is not your jailer.

As you feel the warmth travel from your palms into your heart, whisper to yourself: *"I'm right on time. I'm exactly where I need to be."* Breathe that in, let it settle, and notice how the world softens around you.

PRESCRIPTION FOR YOUR SOUL – TRUTH DROP:
I sip truth slowly. I pour softness into my soul. I'm right on time. I'm exactly where I need to be.

Day 8 – Truth Drop

Tending Your Inner Garden

Through the kitchen window you see a garden bed overrun with weeds. Once it held delicious herbs or colorful flowers you loved, but life got busy and you stopped tending it. Midlife can feel like that — a mind crowded with old worries and other people's needs and stories until your own dreams can't find the light anymore.

The metaphysical law of mind tells us that every change begins as thought. Your subconscious is the soil; your thinking is the planting. When you tend your inner garden with loving, deliberate ideas, your outer world starts to mirror that new growth.

If your mind were a garden today, what weeds — old thoughts, habits, or fears — would you lovingly pull up to make room for new growth? What are you most often watering with your attention?

Pause now. Place your hand over your heart and whisper: *"I release old weeds and choose what grows to nourish me."*
Breathe slowly, imagining clear space opening in your mental garden — rich soil ready for fresh new ideas to take root and flourish. This weeding isn't a fade-out; it's your soul in full color, making space for its brightest bloom yet.

PRESCRIPTION FOR YOUR SOUL – TRUTH DROP:
Every change begins as a tiny seed. You are not too old to plant a new garden — literal or metaphorical.

Day 9 – Surprise Soul Whisper

A Pocket of Delight

Choose a word to bless this season—**_Release._**
Let it meet you like a friend, not a rule.

Whisper Practice

Place **Release** where you'll glimpse it (sticky note, lock screen).
Set one gentle daily reminder (perhaps 2:00 p.m.) for 30–90 days
that simply asks: *Does this serve Release?*
*Little share: I keep this reminder myself—when it pings, I exhale once and let
one thing go.*
Let yours arrive like a bell. Then choose the kinder option.

Soul Whisper:
I choose what serves, release, and let the rest loosen and fall away.

Day 10 – Soul-to-Spirit Meditation

Rest in the Light

Come away with me from the noise for a moment. Find a comfortable place to sit or lie down. Close your eyes. Place one hand gently over your heart and the other over your belly. Feel the rise and fall of your breath — slow, steady, like a quiet tide. This is the rhythm of life moving through you, whispering: *You are alive. You are safe.*

Now imagine above you a soft golden light, glowing like early morning sun filtered through leaves. See it slowly pouring into you — thick and luminous like the most gorgeous Christ like light. Let it flow through your crown, down your spine, and into every corner of your body. With each inhale, draw this light deeper into yourself. With each exhale, release the weight you've been carrying — worries, tension, the fragments of yesterday.

Notice how your shoulders begin to soften, your face relaxes, and the space inside you expands. Stay here for a few moments. Let the light wrap around you like a shawl, filling you with peace. In this stillness you are not doing; you are receiving. You are remembering the truth of who you are — held, loved, and guided.

When you are ready, open your eyes softly, as if returning from a sacred sanctuary. Carry the glow with you into whatever comes next.

Rest is not a luxury. Its how your nervous system resets so you can rise again.

I am alive and well, held in the light of Spirit.

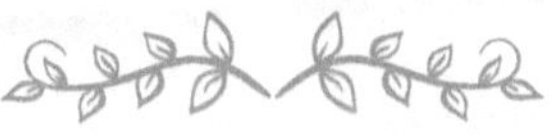

Day 11 – Microdose Laugh-Lift

Laughter Medicine

Your body doesn't always need more pressure or productivity. Sometimes it needs a release and reset — a burst of joy so pure it shakes loose the heaviness you've been carrying. Laughter is not trivial. It is sacred medicine. It opens the ribs like windows, lets the stale air escape, and draws fresh life back in.

Today, give yourself permission to look a little silly, to let sound rise up from your belly without apology. This isn't about performing for anyone else; it's about letting your nervous system know it is safe to play again. Even one minute can shift the atmosphere inside you.

Like this:

- Set a timer for one minute.
- Place your hand on your belly; feel its warmth.
- Begin to laugh — yes, even if it feels awkward at first. Make a small chuckle, then a bigger one, and keep going.
- Let the sound rise, tumble, spill out until it finds its own rhythm. If you can, sway or bounce gently as you laugh, letting your whole body join the release.

Notice how your body softens. Notice how lightness sneaks in through the cracks. That's medicine too — your own built-in healing practice, free and immediate. When you're done, pause for a breath and feel the glow that lingers. Your laughter is medicine. Use it often and without apology.

PRESCRIPTION FOR YOUR SOUL – RX:
My laughter is sacred medicine.

Day 12 – Soul Medicine Quote

"You don't need to fix yourself; you only need to remember yourself."
—Dr. Jennifer Rademaker

For too long the world has whispered a lie to you: that you are incomplete, that you must strive, earn, be perfect, or repair before you are worthy of something. Midlife can amplify that voice. Your body changes, your roles shift, and the old stories rise like ghosts insisting that something is wrong with you. But your soul has never been broken. Nothing essential about you has ever been lost.

What feels missing is not a piece of you gone astray—it is only memory: memory of your worth, your radiance, your original wholeness. Remembering is not nostalgia; it is a homecoming. It is turning inward and hearing, beneath the noise of culture and self-criticism, the steady pulse of Spirit saying, *Beautiful Soul, you are already enough.*

Today, let remembering be your medicine. Pause for a breath. Place your hand on your heart and whisper: *I am whole. I am home in myself.* Each time you do, you re-pattern your subconscious from striving to serenity. You begin to live from the truth that your healing is not about becoming someone new but about reclaiming who you already are.

When you live from remembrance, the pressure to fix dissolves. Your choices become gentler. You act not from desperation but from alignment. This is the quiet miracle of midlife: the chance to shed false stories and inhabit your own soul.

You don't have to prove your relevance. *You already are the relevance.*

Day 13 – Soul Reflection

The Seed Underground

My beautiful soul, there are seasons when nothing seems to be happening. You water, you wait, you pray — and the soil stays silent. Days turn into weeks, and the field of your hopes looks barren. In that silence, it is easy to believe nothing is growing. But the truth is, the unseen is not the same as the absent.

Beneath the surface, life is stirring. Tiny roots are reaching for nourishment. The seed is drawing in minerals, stretching, anchoring, and finding its strength in the dark before it breaks into light. This hidden season is not wasted. The silence is not empty. The waiting is not pointless.

If you could press your ear to the soil of your own life, you would hear a low hum of becoming — stronger, deeper, steadier. Everything that's rooting in you now will keep you from toppling when your next season of bloom arrives.

Today, take a breath and bless your underground places. Let patience be your prayer. Trust that unseen work is still holy work, and that the darkness before dawn is part of your rising. Starting small is not starting late. Every seed begins tiny.

REFLECT:
Where in your life right now does it feel like nothing is happening, and how might that hidden season actually be preparing you for growth?
Even in silence, my soul is growing.

Day 14 – Affirmation + Reflection

I know the world will try to convince you that you're late—late to success, late to love, late to becoming who you're meant to be. Scrolls, calendars, comparisons, social media and timelines shout from every direction, making you believe you're somehow behind. But your soul does not measure time the way the world does. It moves by seasons, by whispers, by divine timing.

Think of the tide: no wave arrives early or late; it comes precisely when it's called by the moon. Think of a flower: no bloom apologizes for when it opens. Every chapter of your life has unfolded exactly as it needed to. Even the pauses, the detours, and the delays have been holy ground, shaping the roots of who you are becoming. Not one moment has been wasted. Where have you been telling yourself you're "behind," and how might this be a season of perfect timing instead? Truthfully, where have you been pressuring yourself to "catch up," and how could you soften into the truth that you are exactly where you need to be?

Today, exhale the lie of "I should be further by now" and inhale the truth of "I am right on time." Feel it settle in your bones. Let your shoulders drop. Let your breath slow. This isn't just positive thinking—it's a return to your own sacred rhythm.

Whisper the affirmation like a prayer until your nervous system believes it. Let it echo through your heart: *I am not behind in my life. I am right on time.* Say it again, softer, until it becomes a heartbeat.

AFFIRMATION:
I am not behind in my life. I am right on time.

Day 15 – Dear God Letter

Dear God,

Some days I rise with certainty and a steady step, feeling the strength of my own spine. And some days, my back feels weak, my heart feels like a single thread holding too much weight, trembling under the strain. On those days, I come to You like this — soft, unguarded, open-handed.

Remind me that even my weakness is holy. That fragility is not failure; it is an invitation to lean. Remind me I don't have to carry everything on my own shoulders. You are the strength beneath my weakness, the light within my darkness, the breath within my weary chest.

As I breathe in now, I imagine Your Spirit flowing into me like fresh air through a window, filling every tired space. As I exhale, I let go of the lies — the illusion that I must do it all, hold it all, be it all. I surrender today — not because I have failed, but because I choose to be carried. I choose to trust Your timing, Your wisdom, Your arms beneath me.

In this surrender there is a quiet relief, a softening of my heart, a remembering that I am held. Thank You for catching me when I fall, for holding me when I tremble, for lifting me when I can't lift myself.

With love, I release

And so it is, Amen.

Day 16 – Breath Practice / Ritual Reset

The Shoulder Release

Your body remembers what your mind tries to carry. Every unspoken worry, every *"I'll handle it myself,"* rests across your shoulders like invisible weight. Over time it rounds your posture and tightens your breath, making you feel heavier than you really are. But your breath can lift what words cannot. Even a few intentional moments can melt tension you didn't realize you were holding.

Before you begin, give yourself a quiet space. Close your eyes and imagine that the air around you is soft and golden, ready to help you release. As you breathe in, picture that light gathering under the weight on your shoulders. As you breathe out, feel it lifting and flowing away like mist.

Practice:

- Sit tall, feet grounded, eyes gently closed.
- Inhale deeply through your nose as you shrug your shoulders up toward your ears. Feel the stretch — the gathering of all that weight.
- Pause for a heartbeat at the top of the breath, sensing the fullness.
- Exhale slowly through your mouth as you roll your shoulders back and down, letting the weight slide off like a shawl.
- Repeat seven times, letting each cycle be a little slower, a little deeper.

When you finish, place your hands lightly on your thighs and take one more soft breath. Notice how your chest feels more open, how your neck feels longer, how your heart feels lighter. This is your body's quiet way of letting go of what your heart doesn't need to hold.

With each breath, I release the weight that is not mine to carry.

Day 17 – Chakra Soul Movement

Root-to-Heart Bridge

At the base of your spine lives your root chakra — your deep well of stability. It's not only about standing still; it's about drawing up what nourishes you so your heart can feel safe enough to open. When this energy flows, you don't just feel grounded — you feel supported and alive, like a tree fed from its roots all the way to its leaves.

My Radiant one, today's practice invites you to bridge your root and your heart, letting the earth steady you as you release what you've been carrying.

Practice:

- Stand with your feet hip-width apart, knees soft.
- Press your soles firmly into the floor, imagining roots spiraling down from your feet.
- Place one hand on your lower belly, one hand on your heart.
- Inhale slowly, drawing a deep red light up from the earth into your belly, then your chest. Pause for a heartbeat at the top of the breath.
- Exhale gently, letting tension flow back down through your legs and into the ground.
- Repeat for seven breaths, feeling each cycle as a root-to-heart exchange — earth steadies you, heart softens.

As you finish, stand tall and sense the quiet strength rising from your feet into your heart. This is your foundation feeding your compassion.

Mantra:
Rooted below, open above — the earth steadies me, my heart rises free.

Day 18 – Soul Whisker

Hello, my two-legged soul sister.

I've been batting my toy around the room for ages — claws, leaps, swats — then suddenly I stop. I let it roll away, stretch my back, flick my tail, and glide off without a second thought.

No guilt. No tally.
No *"should I finish?"* I just release.

I see you. That thought you've been batting around in your mind — the conversation you keep replaying, the to-do list — simply let it roll away.

In this Release season, even a small letting go softens your nervous system and frees your spirit.

Soul Whisker:
Release the toy, flick your tail, and stroll off lighter. Bonus points if you also knock something off a shelf.

It's medicine.

Day 19 – Sacred Sips Moment

A Cup of Stillness

Imagine yourself pouring tea slowly, the sound like a whisper in a quiet room. Watch the steam rise like a soft prayer curling upward, carrying your worries with it. Feel the warmth of the cup steadying your hands, bringing you back to the present moment. This isn't just tea; it's a sacred pause, a microdose of soul medicine.

Life will always try to pull you into its rush — lists, noise, and endless doing. But truth doesn't always shout. Sometimes it comes as a hush, a nudge, a breath. In stillness, your soul remembers its own voice. In stillness, you can hear God's timing instead of the world's timelines.

Take one sip. Let the warmth travel down your throat and into your chest. Breathe. Feel how your shoulders drop, how the room seems to widen. Let this moment be enough. As you sit in this softness, know that you're not falling behind; you're filling up. You're making space for the goodness ahead.

My darling, God hasn't forgotten you. Even now, in the quiet, something good is unfolding. Stillness isn't wasted time; it's where your roots drink the water they need so you can bloom when it's time.

"Be still and know that I am God." — *Psalm 46:10*

Day 20 – Truth Drop

As Within, So Without

A soul sister stands at the window before sunrise, coffee warm in her hands, staring at the garden she planted years ago. Some corners are wild with weeds; others bloom without effort. She notices how the garden mirrors her inner life — seasons of care, seasons of neglect, bursts of color, patches of bare soil. *No wonder it looks like me,* she thinks. *This is exactly how I've been feeling inside.*

Every moment your inner life is shaping the outer life you're living. Thoughts, beliefs, and emotions are not just private — they are subtle architects of your experience. When your mind races with fear, everything feels urgent and unsafe. When your heart softens into love, the world reflects that softness back to you. This isn't punishment or reward; it's resonance. Spirit mirrors the vibration you hold inside.

Midlife can be a mirror-storm — old roles, changing bodies, and hidden griefs rise to the surface. You may feel at the mercy of circumstances, but you are not. The metaphysical truth is that you are a co-creator with God, and your inner atmosphere is powerful enough to shift your outer weather.

Begin where your power lives — inside. Tend your thoughts like a sacred garden. Breathe peace into your body. Let gratitude and self-compassion be the seeds you plant. Watch how your life begins to echo the beauty you're cultivating within.

TRUTH DROP:
I tend my inner world with love. As I shift within, my outer world responds with grace, ease, and beauty.

Day 21 – Surprise Soul Whisper

The Barefoot Reset

Sometimes the quickest way back to yourself is also the simplest. Spirit doesn't always ask for hours of meditation or elaborate rituals. Sometimes it only asks for your feet to touch the earth — to come back to the place where you began.

We spend so much time in shoes, in cars, in buildings, sealed off from the ground that steadies us. Yet beneath everything is a living, breathing planet humming with support. When you step out barefoot, you're not just touching dirt or grass; you're plugging back into the heartbeat of creation. It's a quiet, immediate medicine — free, ancient, and always available.

Whisper Practice:

Step outside barefoot. If you can, choose a small patch of ground that calls to you: cool grass, warm stone, soft soil, or even the edge of a wooden porch kissed by the sun. Pause before you place your feet down. Breathe. Feel the temperature, the texture, the pulse beneath you. With each inhale, imagine the earth's strength rising into your body; with each exhale, let any tension or worry sink back down into the ground like roots releasing old water. Stand there for a minute or two, eyes open or closed, letting the earth hold you. Let your body release it all and remember that you belong here.

Even two minutes of this can release and reset your nervous system, calm your mind, and remind you: you are supported. You are not floating untethered; you are held.

Soul Whisper:
Mother Earth holds me. I am safe. I belong.

Day 22 – Soul-to-Spirit Meditation

The River Within

Maybe it's you, standing by the edge of a quiet river, and the water moves without noise or hurry. It carries twigs, leaves, and bits of yesterday downstream — perhaps it does that to make space for what is new. The river keeps flowing, steady and sure, not asking anything of you but presence. Watching it, you realize how much you've been holding your breath, gripping your own "debris" inside. A single exhale softens your shoulders.

This is your invitation today. Peace is already moving through you like a current. All you need is a moment to notice — to step to the edge within and let it carry what you're ready to release.

Meditation:

Close your eyes. Imagine a gentle river flowing through you. It begins at the crown of your head, streaming slowly down your spine, pooling softly in your belly. With each inhale, the water brightens, clearing away fear. With each exhale, it carries the weight downstream — old thoughts, tension, self-criticism. You don't need to force it. Simply breathe and let the current do the work. Feel yourself floating inside your own body, being cleansed and supported at once.

Stay with the river for a few breaths. Notice how peace feels when it flows rather than when you chase it. Let your nervous system learn this softness — less striving, more allowing. The universe meets you where you exhale.

AFFIRMATION:
I release the weight of yesterday, I trust the current.

Day 23 – Microdose Laugh-Lift

The One-Minute Reset

Sometimes the body holds heaviness longer than the mind does. Worry, tension, and fatigue settle into your chest like stones. But laughter shakes them loose.

Try this:

- Set a timer for one minute.
- Place your hand on your heart and the other on your belly.
- Begin laughing — softly at first, then louder. Even if it feels forced, keep going.
- Notice how your body vibrates, how your breath deepens, how the stones begin to tumble away.

When the timer ends, sit in the silence after laughter. That silence is freedom.

I laugh myself into freedom.

PRESCRIPTION FOR YOUR SOUL – RX:
Joy is not a reward; it's a daily vitamin

Day 24 – Soul Medicine Quote

"With love, I release, reset, and rise and find the medicine inside."
—Dr. Jennifer Rademaker

A soul sister sits at the end of a long day, shoulders tight, scrolling through her phone for answers. She thinks, *If I could just find the right book, the right plan, the right fix… then I'd finally feel whole.* Decades of caring for others and pushing through have taught her that healing lives somewhere "out there" — in another person, another program, another future version of herself. But under the noise, a quieter truth is already waiting.

My beautiful soul, your healing doesn't live outside of you — it lives within. It's easy to believe that wholeness is something you must chase, fix, or earn. But the truth is, every breath you take, every thought you shift, every moment you choose love over fear, you are practicing medicine for your own soul. When you release what no longer serves, you create space. When you reset into the calm that is your birthright, you return to the quiet place inside that has always been whole. And when you rise into the truth of who you really are, you embody the medicine you've been searching for. It has always been here, pulsing quietly beneath the noise, waiting for your attention.

Pause now. Take a slow breath in, placing your hand over your heart. As you exhale, imagine everything heavy sliding off your shoulders.

WHISPER YOUR AFFIRMATION:
With love, I release, reset, and rise and find the medicine inside, as if it's a key unlocking your own inner pharmacy of peace.

Day 25 – Soul Reflection

No Longer Half

Have you ever felt loved but not respected? Or respected, but not truly loved?

It happens quietly sometimes. Someone may tell you they love you, yet their actions don't honor your dignity. The affection is there, but without respect, that love feels unsteady—like sunlight dimmed by shadow.

Other times, you may be respected for your strength or integrity, yet never truly cherished. Respect alone can feel like a tall gate—safe, but distant. Solid, but never tender.

Both leave the soul hungry. Love without respect feels unsafe. Respect without love feels cold. But when love and respect walk hand in hand, something sacred unfolds.

To walk hand in hand, we must first soften our sight. It begins by seeing beyond another's actions into their essence—to look not through judgment, but through soul. Sometimes that means whispering, *"They're doing the best they can with the light they have."*

This doesn't excuse harm; it restores compassion where resentment once lived. It lets us see the soul instead of the struggle. When we ask, *"God, help me see through love today—not fear,"* miracles begin quietly in the mind. The shift happens inside first.

And if you've stayed too long in what didn't honor you, forgive yourself. You were learning the difference between crumbs and nourishment. That lesson was sacred medicine, preparing your heart to receive more.

Pause here, my darling. Rub your hands together until you feel warmth. Place them over your cheeks, melting away doubt. Inhale softly, exhale slowly.

WHISPER WITHIN:
I am worthy of love that honors me and respect that warms me.

REFLECTION QUESTION:
Where am I still accepting half-love—and what am I ready to release today so I can honor both love and respect?

Life piles up in layers — responsibilities, regrets, fears you never asked to carry. Some of it belongs to you. Much of it does not. And yet you've held it, trying to be strong.

But strength is not in carrying everything. Strength is in choosing what to put down. Today, trust that you are allowed to release the weight that isn't yours. Lay it down — soul sister, lay it down. When you let go of what is heavy, your hands are free to receive what is light.

Less striving, more allowing. The universe meets you where you exhale.

Peace is the new success, and it fits you perfectly.

Affirmation (repeat):
I release what is heavy and welcome what is light.

Reflection:
What are you carrying today that no longer belongs to you — and how might you set it down?

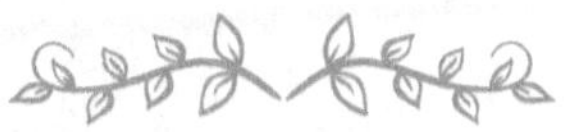

Day 27 – Dear God Letter

Dear God,

I am tired of carrying what is not mine —
the worries that are borrowed,
the expectations that never belonged to me,
the voices that tell me I must do more to be enough.

I lay them down at Your feet today.
Take them, for they weigh more than my soul can hold.

Fill my empty hands with what is true —
peace instead of pressure,
love instead of fear,
lightness instead of shame.

Teach me that surrender is not weakness,
but a doorway to freedom.

With love, I release what was, reset my mind, and rise new.

And so it is, Amen.

Day 28 – Breath Practice / Ritual Reset

The 4-4-4 Calm

When the world feels loud and scattered, your breath can be your anchor. Like waves returning to shore, it brings you back — steady, reliable, faithful. This simple practice becomes a way of saying to yourself: *I'm here. I'm safe. I'm steady.*

Before you begin, find a quiet space. Place one hand on your heart and one on your belly to remind your nervous system you are present and held. Let your shoulders soften. Notice the rise and fall under your palms.

Then try this:
- Inhale through your nose for a count of 4.
- Hold the breath gently for a count of 4.
- Exhale slowly through your mouth for a count of 4.
- Repeat 4 times.

As you move through the rhythm, feel how your body begins to settle. This practice drops you down into your body, into your nervous system, centers your mind, and reminds your spirit: peace is always one breath away. Let each cycle be an act of kindness toward yourself — a small release and reset you can carry anywhere.

In the quiet after your last exhale, pause. Feel the stillness around you and within you my love.

Silence can be more powerful than explanation

SOUL WHISPER:
With each breath, I return to silence and calm.

Day 29 – Chakra Soul Movement

Solar Plexus Fire

Your solar plexus, just above the navel, is your center of confidence and courage — where self-trust, personal power, and inner fire live. When this energy is dim, fear sneaks in and takes over; you shrink, second-guess, and forget your own brilliance. But when it glows bright, you feel strong, capable, unstoppable — moving through the world with a quiet knowing that you can handle what comes.

My radiant one, today is an invitation to tend that inner fire. You don't have to force it; you simply remember it's there. This flame isn't something you create from scratch — it's your birthright. Every breath can make it brighter. Every exhale can release the doubt that tries to smother it.

Practice:
- Stand tall with your feet grounded, toes spreading slightly for balance.
- Place your hands gently on your belly, just above your navel. Feel its warmth.
- Inhale slowly as you imagine a golden flame igniting inside you — bright, pure, steady. Pause for a heartbeat at the top of the breath, sensing its glow.
- Exhale as that flame spreads warmth through your chest and arms, melting hesitation, softening fear.
- Repeat for seven breaths, letting your body sway or move if it wants to — as though your flame is dancing inside you.

With each cycle, feel your posture becoming taller, your shoulders back, your heart open. Notice the heat in your palms, the steadiness under your feet. This is your fire, steady and strong. Let it burn away doubt and call forth your courage.

There is nothing small about a woman reclaiming herself.

The fire within me is steady, strong, and unshakable.

Day 30 – Soul Whisker

Curiosity at the Window

Hello, my two-legged soul sister.

I sit at the window and don't worry about yesterday's pawprints or tomorrow's chase.
I simply watch — the flutter of a bird, the sway of a branch, the dance of the wind. This is my gift to myself: presence.

You could do this too. Notice instead of analyze. Be curious instead of critical. Watch your own life unfold the way I watch the garden — with soft eyes and an open heart. Nothing to fix. Nothing to grip.

Sometimes the medicine isn't in doing more. It's in letting a single moment land on your whiskers and feeling it fully. That's how you stay alive to your own magic.

SOUL WHISKER:
I give myself purrmission to be present and curious.

Bonus paw-tip: if a bird stares back, blink slowly and pretend you planned it all along.

Day 31 – Sacred Sips Moment

The Pour

Listen as the tea pours into the cup. Notice the sound — soft, steady, certain. Watch the gentle stream swirl and settle, steam rising like a quiet prayer. The cup does not question if it is worthy to be filled. It simply receives. In this simple act there's a whole teaching: receiving is not taking, and it's not weakness. It's holy.

You are the same. You do not have to earn love, peace, or rest. You only have to open and allow yourself to be filled.

So many of us have been taught to pour and pour for others, to earn every drop of care. But here, with this cup in your hands, you're invited to remember you are already being poured into. God's love, grace, and timing are flowing toward you even now.

The same way the tea fills the cup without question, divine love is flowing into your life. You are not overlooked. Even now, in the quiet, something good is unfolding for you. This is your moment to receive without apology.

Take a slow sip. Breathe in the scent, the steam, the silence. Whisper your affirmation like a prayer. Let it settle into the places inside you that may have felt empty.

"My cup overflows." — Psalm 23:5

Day 32 – Truth Drop

Energy Never Lies

A mid-life sacred friend walks into the room before she even speaks. People glance up, sensing something — a heaviness, a brightness, a subtle pull they can't quite name. It isn't her clothes, her words, or her posture. It's her energy. It drifts ahead of her like a scent, announcing her mood without a single syllable.

You do this too. Every woman does. You might say, *"I'm fine,"* because it feels easier than unpacking the ache. You smile through tears, keep busy, and hope no one notices. Yet even when your lips stay silent, your energy tells the story — the quiet echo of your inner world, the hum beneath the smile. When you're hurting, it feels heavy. When you're hopeful, it becomes soft and bright. Your energy is a lighthouse others sense, even in the dark.

The good news is that your vibration is not fixed. Each breath, each thought, each prayer can shift it. This is why you feel different after you breathe deeply, pray, or pause — you are recalibrating your field. In midlife, as you shed old stories, this becomes one of your greatest powers: the ability to choose what you radiate instead of being ruled by what you've absorbed.

Right now, place your hand over your heart. Inhale slowly, imagining a soft glow expanding inside you. Exhale what feels heavy. Inhale love. You're not pretending; you're reprogramming. Love, gratitude, and truth are frequencies that change the room you walk into. As you realign your energy, watch how life responds. This is the subtle alchemy of the soul: when you choose to release love, the world mirrors it back.

Day 33 – Surprise Soul Whisper

Name the Woman You're Becoming

Upgrade your identity—not your to-do list.

Brave one… I see you. You've carried so much—quiet lists no one applauds, a heart that keeps showing up, even when it's tender. If you agree, maybe something in you is whispering, *Enough of who I'm not. Let me breathe into who I am.*

Write one tender truth line: **"I am the woman who _______."**
(*…speaks her truth, chooses peace before proving. …nourishes her body.*)

Micro-practice: Pick one identity and take one small, aligned action today.

Soul Whisper:
I lay down what isn't true of me and live one sacred truth that is.

Day 34 – Soul-to-Spirit Meditation

The Quiet Flame

My soul sister, you are safe here. Allow me to drape a soft shawl over your shoulders. Here, there are no lists to carry, nothing to prove— only the quiet light you already hold. Let's meet that light together.

If it feels good, let your eyes soften or close and take a slow, generous breath… As the outer world fades, imagine a small flame inside your chest — steady and golden. It does not flicker with fear. It does not vanish in the dark. It holds, quiet and certain, like a lantern left burning for you in the night.

Bring your awareness to that flame. With each inhale, feel it grow warmer, brighter, a little taller. With each exhale, imagine its glow spreading softly through your body — down your arms, into your hands, all the way to your fingertips, until you feel a subtle tingling of warmth. Allow your shoulders to drop, your jaw to loosen. You don't have to force this light. It was never gone. It is simply waiting for your attention.

If you'd like, place one hand on your heart and one on your belly, as if cradling that flame between your palms. Breathe gently. Sense how the light fills even the spaces you once called empty. This is your inner spark — resilient, alive, eternal.

Rest here for a few moments. Feel the warmth. Let your soul remember its own glow. When you're ready to return, open your eyes softly, as you move through your day, imagine that quiet flame glowing gently behind your heart with each step you take.

Affirmation:
My inner flame is steady, alive, and eternal.

Day 35 – Microdose Laugh-Lift

Have you noticed how laughter changes a room? One chuckle ripples into another until even those who weren't part of the joke find themselves laughing too.. Laughter is contagious because it carries freedom. It shakes loose what words can't, it opens windows in the soul where stale air has been trapped.

Your body longs for that release — not the polite laugh you offer at a meeting or the little smile you paste on for others, but a raw, belly-born burst that lets the weight shake off your shoulders. Even one minute of unselfconscious laughter can loosen sorrow lodged in your chest and remind you that you're alive.

Think of this practice as a spiritual reset. When you laugh on purpose, you're telling your nervous system, *"I am safe enough to play."* You're letting your inner child stretch, and breathe again.

Find a small, ordinary moment today — like washing the dishes — to laugh on purpose and watch how lightness spreads into everything else.

Set a timer for one minute. Place your hand gently on your belly. Begin to laugh — even if it feels awkward at first. Make a small chuckle, then a bigger one, and keep going. Let the sound rise, tumble, spill out until it finds its own rhythm. If you want, bounce as you laugh, letting your whole body join the release.

Notice the shift in your mood. That is freedom in motion — your own sacred medicine.

Prescription for Your Soul – Rx:
Forced laughter is a youth serum no cream can match.

Day 36 – Soul Medicine Quote

"The soul is not in a hurry — only the mind is."
—Dr. Jennifer Rademaker

My beautiful soul, the mind races with deadlines, expectations, and fears of running out of time. It sprints from one worry to the next, whispering that you're behind, that you're late, that you should have done more by now. But the soul moves at the pace of eternity. It breathes in seasons, not seconds. It knows that nothing real can be rushed, and nothing meant for you can be missed.

When you feel behind, pause for a moment. Place your hand on your heart and feel its steady beat. This is the rhythm of your soul — unhurried, unwavering. Notice how, beneath the noise of the mind, your inner self is not anxious. It is steady. It is sure. It is waiting for you to trust its timing.

Any time you catch yourself hurrying today, place your hand on your heart, breathe once slowly, and remind yourself: *"I move at the pace of my soul."* Take a few slow breaths — inhale patience, exhale pressure. Whisper the words like a prayer until you feel their truth sink into your body. Let the edges of your day soften. Let the rush drain away. This is not idleness; it is alignment. You're not falling behind — you're falling back into rhythm with your own life.

Prescription for Your Soul – Truth Drop:
I move at the pace of my soul, not the pressure of the world.

Day 37 – Soul Reflection

The Weight of the Sky

Let me ask you, have you ever laid on your back in the grass and stared at the endless sky above you? At first it feels light, infinite, full of possibility. But if you linger long enough, you begin to imagine how heavy it would be if you had to hold up the whole sky yourself. It's impossible — yet that's exactly what so many of us try to do in our inner lives.

That's what you've been doing — trying to carry what was never yours to hold. Responsibilities, expectations, outcomes, other people's emotions… you've been bracing your shoulders as if the sky itself might fall if you stopped supporting it. But the truth is, the sky can hold itself. You are only asked to breathe beneath it, to live, to be.

Today, let this be your quiet release. Close your eyes, inhale deeply, and picture the vast blue stretching above you — limitless and self-sustaining. With each exhale, imagine setting down what is not yours — one piece at a time — until you feel the ground holding you and the sky above holding itself. My darling, you were never meant to carry everything. You were meant to be carried by love.

As you sit with this question — *what part of the "sky" in your life are you trying to hold up that could be released to God, love, or the universe today?* — place your hand on your heart and softly whisper: *I am held by something greater than myself.*

Day 38 – Affirmation + Reflection

Rest Without Earning

For so long you've measured your worth by what you produce, by how much you do, by who you take care of. You've poured out for others until the very idea of pausing felt like a luxury you couldn't afford — or worse, like laziness. But that's not the truth.

Rest is not a reward. It is a birthright. It is medicine. It is the soil where strength regenerates. The God who made the oceans ebb and flow also wove seasons of stillness into every living thing. Even the sun sets. Even the earth sleeps under winter's blanket. You were designed to move in the same rhythm — pouring out and filling back up. You don't have to do one more thing to deserve it.

Before you end this reading, set a timer for five minutes, close your eyes, place your hand on your heart, and simply rest without doing — let the world wait and let your body feel the permission. Imagine your rest as sacred ground. When you close your eyes, breathe in softness. When you exhale, let the pressure roll off your shoulders like a heavy cloak. **Ask yourself gently, "What would change in my spirit if I gave myself rest today without guilt?"** Trust that as you honor your body's need to rest, your soul rises to meet you with renewed strength. This is not laziness. This is alignment.

As you sit with this, softly whisper over yourself:
"I am allowed to rest without earning it." Say it until the guilt begins to loosen and a quiet permission starts to bloom inside you.

Affirmation:
I am allowed to rest without earning it.

Day 39 – Dear God Letter

Dear God,

I am weary of my own weariness.
I have carried so much, given so much,
and I wonder if You see me here—
not longing for more strength,
but longing for a holy exhale.

Teach me, God,
that I do not have to earn my rest,
that I do not have to prove myself worthy of laying it all down.
Whisper to my spirit that You created night for sleeping,
seasons for pausing,
and silence for listening.

Wrap me now in the assurance
that when I stop striving,
nothing essential will collapse.
That while I breathe, You are holding it all—
the world, the weight,
and me—together.

Let my surrender be not a sign of failure
but an act of faith.
Let my stillness become a sanctuary
where Your strength rises quietly within me.

With grace, I release.

And so it is, Amen

Day 40 – Breath Practice: The Soft Exhale

How is your breathing?

Do you breathe from your chest or your belly? When breath stays high in the chest it's usually shallow — the body's stress mode. When breath begins low in the belly it signals safety, calm, and presence. So often we breathe just enough to survive, not enough to feel alive. Our inhales rush in, but our exhales cut short — as if we're afraid to let go all the way.

Try this: close your eyes and soften your jaw. Let the weight drop off your shoulders. Inhale gently through your nose from your belly, not your chest. Then let your exhale spill out longer, slower, like a sigh of relief. Feel how the body melts when the breath is no longer forced.

This is your soul's reminder: release is not a push — it is a surrender.

Soul Whisper:
With every exhale, I release and return to peace.

Day 41 – Chakra Soul Movement

Heart Opening

Your heart is more than an organ — it is the center of your love, your compassion, your connection to life. When it closes, the world feels heavy and small. When it opens, even for a moment, everything softens; colors brighten; your breath feels wider. You were created to give and receive love freely.

Before you begin, create a small atmosphere of softness. If it helps, put on music that feels like a gentle embrace — a slow instrumental, flowing strings, a soft piano, or the sound of ocean waves. Later today, if you feel yourself closing, pause for one breath, open your arms slightly, and recall this practice to invite softness back in. Let the rhythm become the backdrop for your heart-opening ritual.

Invitation:
- Stand tall, feet rooted to the ground, toes spreading slightly for balance.
- Place both hands gently over your heart. Feel its warmth under your palms.
- As you inhale, slowly open your arms wide, as if embracing the sky. Pause for a heartbeat at the top of the breath, sensing your chest expand.
- As you exhale, bring your hands back to your chest, returning to yourself, as if gathering the love you've just welcomed in.
- Repeat for seven breaths, letting your chest expand with each opening and letting the music guide you if you've chosen to play it.

This is not just movement — it is a remembering. It's your body teaching your soul that it's safe to open again.

I open my heart to love, and love flows freely through me.

Day 42 – Soul Whisker

The Empty Bowl

You, soul sister: "My cup is empty. I'm so stressed, I'm overwhelmed, and I want to fix everything. My mind right now is spinning—How? When? What if?"

The Cat: "I add a little flair, sure, but underneath I trust. I make my request (meow), then I stretch, nap, and taste the feast on its way.

My two legger, try this: less 'How will it happen?' and more 'I know it's coming.' Place your request, then do something gentle—, watch the birds, call a friend. Let life fill your cup in its own time."

SOUL WHISKER:
Order placed. Lounge like a queen while the universe prepares your dinner.
Bonus paw-tip: add a dramatic side-eye to the sky — it speeds up service.

Day 43 – Sacred Sips Moment

The Pause Between Sips

Notice what happens after the sip. The warmth spreads through your chest, your hands relax around the cup, and in the pause before the next taste a quiet appears. That pause is not empty; it is where your body receives.

So often we rush from one thing to the next, never honoring the sacred pause. Yet it is in the in-between moments where integration happens, where the soul catches up, where peace settles in. In the same way your tea must steep to draw out its flavor, your life needs space to draw out its meaning. You are not falling behind in the pause; you are being filled.

Even in the stillness between sips something good is unfolding. The pause is not a void — it's a cradle. You're not empty; you're being poured into.

Take a slow sip now. Feel the steam rise against your face. Let the warmth slip down into your chest. Rest for a heartbeat before the next taste. Breathe. Whisper your affirmation. Imagine your soul expanding in that space, ready to hold more love, more clarity, more joy.

SACRED TRUTH DROP:
Right here, right now, I honor the pause as sacred space.

Day 44 – Truth Drop

What You Focus on Grows

Energy flows where attention goes. Your thoughts and feelings are like water in a garden — whatever you pour them on will bloom. When you dwell on fear, it multiplies like weeds. When you nurture gratitude, it expands like flowers reaching for sunlight. The universe is always listening to the vibration of your focus and responding in kind.

You are not powerless. You are a gardener of energy. Every thought is a seed. Every feeling is water. What you water with your attention will grow strong roots. Choose with care, and choose with love. Before your next task or conversation, close your eyes for one breath and silently ask yourself: *"Which seed am I watering right now?"* — then pour your attention where you want it to bloom.

Pause for a moment and picture your inner world as a small garden. Notice which plants have been getting the most water from you — worry or hope, doubt or trust. Without judgment, shift your watering can. My beautiful sunflower, turn your attention toward the blooms you want to see flourish. This is how you become an intentional creator of your life's atmosphere.

PRESCRIPTION FOR YOUR SOUL – TRUTH DROP:
I water what I want to grow.

Day 45 – Surprise Soul Whisper

The One-Word Reset

Sometimes a whole prayer can be too much. Sometimes the heart is too heavy for long sentences. In those moments, all you need is one word.

Choose it now — Peace. Love. Freedom. Light. Whisper it softly under your breath, again and again, until your body remembers what your mind has forgotten.

One word can reset the whole day.

Truth Drop:
Even a single word can shift my spirit.

Day 46 – Soul-to-Spirit Meditation

The Ocean Within

Have you ever stood at the edge of the sea and felt its breath on your skin — the emotional pull of the tide, the endless rhythm of waves arriving and retreating — and wondered about your own life?

In midlife it's easy to believe you've lost that steadiness. Responsibilities rise like storms, emotions shift like currents, and your subconscious whispers that peace is something you have to earn, control, or schedule.

But the ocean tells another story. It moves without apology, faithful to its inner moon. It never asks permission to ebb or flow. And here is the hidden truth: the infinite ocean of Love moves through you. Beneath the surface noise of your days, a vast and steady tide already lives inside you. It cannot be rushed. It cannot be broken. It is your birthright.

Today you're invited to remember that rhythm. Find a quiet spot. Close your eyes. Place one hand over your heart and one on your belly. Inhale slowly through your nose, feeling a wave rise from your belly to your chest. Pause for a heartbeat — a float at the top of the wave — then exhale longer than you inhaled, letting the wave return to shore. Repeat for several breaths, letting the movement rock you like water.

As you breathe, whisper inwardly: *"The infinite ocean of Love moves through me."* Let that truth wash over you.

AFFIRMATION:
The infinite ocean of Love moves through me. I move with the rhythm of the eternal within me.

Day 47 – Microdose Laugh-Lift

The Giggle That Escapes

Do you remember the last time laughter slipped out before you could stop it? The kind that starts as a sparkle in your chest, spills through your lips, and shakes your shoulders until you can't hold it back. That giggle is holy. It doesn't ask permission. It doesn't care if the timing is right. It reminds you that joy lives inside you, waiting to break free.

Over time we become careful with our joy. We save it for "appropriate" moments. We mute our giggles so we won't draw attention. But your body longs for that spontaneous burst — a raw, unedited sound that lets the weight tumble off your heart and makes room for lightness to enter again.

Sometime today — even in a mundane moment like folding laundry or driving — let a small giggle escape without reason, and notice how the air around you shifts. Think of this practice as an inner jailbreak: letting joy slip past the guard of your mind and run out into the open.

Practice Whisper:
Find a quiet spot. Place a hand on your belly. Close your eyes. Begin with a soft chuckle — even if it feels silly at first. Let it bubble up, unforced, until you hear your own giggle escaping. Allow your shoulders to shake, your face to soften. Keep going for a minute or two, riding the sound like a wave.

When you finish, take a slow breath. Notice the warmth, the lightness, the small lift in your mood. That's your inner freedom, remembered.

Prescription for Your Soul – Microdose Rx:
Joy taken seriously is a radical act.

Day 48 – Soul Medicine Quote

"Release is not weakness — it's wisdom.
Letting go is not the end of your strength — it is the beginning of your freedom."
—Dr. Jennifer Rademaker

Somewhere, a woman stands in her bedroom at the end of the day, holding a stack of papers she no longer needs — old notes, goals, and faded reminders. She's been meaning to sort them for months, but each time she hesitated, thinking, *what if I need this someday?* The pile has grown heavier in her hands, and in her heart.

Midlife carries piles like this: relationships we've outgrown, obligations that once made sense, identities that no longer fit. We've been taught to grip, to cling, to hold on no matter what — equating perseverance with worth and imagining that letting go must mean we've failed.

Sometimes the holiest act is the letting go — not because you've given up, but because your soul has learned what it came to learn. Release is not the end of your strength; it's the beginning of your freedom. It's a conscious choice to stop carrying what has become too heavy, to trust that love will hold what you've set down. What you release doesn't vanish into nothingness — it creates space for what is meant to rise.

Today, breathe in deeply. As you exhale, imagine opening your hands and letting one small burden slip away. This is not weakness; this is wisdom. Each time you practice release, your nervous system learns safety in surrender and your soul remembers its wings.

The cage was never locked.

Day 49 – Soul Reflection

The Stone You've Been Carrying

There's a stone you've carried for so long, you almost forget it's there. Heavy, tucked inside your chest, weighing you down with memories, regrets, or fears. Maybe it started as a pebble, then grew as the years added their layers. You've adjusted your posture around it. You've built routines to manage its weight. It has become so familiar you've begun to believe it's part of you.

And yet, if you pause, you may notice — it's smooth now. Time and endurance have softened its edges. What once cut you sharp has become round in your hands. The ache you've felt has shaped you, but it no longer defines you. What was once a wound has been transformed into wisdom.

Maybe it's time to set the stone down. It has served its purpose. It has taught you what it came to teach. You don't have to carry it into the next season. Releasing it isn't abandoning your story — it's acknowledging that part of the journey is complete. In letting go you're not losing anything; you're making space for something new to arrive.

Close your eyes for a moment and picture yourself holding that stone. Feel its weight, its smoothness, the history in its surface. Then imagine gently placing it on the earth, whispering gratitude for what it gave you, and stepping lighter into your life.

REFLECT:
What stone have you carried long enough, and how might it feel to finally set it down?

Day 50 – Affirmation + Reflection

For much of your life you've been catalogued by your scars — the betrayals you endured, the children you raised while carrying your own pain, the losses that left you standing in kitchens or offices or bedrooms wondering if there was anything left of you at all. You became strong, resourceful, and competent. You survived. But somewhere along the way the label *"survivor"* started to sound like your whole name.

Survival is not your identity. It was a chapter — an important one — but it is not your essence. You are not just the ashes; you are the fire that still burns. You are the one who dared to keep loving, keep creating, keep hoping even when it hurt. You are the healing, the becoming, the rising.

Midlife is not the end of your story; it's the threshold where you can lay down the heavy cloak of survival and step into your soul's true name. If you released the identity of *"survivor,"* what new name or image might your soul choose to describe who you truly are today?

Take a breath with me right now. Feel your chest soften. Breathe through the belly. Whisper to yourself: *I am more than what I endured. I am who I am becoming.* Each time you say it, your subconscious begins to loosen its grip on the old identity and make room for a new one — one defined by freedom, joy, creativity, and wholeness.

Every season of your life has prepared you for this one.

Affirmation:
I am no longer defined by what I have survived. I am defined by who I am becoming.

Day 51 – Dear God Letter

Dear God,

There are mornings when I look into the mirror and my eyes go first to the lines, the weight, the soft changes that tell me time is moving. I confess — too easily I forget to see the beauty, the story, the strength written in those same lines.

Teach me to see myself as You see me:
not aging, but ripening,
not fading, but deepening,
not less, but more.

Help me bless this face, this body, this temple — exactly as it is right now. Let every mark become a testament of love, every curve a witness to life, every change a signature of grace.

Let me see that aging is not loss of beauty. It's beauty evolving into wisdom.
Let my reflection be a reminder of mercy, not a verdict of loss.

Restore in me the eyes of compassion. Let my gaze become an embrace. Let my heart recognize the sacredness of what I see staring back at me.

And so it is, Amen.

Day 52 – Breath Practice / Ritual Reset

You don't have to earn your right to be comforted. You don't have to finish the list, fix the world, or hold yourself together to deserve soft love. Through late nights, caretaking, quiet tears, and brave smiles, your body has been faithful. Today, lay it all down. Let your body be the one held and try this..

Place one hand on your heart and one on your belly—two centers speaking at once: the wisdom that knows and the ground that holds. This simple posture tells your nervous system: *I am safe now.* It's the embrace you've given everyone else, finally returning to you. As you breathe, whisper: *Beloved body, thank you for carrying me. Beloved heart, thank you for beating every day.* Imagine warm light pooling beneath your palms, draping you in a warm shawl of peace.

Your heart isn't scolding you for being behind; it's blessing you for arriving. Your breath isn't a task; it's a homecoming. With each inhale, you gather yourself. With each exhale, you release what was never yours to carry. Before sleep tonight, take three more breaths. My love, tell yourself: *I am not behind. I am held. I am safe. I am home*

You don't have to prove you are worthy of rest. You already are.

Day 53 – Chakra Soul
Movement: Speaking Truth

Let yesterday's warm shawl of peace stay around your shoulders. Breathe. Nothing to prove. Place a hand near your throat and notice how your pulse keeps time for you—faithful, steady. We'll meet that rhythm with a quiet hum and let your truth remember the way out.

Invitation:
- Stand tall with your feet grounded.
- Place your fingertips lightly at your throat.
- Inhale through your nose, feeling your chest expand.
- As you exhale, gently hum — a soft vibration awakens your voice.
- Repeat for seven breaths, letting the hum grow steadier each time.

This is your reminder: what you have to say matters. The world needs the sound of your truth.

MANTRA:

My voice is sacred. My truth is a gift, and the world is blessed when I let it be heard.

Day 54 – Soul Whisker

Permission to Curl Up

Some days your body whispers, "enough."

Cat: You don't have to chase shadows—tuck into the softest spot and let the world keep spinning without you.

"Curl first, explain never. Rest doesn't make you less; it makes you ready."

Soul Whisker:
Curl up without apology; the world can wait while you purr.

Day 55 – Sacred Sips Moment

The Warmth in Your Hands

Before you even drink, notice the warmth of the cup in your hands. Let it seep into your palms, your fingers, your skin. This simple warmth is a reminder — you are alive, you are here, you are being held.

The tea itself is medicine, yes. But so is the comfort of touch, the reassurance that warmth is always within reach.

My darling, let today's sip remind you: you don't have to search far for love — it can be felt in the palms of your hands.

TRUTH DROP:

I no longer pour all my warmth outward and leave myself empty. I cup my own heart first and fill it with love. What I have been giving to another, I now give to myself — freely, tenderly, without apology.

Day 56 – Truth Drop

Words as Wands

At the heart of her morning, something shifted. A woman catches herself mid-sentence at the kitchen table, saying something harsh about her own body without even thinking. Her daughter looks up, startled, and for a moment she realizes how easily words slip out like sparks from a fire — and how quickly they land. Midlife has taught her that the self-talk she thought was private actually shapes her mood, her energy, even the atmosphere in the room.

Every word you speak is alive. It carries energy into the room, into your body, into the ears and hearts of those who hear it. Words are medicine — or poison. They can heal, bless, soothe… or wound and diminish. Most of us toss words out like pebbles, unaware of the ripples they create. But in truth, you hold a wand in your mouth. Each phrase you whisper over yourself becomes a spell, shaping the way you feel, the way you rise, the way you see the world.

This isn't about perfection; it's about remembering your power. Even small shifts — replacing one self-criticism with one blessing — can redirect the current of your day. Midlife especially invites this reprogramming: to stop rehearsing self-attack and start practicing self-blessing.

Pause with me now. Inhale slowly, exhale gently, and whisper: *"My words are spells of love."* Feel the vibration move through your chest and out into the space around you.

TRUTH DROP:
I choose my words as medicine — weaving love first over myself, then into the world around me.

Day 57 – Surprise Soul Whisper

The Note on Your Mirror

Morning light slides across the bathroom sink. Steam curls up from your tea. You lean close to the mirror and pause — catching the face you've lived inside for decades. The jowls you never imagined would soften. The lines you didn't ask for. A stranger, and yet still you. For a moment you want to look away.

But wait. Place a hand flat against the glass. Feel the cool surface. Feel your own warmth beneath it. This is the woman who has carried children, dreams, disappointments, and secret hopes. This is the one who kept going when she didn't think she could. Time has touched her body, but it has not dimmed her soul. That light still flickers behind your eyes, waiting to be named.

Today, speak to her in writing. Just one line — a sentence you have longed for someone else to whisper to you:

"I honor the woman I've become."
"My beauty has grown roots deeper than skin."
"My soul is radiant and cannot be undone."

Write it on a sticky note. Tape it to the mirror. Slip it under your pillow. Or schedule it as a daily reminder for the next 30 days. My Darling, let your own words surprise you tomorrow, like a tender loving hand on your back reminding you what is true.

SOUL WHISPER:
My beauty has grown roots deeper than skin. My soul is radiant and cannot be undone.

Day 58 – Soul-to-Spirit Meditation

The Light Behind Your Eyes

Have you ever sat through a sudden power outage—one second the room is ordinary, the next it's swallowed by dark—and noticed how the smallest flame can redraw the whole world? You strike a single match and the edges return: the curve of a cup, the outline of a chair, your own hands. Nothing in the room changed; only the light that let you see it.

Midlife can feel like that blackout. Hormones shift, roles change, the map you used to trust blurs—and a quiet fear whispers that your glow has dimmed. But hear me, my beautiful soul: your light has not gone out. It's simply waiting for you to turn toward it. The illumination you're seeking isn't out there; it's the steady flame within—patient as a pilot light, faithful as dawn.

Close your eyes. Feel the quiet there. Behind your lids, there is a soft glow—a light that is always present, whether or not you notice it. It doesn't dim when you are weary. It doesn't vanish when you doubt yourself. It simply waits—steady, patient, eternal.

My Radiant one, this is your soul's flame—the light behind your eyes. You don't have to make it brighter. You only have to remember it is there.

Breathe here. Inhale and let the light expand. Exhale and let it soften into every corner of your being.

AFFIRMATION:
All I need is the light within.

Day 59 – Microdose Laugh-Lift

The Unstoppable Smile

Have you ever tried to hold back a smile and found it impossible? The corners of your mouth betray you, your cheeks ache, your eyes crinkle until laughter bursts through. That smile is medicine. It sneaks past the mind's heaviness and reminds the body of joy. Even science confirms it: when you smile, your brain releases feel-good chemicals that lift your mood, soften your breath, and calm your nervous system. You don't have to fake it — you only have to allow it.

We've all been taught to "keep it together," to save our smiles for the right moment. But your body longs for the opposite: spontaneous warmth, a softening of the face, a signal to your heart that it's safe to feel good. Smiles are contagious because they carry freedom. They ripple outward like sunlight spilling across a room, reminding everyone nearby that joy is not scarce — it's always within reach. Each smile is a quiet revolution against heaviness, a tiny rebellion of grace.

Today, give yourself permission to let the smile win. Even if it starts small, let it spread until it becomes laughter. Notice how your spirit lifts when you stop resisting joy. Watch how the atmosphere shifts — first inside you, then around you.

At some point today, pause, soften your jaw, and let a smile rise — at your reflection, at a stranger, at the sky itself. A smile is laughter's first language. Let it be your micro-dose of soul medicine

TRUTH DROP:
Go on- let your face misbehave. It's holy rebellion.

Day 60 – Soul Medicine Quote

"You are not behind—you are right on time for your own becoming."
—Dr. Jennifer Rademaker

A soul sister scrolls through her feed late at night. She cant sleep. Someone just got a promotion, another just launched a business, a friend posts photos of a perfect vacation, someone else is holding a newborn. In the quiet glow of her screen, the old thought surfaces: *I'm so behind. I should be further ahead by now.* Her shoulders tense. Her breath turns shallow. She forgets that her own life has been ripening beneath the surface — quietly, faithfully, in ways no one on a screen could ever see.

The world will try to convince you that you've missed it — that you're too late, too old, too far gone. Deadlines, social media, comparison, and regret whisper that everyone else is ahead of you. But your soul knows better. Beneath the noise it keeps whispering: *You are unfolding exactly as you should.*

The timing of your life is sacred. Every delay, every detour, every pause has been part of your ripening. What felt like wasted years were actually seasons of root and foundation. What felt like a setback was preparing you for the path opening now. You are not late. You are ready. Even the waiting has been a kind of midwifery, shaping you for what you are becoming.

Today, let yourself exhale the pressure to catch up. Feel your feet on the ground. Imagine roots from every season of your life weaving strength beneath you. Breathe in patience; exhale comparison. My beautiful soul sister, midlife isn't a finish line; it's a threshold into your fullest becoming.

TRUTH DROP:
You're not behind — you're right on time.

Day 61 – Soul Reflection

The Living Reminder

There are seasons when midlife can feel like a long stretch of grey—too much sameness, too much weight, too much loss of color. You wake up and the days blur together, heavy and unremarkable, and somewhere inside you wonder, *Have I gone missing from my own life?*

In those moments, your soul doesn't always need a grand solution. Sometimes, it longs for something as simple as bringing a little life home. A plant—green, alive, rooted. Not to decorate a corner, but to remind you that growth is still happening.

Imagine yourself walking into a nursery, pausing in front of rows of small plants. One will call to you. You'll carry it home, place it somewhere with light, and every time you walk past, it will whisper back: *I am growing. So are you.*

Today I opted for something fresh and new—something out of the ordinary. My soul gravitated to a lotus for what it represents. *Why not?* I thought. And when I brought her home, I realized: it's not about gardening—it's about presence. About creating a mirror in your home that reflects your own becoming. On the low-mood days, that little plant becomes a truth-teller, reminding you that what is tended thrives, and what thrives reflects back your own possibility.

Your lotus will thrive most where she is not only fed by sun and water, but where you feel her presence every day as a mirror of your own becoming—your own blooming

Day 62 – Affirmation + Reflection

The Ripening

Think of how fruit ripens on the branch. Some come early, some late; some need more sun, some more rain. None are "behind." Each carries its own season inside. The world may be loud with clocks and deadlines, whispering that you've missed your chance, that the best days are behind you. But your soul does not run on the world's time — it moves by its own sacred rhythm.

You are like that fruit on the branch, quietly gathering sweetness unseen. Every pause has been a season of deepening. Every delay has prepared you. Every detour has drawn out a flavor, a strength, a wisdom you could not have gathered any other way. You're not late — you're ripening. You're arriving right now, in this moment, and it is holy.

Take a breath. Place a hand over your heart. Whisper your affirmation and imagine your life as an orchard — each moment arriving in its perfect season, nothing rushed, nothing wasted. Feel the relief of stepping out of the world's clock and back into your own.

AFFIRMATION:
I am not too late. My soul is always on time.

Day 63 – Dear God Letter

Dear God,

There are moments when I feel invisible — as if my voice is swallowed by the noise of the world, as if my presence does not matter. My heart whispers that I'm here, but my mind wonders if anyone notices. And yet, somewhere deeper, I know this cannot be true.

Remind me that You see me. Remind me that my breath, my life, my soul are holy to You. Remind me that even when others overlook me, I am never hidden from Your love.

Teach me to honor my own presence as You do — to stand in the quiet confidence that I belong here, exactly as I am. Let me walk today knowing that my life carries a light only I can bring, a song only I can sing. May my invisibility become an invitation to turn inward, to find You, to find myself, and to know that being unseen by people is never the same as being unseen by Love.

For invisibility to another can become intimacy with You — and that is greater than any spotlight the world could ever offer.

With love, I release, reset, and rise.

And so it is. Amen

Day 64 – Chakra Soul Movement: Vision Within

"Where do you go to hear the whisper that knows?"

When the world feels loud, your inner voice can grow faint. You long for clarity but only hear static. The third eye — the *Ajna chakra*, resting between your brows — is your lantern of intuition. When you tend it, confusion softens. The veil lifts. Your guidance shines.

Today's practice is not about figuring it all out. It is a soul movement, a way of remembering.

Invitation:
- Choose soft music without words — something that feels like breath, like flowing water.
- Sit tall or stand steady on the ground.
- Close your eyes. Bring your focus gently to the space between your eyebrows.
- Inhale slowly, picturing a violet light glowing there — your intuition awakening.
- Exhale and let your body sway gently from side to side, as if moved by an unseen rhythm.
- With each sway, imagine Spirit meeting you here, sending love, wisdom, and guidance.

Breathe and move like this for a few minutes. Let the rhythm of the music, the breath, and the sway carry you. Each inhale brightens the indigo light. Each exhale clears away doubt. Feel how this gentle dance connects you back to your own knowing. When you turn away from the outer world and turn within here, what might this higher guidance be offering you?

I see with the eyes of my soul. Guidance flows to me with ease and love.

Day 65 – Soul Whisker

The Door Crack

Hello, my two-legged soul sister.

The second a closed door opens — even a whisker's width — I'm not sitting around. I slip through.

You've got doors too — tiny cracks of possibility. Don't overthink them. When life opens even an inch, slide through like me and run like a bandit. *Woohoo!* There's a whole world waiting on the other side: adventure, freedom, surprise.

SOUL WHISKER:
When a door cracks, squeeze through like a legend. Explore what's beyond, and play the game of- Catch Me If You Can.

Day 66 – Sacred Sips Moment

Pouring Out

Have you ever felt poured out — like there was nothing left to give? You've carried your husband, your children, your grandchildren, maybe even your aging parents, your coworkers, your home. You've given so much that by the time night falls, you wonder if there's anything left of you. I see you. I feel you. And I know the weariness in your bones.

Take a breath. Place your hands around the cup and feel its warmth seep into your palms. That warmth is a reminder — you are here, you are alive, you are being held. Let it soften your shoulders. Let it remind you: you have already done enough today. You are enough.

The world tells you to ration love, to guard it, to give it all away. But love isn't a bucket that runs dry. Love is a spring, steady and eternal, rising from within. And it flows not just for others, my darling, but for you. You are called to receive it, too.

So tonight, do something gentle for yourself. Take your cup into the bath. Wrap a shawl around your shoulders. Light a candle. Whisper to yourself: *"I did my best today, and that is enough."* Let the warmth of the tea and the water remind you — you are deserving of rest, of tenderness, of your own love.

Truth Drop:
Love within me is endless, rising to fill me as tenderly as I have poured out for others.

Day 67 – Truth Drop

The Present Moment Is the Only Power

When was the last time you truly felt yourself here — not replaying yesterday, not rehearsing tomorrow — just breathing the air of now?

The mind is a restless traveler. It sprints ahead into tomorrow, dragging bags of worry. It loops backward into yesterday, clutching regret. In between, you are left restless and scattered, as if life is happening somewhere else. But your soul whispers: *Now is where eternity lives.*

The present moment is not a waiting room. It is creation itself. Every breath, every heartbeat, every thought born in the now carries the power to shape your life. Here, in this instant, you are not late, not behind, not incomplete. You are a living seed of possibility, rooted in the only soil where anything can grow — the soil of this moment.

Pause and feel it. Place a hand over your heart and one on your lower belly and breathe deeply. Let your shoulders drop. Let your jaw unclench. Listen to the sounds around you. Feel the support beneath you. This is not a pause between "real" life. This is life. This is your point of power.

You don't have to fix the past or control the future. You only have to inhabit this holy moment fully. This is where your power lives, and where Spirit meets you with new strength.

TRUTH DROP:
I return to the now, where my soul's power waits for me.

Day 68 – Surprise Soul Whisper

The Pebble in Your Pocket

Yesterday reminded you: the present moment is the only power. What if you could carry that presence in your pocket today?

Slip a small stone or pebble into your pocket today. It doesn't have to be perfect or polished. A simple, ordinary stone picked up from the driveway or the edge of a path will do. The soul has a way of making the ordinary sacred.

Each time you feel its weight against your hand, let it whisper: *You are grounded. You are steady. You are here.* This tiny stone becomes a secret touchstone — a quiet anchor in the middle of your busy day. No one else has to know it is there. It's yours alone.

Every time your fingers brush the pebble, pause for one slow breath and silently repeat your whisper: *I am grounded in this moment, steady and whole.* Let its weight draw you back to yourself. Let it steady your nervous system and remind you that you belong here, exactly as you are.

You don't need a perfect meditation or a long retreat to reconnect with yourself. My darling, Sometimes the simplest object becomes holy when you allow it to carry truth. Each time you touch that stone, breathe — and remember: *I carry the glow of every woman who came before me.*

SOUL WHISPER:
I am grounded in this moment, steady and whole.

Day 69 – Soul-to-Spirit Meditation

The River of Calm

When was the last time you let go of control and simply allowed yourself to be carried by life's flow?
When was the last time you lay on the earth and felt it holding you, rather than you holding the weight of the world?

Close your eyes, my luminous one. Picture a wide, gentle river winding through a quiet forest. The water is clear and slow, glinting with soft light. Birds sing beyond the banks. A breeze moves the leaves but does not disturb the water's surface.

Now imagine that this river runs through you. It isn't rushing. It isn't storming. It's simply there — a steady stream of peace flowing from your crown to your toes. Each inhale draws from its waters. Each exhale releases into its flow. With every breath, you merge with its rhythm.

At some point today, run your hands slowly under cool water, imagining the energy of that river is part of you. Let its calm move through your body and into the rest of your day.

This river is your soul's calm — eternal, unbroken, always replenishing itself. No matter the noise of the world, no matter the weight of your thoughts, the river remains. Always there. Always enough. Its banks hold you. Its waters cleanse you. Its current carries you toward stillness.

You don't have to fix, force, or strive. You only have to float. Let your body soften as if you're being held in water. Feel the current moving under you, around you, through you. Rest here for a few breaths, remembering.

AFFIRMATION:
I surrender into the calm river of my soul.

Day 70 – Microdose Laugh-Lift

"Joy is not a performance; it's a release"

Midlife teaches us to "hold it together"—face composed, shoulders tight. But what if the medicine today is to let one thread loosen so the whole knot can breathe?

Think of a summer storm: heavy air, cloudy sky, dreary mood— and then, right out of the blue, a sudden break of sun makes the street gleam and the children laugh. Laughter does that inside you. It's the sun-break after the storm.

Try this with me:
Find a private spot. Place one hand on your belly and one over your heart. Inhale gently through your nose. As you exhale, let a small "ha" escape—awkward is fine. Inhale again, let it grow: *ha-ha…* shoulders bouncing. On the third breath, intentionally let out a *hahaha*—let the laugh roll, unpretty or real, body-shaking. Try to keep it going for about a minute, as if you're shaking rain from a coat… *haha*.

When it settles, notice the warmth in your chest, the space behind your eyes, the glistening afterglow. Thank God for intentional, out-of-the-blue laughter. It feels good, doesn't it? We all long to feel good.

Each on-purpose laugh tells your nervous system: *I am safe to feel good*.

Laugh on purpose and let joy loosen what worry has knotted.

Day 71 – Soul Medicine Quote

"Like any flower, the soul does not bloom under pressure — it blooms in presence."
—Dr. Jennifer Rademaker

We've been taught to push, to hustle, to force our way forward. We measure our worth by our productivity and our pace. But the soul doesn't bloom like that. A flower never strains to open; it simply unfolds when the light and warmth are right. Its roots reach quietly for what nourishes them. Its petals unfurl when the time is kind.

My darling, your becoming is no different. You don't have to force your growth. You don't have to grip or strain or meet some invisible deadline. You only have to rest in presence — to root where you are, to breathe in the moment, to trust that what is meant for you will rise in its season. Presence, not pressure, is the sunlight your soul needs.

Pause now. Imagine yourself as a sunflower turning softly toward the light, opening at exactly the right moment… simply because you are.

TRUTH DROP:
I bloom in presence, not pressure.

Day 72 – Soul Reflection

The Old Swing

There was an old swing in her backyard — the ropes frayed,
the wooden seat weathered by years of rain and sun.
She hadn't touched it in decades. It had become part of the
scenery, a forgotten relic of a younger time.

One warm afternoon she walked past it, distracted by her
list of errands. But something stirred. She brushed off the
seat, sat down, and pushed off gently. The ropes creaked,
the ground tilted away, and a soft rush of air touched her
face. For a moment, she was a child again — toes reaching
for the sky, hair flying back, heart wide open.

In that moment, she remembered: the dreams she once
carried, the freedom she thought she had lost, the giggle
hiding behind her ribs. It was all still there — waiting for her
to sit down and move again.

Your soul hasn't forgotten joy. It waits patiently,
like that swing, until you return. Joy isn't gone; it rests inside
you, like sunlight within a seed, ready to awaken.

Brush off your own "old swing" — whatever simple thing once
lit you up — and let your spirit feel the wind again. Skip a
stone, swing your arms while you walk, or revisit one small
pleasure from your younger self. Let your body remember
what unforced joy feels like.

REFLECT:
*What simple thing from your past could you revisit today to
remind your soul that joy is still alive in you?*

Day 73 – Affirmation + Reflection

The Lantern

In the dark, it's easy to stumble, to feel lost, to forget the path.

We think if we could just see the whole road we'd feel safe. But the soul is like a lantern — you may not always see far ahead, but the glow you carry is enough for the next step. Where in your life do you need to trust the lantern you already hold, instead of waiting for a floodlight to show the whole way?

Picture yourself holding that lantern. Its light may seem small, but notice how it softens the darkness nearest you, how it warms your hands, how it makes each step clear as you walk. That is how guidance works. It rarely arrives as a floodlight showing the entire map. It comes as a quiet glow, just bright enough for the present moment.

You don't need tomorrow's answers today. You don't need the whole map to begin. Your light — even if it feels fragile — is a living flame within you, and it will always be enough to guide your next move. Trust it. Lift it. Walk by it. One step at a time, your way will appear.

Today, when you feel unsure, pause. Close your eyes, and with one slow breath, imagine a small lantern glowing in your hands. Silently repeat your affirmation before you take your next step.

AFFIRMATION:
I trust the light within me. It always guides me on the right path.

Day 74 – Dear God Letter

Dear God,

There are days I feel small—like my voice won't matter, like my steps won't leave a mark. And yet, when I turn to You, I am reminded: I am not here by accident. I am here because You breathed life into me.

Release me from what I cannot do, and reset my mind to focus on what I can do. Lift my eyes from what I lack and steady them on what I carry—Your Spirit, alive within me.

Help me trust that even the smallest seed planted with love can grow into something eternal. When I forget my worth, remind me: I am Yours. When I question my path, remind me: You walk with me.

With love, I release, reset, and rise.

And so it is. Amen.

AFFIRMATION:
I am not small—I am a vessel of divine life.
You are the light of the world. —Matthew 5:14

Day 75 – Breath Practice / Ritual Reset

The Cleansing Exhale

Yesterday you prayed for release and remembered your light. Today, let that prayer move through your body—one breath at a time. Your body knows how to release what the mind tries to hold. Each exhale is a letting go, a natural surrender. When you breathe with intention, you give your soul permission to unclench and make room for what nourishes you now.

Here's a simple way to try it:

- Sit or stand where you feel supported.
- Inhale slowly through your nose, filling your lungs fully and completely; hold for a few seconds.
- Open your mouth and exhale with a soft sigh, as though fogging a window.
- Repeat this for seven breaths, each exhale carrying away what no longer nourishes your soul and what your heart is ready to lay down.

Each sigh is a cleansing stream, carrying tension back into the earth. Every breath out creates space for Spirit to move in. Feel how, with each release, your chest softens and your body remembers its natural rhythm.

SOUL WHISPER:
With each exhale, I release what weighs me down. I reset in truth, and I rise in freedom.

Day 76 – Chakra Soul Movement

Fire in the Belly

When you've laid down the weight of what isn't yours, what begins to rise within you? The Solar Plexus, just above your navel, is the center of your personal power—your courage, confidence, and inner fire. When this flame burns steady, you remember who you are.

Here I invite you to:
- Play music without words. Stand tall, feet grounded.
- Place both hands just above your belly button.
- Inhale, pulling your elbows back, chest lifted.
- Exhale, pressing your palms forward, as though pushing away fear.
- Repeat 7 times, moving with strength and intention.

Visualization:

With each inhale, imagine a golden flame glowing brighter in your belly. With each exhale, see it expand, filling your whole body with warmth and light. Let it remind you: your power is not outside of you—it has always been within.

Your fire is steady, your light is unshakable

Mantra:
The flame of my soul is strong, and it fuels my life.

Day 77 – Soul Whisker

The Cat Who Waits

Hello, my two-legged soul sister.
I can stare at a door for twenty minutes… then walk off like I never cared. That's my secret: I move when I'm ready, not when the world expects me to.

Try that. Stop pacing. Stop panicking. What's meant for you will come — and if not, take a nap. Another sunbeam always shows up.

Soul Whisker:
Patience is power — nap now, pounce later.

Bonus paw-tip::
If anyone asks what you are doing, flick your tail, look away and let them wonder.

Day 78 – Sacred Sips Moment

The Steam Rising

If your anything like me, some days you may feel worn down, as if rising takes more effort than you have. Maybe you're standing at your kitchen counter right now, hands wrapped around a mug, longing for something — anything — to lift you.

On a cold day, have you ever watched steam rise from a cup of tea? It curls upward in graceful swirls, dancing with the air. It doesn't force itself. It doesn't strain to be noticed. It simply lifts, warmed by the source within it.

Your soul is the same. When you are warmed by love, compassion, and truth, you rise without struggle. You don't have to push your way up; you are lifted by what fills you. Just as the steam rises effortlessly, so do you when your heart is heated by God's presence, Spirit's truth, and kindness poured back into your own cup.

Pause now. Breathe in slowly, inhaling the scent of the tea. Hold the cup closer to your heart and notice the warm comfort it gives — like a quiet embrace, reminding you that you are held, too. This simple act of sipping is not just tea — it's a reminder: rising is not an act of willpower; it's a natural response to being filled.

The same God who warmed the sun and set the steam placed His warmth inside you. Keep filling yourself with what lifts you. You won't have to strive your way upward; you'll be carried on the updraft of grace.

TRUTH DROP:
I rise with ease when I am filled with love.

Day 79 – Truth Drop

The Mirror of Thought

Have you noticed how your thoughts speak to you when you look in the mirror? Do they lift you the way the steam did, or do they weigh you down? Every thought you think is like light hitting a mirror; it reflects back to you, shaping what you see and how you feel. When you linger on fear, fear seems to grow. When you linger on love, love multiplies. This isn't magic or punishment, it's a principle of creation. The universe is a mirror. It returns what you pour into it.

Midlife, often feels like standing in a mirror-filled room. The body changes. The seasons shift. You see new lines on your face, a different rhythm in your energy. Menopause can feel like a breaking—but it's also a becoming. These years are not a signal that you're fading; they're an invitation to reflect differently. When you change your inner dialogue—what you think about your worth, your beauty, your timing, the reflection changes too. What you bless, blesses you. What you curse, becomes heavier.

This is not about pretending everything is perfect. It's about gently choosing the thoughts you want mirrored back to you. If you want to see peace, sow peace. If you want to see joy, tend to joy. If you want to see strength, speak to yourself as if you are already strong. This is how Spirit's goodness manifests in your body and your world.

Pause now. Place a hand over your heart and one over your lower belly, the seat of your creative power—and whisper your affirmation. Feel how even in this season, you are creating a new reflection with each thought.

"Ask, and it will be given to you; seek, and you will find; knock, and it will be opened to you." —**Matthew 7:7**

Day 80 – Surprise Soul Whisper

Release what no longer fits

Sometimes the most sacred growth isn't what we add—it's what we finally allow to fall away.

Midlife reinvention is a subtraction game.

Micro-practice:
Create a "Stop-Doing" list (3 items). Circle the easiest one and stop today—with love.

Day 81 – Soul-to-Spirit Meditation

The Garden Within

When was the last time you paused long enough to feel the garden of your own heart — the place where life is quietly blooming inside you?

Close your eyes, my beautiful soul, and picture a secret garden nestled within your chest. The soil is dark and rich, warm to the touch. Paths of moss wind between beds of flowers. Some blossoms open brightly to the sun; others are still tucked in their little buds, waiting for their time. You can almost hear the soft hum of bees, the whisper of wind moving through leaves.

Breathe slowly. As you inhale, imagine drawing in the fragrance of fresh lavender from this inner garden — its calm, clean scent filling your lungs. As you exhale, picture yourself gently watering the flowers. With each breath, the garden stirs, alive with quiet beauty. Maybe you even notice a butterfly drifting past, reminding you how transformation is always happening, often in silence, often unseen.

Stay here for a few moments. Let your shoulders soften, your belly loosen, your mind quiet. Notice how, as you release tension, your soul is even more open for Spirit to move through.

When you open your eyes, carry this truth: the garden within you is beautiful, and alive.

AFFIRMATION:
My soul is beautiful and whole, blooming with Spirit's life.

Day 82 – Microdose Laugh-Lift

The Intentional Laugh

When was the last time you laughed on purpose, not because something was funny, but because your body needed to remember joy. So often the weight of midlife rests heavy in your shoulders, your chest, even your jaw. You carry so much, and laughter slips quietly to the side. But intentional laughter — chosen laughter — is medicine for your soul.

Close your eyes and take a slow breath in. As you exhale, let the sound come out — not as a sigh, but as a laugh. Even if it feels awkward at first, let it rise. Start with a soft *ha… ha…* and let it grow louder, fuller, freer. Imagine the sound bouncing off the walls, shaking loose the heaviness you didn't even realize you were holding.

Keep going for a minute. Feel your shoulders soften, your chest lighten, your spirit begin to glow. This isn't forced — it's remembering. Laughter is a natural reset, coded into your being. It tells your nervous system: *It's safe to release. It's safe to feel good.*

Laughter with intention turns heaviness into light. It's like a soul massage — untying the knots of your heart without a single word. Let this practice remind you: joy is not gone. Joy is still here, waiting for you to let it out.

Truth Drop:
At midlife, fun is no longer optional — it is soul medicine.

Day 83 – Soul Medicine Quote

"The light you seek has always been inside you — it was never missing."
—Dr. Jennifer Rademaker

There was a time you thought you had to earn your glow. You looked for it in the best social media posts you could share, in relationships, or in someone else's eyes. You tried to be a certain weight, hold a certain title, wear the right mask. Each time you found a little flicker of validation, it felt good for a moment, but it faded — because it wasn't rooted in you.

Your soul has been whispering all along: *look within.* The light you've been chasing is not out there. It burns in you still — steady, unbroken, waiting for your gaze to turn inward. Like a candle hidden behind your own hands, its glow has never gone out; it's only been shielded from your view by layers of expectation, lies, and self-doubt.

In midlife, when old roles shift and external markers fall away, you're invited to discover what was always true. This is the gift of this season: the chance to stop outsourcing your worth and start remembering your radiance. When you live from that place, you stop chasing and start radiating. Answers rise naturally, like dawn inside you. Your energy softens yet grows stronger at the same time.

Pause now. Imagine turning away from the outer world and its noise. Step inward as if opening a door to a quiet room where your light waits. Feel its warmth on your skin, its steadiness in your chest. This is your true guidance system — the flame that no loss, no season, no opinion can ever extinguish.

TRUTH DROP:
Our radiance is not something to find — it is something to remember.

Day 84 – Soul Reflection

The Broken Cup

One quiet morning a soul sister dropped her favorite cup — the one she held every day for tea, the one that had become part of her daily ritual. It hit the floor and cracked cleanly down the middle. Her first impulse was to sweep it up and throw it away. That's what we do with broken things, isn't it? We hide them. We discard them. We pretend they never existed.

But something in her hesitated. She picked up the pieces carefully, as if they were still precious. She rinsed them, dried them, and set them on the table. Later she learned of an old Japanese art called *kintsugi* — the practice of mending what's broken with gold. Instead of disguising the damage, you honor it. The seams become veins of beauty, the history of the object turned into its most treasured feature.

Your soul is no different. And neither is your body. Just as a cup's cracks can be filled with gold, so can the lines on your face hold the gold of experience — laughter etched at the corners of your eyes, resilience carved softly into your skin, silver in your hair- like threads of light. These are not flaws. They are shimmering seams of wisdom, proof that you have lived and loved and risen again.

Pause for a moment and place your hands over your heart. Imagine your own cracks and lines lined with warm, glowing gold — each scar a shimmering thread of wisdom. You are not diminished by what you've survived. You are illuminated. You are a living *kintsugi*, a masterpiece in progress.

My broken places are filled with gold and light

Day 85 – Affirmation + Soul Reflection

The Open Hand

Have you ever noticed how hard it is to hold anything new when your fists are clenched around what you already have? We grip so tightly — a role, a relationship, a way of doing things — thinking that if we loosen our hold, it will all slip away. But a closed fist can only keep; it can never receive. Where are you clinging too tightly in your own life right now, and how might opening your hands change what flows toward you?

An open hand is not a sign of weakness; it is a sign of trust. It says: *I believe there is enough. I believe what is truly mine will stay. I believe more is on its way.* Living with open hands doesn't mean you never feel fear or loss. It means you choose to let Spirit place new blessings where you've made space. It means you stop trying to control the outcome and start welcoming the unfolding.

Your life, like your hands, is not meant to stay clenched. It's meant to open and close with the rhythm of giving and receiving — a holy circulation. The more you open, the more you discover that what is yours will always find its way back, and what is ready to leave will do so with grace.

Pause now and literally open your hands, palms up. Feel the air, the soft stretch in your fingers. Imagine a gentle breeze moving across your palms, clearing away what no longer nourishes you and making room for something new. Breathe in deeply, exhale slowly, and whisper your affirmation.

AFFIRMATION:
I live with open hands- an open heart. I am ready to divinely receive.

Day 86 – Dear God Letter

When the world grows noisy, my soul feels like a bird fluttering against a windowpane — wings beating, searching for a way out, forgetting there's a sky already above me. I reach for more doing, more control, more proof, as if peace lives somewhere out there. And yet, deep inside, I know: You are my wholeness. I can never be separated from the Source of my life.

So, I pause now. I close my eyes and feel the warmth of Your presence — not distant, but here, moving through my breath, steady beneath my heartbeat. Like a gentle tide rolling in, you quiet my restless waves. Like sunlight pouring through closed blinds, you find the cracks and soften the room.

Teach me to return to this remembering. Quiet my mind when it wants to grasp, to fix, to prove. Steady my heart when it forgets that love is already flowing, already enough. Let me see the world today not through the eyes of uncertainty, but through the lens of Your eternal love.

Help me remember there is no separation. You and I are one. When I abide in that truth, I do not chase wholeness — I live from it.

With love, I release what was, reset my mind, and rise anew.

And so it is, Amen.

"My Father and I are one." —John 10:30

Day 87 – Breath Practice / Ritual Reset

The Pause Between

Have you ever noticed the quiet that lives between your breaths? Breath is more than the inhale and the exhale. It is also the pause in between — the stillness, the gap, the space where nothing happens and yet everything is held. In that quiet, your nervous system softens, your mind is soothed, and Spirit whispers.

Today, let your breath teach you how to rest inside the pause:

Invitation:

- Inhale gently through your nose for a count of 4.
- Hold softly at the top for a count of 2 — the sacred pause.
- Exhale slowly through your mouth for a count of 6.
- Let your breath return to its natural rhythm for a moment — resting in the sacred pause — before beginning again.
- Continue this rhythm for 7 breaths, noticing how your body settles deeper with each cycle and how much stiller you are after.

You don't have to fill every silence. The pause is sacred. It holds you as surely as the breath itself. In that stillness between movements, grace meets you and helps you let go. My love, rest in knowing that as you release, you are being held.

Soul Whisper:
I honor the pause; it is my sacred rest, and rest is holy.

Day 88 – Chakra Soul Movement

Opening the Heart

When was the last time you gave your heart a moment to breathe — to open, soften, and feel calm again?

Your Heart Chakra is the bridge between earth and Spirit — the meeting place of human and divine love. When it opens, forgiveness flows, compassion deepens, and connection feels safe again. This is not about forcing yourself to "be loving." It's about allowing the love within you to rise and move through you.

Before you begin, put on gentle, heart-opening music — something that feels like green light in sound: soft strings, piano, or a hymn you love.

Invitation:

- Stand or sit with your shoulders relaxed.
- Place your palms together at your heart center.
- Inhale as you press your palms gently into one another, feeling the warmth between them.
- Exhale as you open your arms wide, chest lifted, as if embracing the world.
- Repeat 7 times, moving with tenderness and letting the music carry you. When you finish, bring your palms softly back to your heart.

  Feel the quiet pulse beneath them — the reminder that your heart still beats in rhythm with the divine. Let that be your closing breath before the visualization begins.

Visualization:

With each inhale, see a green light glowing in your chest. With each exhale, imagine it radiating outward, wrapping you — and those you love — in warmth and compassion. Let it soften old walls around your heart, creating space for new connections and self-acceptance.

My radiant one, your heart is not fragile. It is resilient, radiant, and designed to expand. Even after loss, even after hurt, it knows how to open again.

Day 89 – Soul Whisker

The Curious Cat

You, soul sister: "I want to try something new, but I don't know, I feel like it's too late—and a little foolish. What if I don't belong there?"

Cat: "Put me in a new room and I sniff every corner. I don't ask permission; I explore. Curiosity isn't childish, it's sacred. Take one tiny step of wonder: read the note, send the message, peek through the doorway. If it leads nowhere, no shame—stretch, nap, and call it scouting. Let curiosity, not worry, lead."

SOUL WHISKER:
A tail flick from the universe: slow down, play more

Reset — Winter

*My **beautiful soul**...*

You've stepped into the season of Reset.

Like the hush of fresh snow blanketing the earth, this is your sacred pause — a time to slow the rhythm of your days and let your inner world grow quiet enough to hear its own wisdom.

In midlife, the world may tell you to keep pushing, but Spirit whispers *rest is holy; stillness is fertile.*

As you walk this path, give yourself a gentle wintering moment. Close your eyes. Inhale softly through your nose. Place a warm hand over your heart, feeling the steady pulse beneath. Exhale as if you're melting the ice of old tension. Whisper, *"I am safe to reset."* When you're ready, let your hand fall softly back to your lap, trusting that the warmth remains, quietly renewing you from within.

Here you'll find prayers, reflections, and rituals to soothe your nervous system and rewrite-tired patterns. Each entry is a hearth-fire for your soul, inviting you to be held, not hurried.

Even now, life is working quietly beneath the surface. Trust the pause. Trust the unseen roots.

AFFIRMATION: *I am safe and calm to reset and let stillness renew me.*

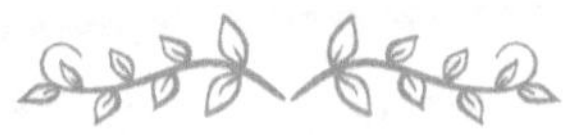

Day 90 – Truth Drop

Maybe lately you've wondered if your best years are behind you… if what's possible for you has already passed. Perhaps you've felt invisible, or that what you most need lives somewhere outside of you.

But even Scripture whispers the truth: *"God is love."* (1 John 4:8)

That Love is not only what God gives — it is who God is. And because God is the Source, you were manifested out of that same essence. You are a daughter of the Divine, created from the fullness of God's being.

When the masks of fear creep in, they try to convince you of separation, lack, or limitation. But metaphysical truth says otherwise: there is only One Presence and One Power. That One lives in you, as you. Which means your second half of life is not empty, but overflowing with possibility.

Today, pause for one slow breath. Place a hand over your heart and whisper: *"I was manifested by God — my Source is within me."* Let this remembering loosen doubt, soften uncertainty, and expand your imagination for what is still to come.

PRESCRIPTION FOR YOUR SOUL – TRUTH DROP:
I was manifested by God. I am an expression of the One Presence, unlimited in possibility.

Day 91 – Surprise Soul Whisper

The Candle Flame

Yesterday you remembered where you came from — Love itself. Today, let's remember what that Love looks like when it burns inside you.. Light a candle and watch the flame. Notice how it flickers with the air, yet never forgets its purpose — to shine.

Soul sister, you are the same. Life may bend you, winds may swirl around you, but the light within remains faithful. You don't have to be unshaken to be radiant; you only need to stay in touch with the flame God placed inside you.

This tiny fire is a teacher. It shows you how to be soft and strong at once — responsive, but never extinguished. It reminds you that warmth travels farther than words, and that a steady glow changes a whole room without raising its voice. Midlife asks for this kind of luminosity: less proving, more presence; less fuel spent on fear, more oil saved for light.

Micro-Practice: Tending Your Inner Flame (3 minutes)

Kindle — Strike the match. As the wick catches, whisper, *"I choose light."* Let your first breath be slow and generous.

Steady — Bring one hand to your heart, one to your belly. Inhale for four, hold for two, exhale for six — three times. Imagine your breath feeding the flame, fanning your fears.

Carry — Cup the candle with your hands (without touching the glass) and ask: *"Where will I bring this light today?"* Name one small act — an honest word, a gentle boundary, a moment of kindness — and commit to it.

Let the glow remind you: you don't have to blaze to bless. A steady flame is enough.

Day 92 – Soul-to-Spirit Meditation

The Gentle Snowfall

The steady flame within you softens into another kind of stillness — a quiet that drifts, cool and slow, like snowfall for the soul. I grew up in Newfoundland and Labrador, an island held by the cold North Atlantic. Winter didn't just visit for a season; it moved in and stayed. January through May — snow upon snow. By midsummer, icebergs still floated in the water, remnants of winter's grip.

I remember pulling a snowsuit over my Halloween costume before heading into the night air. Those winters were harsh, yet also magical: the way snow could hush everything, even the noise inside you.

Now, living in Florida, there is no snow outside my window. But my soul still remembers. And I want to share that memory with you as a meditation.

Close your eyes. Imagine a gentle snowfall happening inside you. Each flake is a thought, drifting slowly down, quieting as it lands. No rush. No noise. Just a hush of white silence — a tender stilling of everything that felt urgent. With every inhale, picture more snowflakes falling softly. With every exhale, feel the air grow calmer inside your chest.

Then, imagine yourself stepping into a warm room. A fire glows. A mug rests between your palms. A soft blanket wraps your shoulders. A candle flickers nearby. Outside may be ice and wind, but inside it is quiet and warm.

This is what your inner winter feels like — a hush that welcomes you back to yourself. You don't have to wait for a snowy day; you can create this refuge anytime you close your eyes and breathe.

TRUTH DROP:
No matter where I live, no matter what season I'm in, peace is always present within me

Day 93 – Microdose Laugh-Lift

The Fire of Laughter

When winter settles in, everything slows. The trees stand bare. The light fades early. The air feels still and heavy. In these months it's easy to let your own warmth dim, to forget that joy lives inside you like a small hearth fire waiting to be stirred.

My darling, laughter can be your fire. Even in the stillness of winter, a single chuckle can thaw the ice around your heart. Think of a cat stretching in a sunbeam, or a friend's unexpected joke that makes you snort your drink through your nose — the body can't help but respond. Shoulders drop. Chest softens. Eyes crinkle. Spirit brightens.

Today, give yourself permission to light that fire intentionally. Sit comfortably and take a slow breath in, holding it for a sacred pause. Then let it out with a sound: *ha… ha…* Begin with a quiet chuckle. Let it rise into a giggle. Let it grow into a full belly laugh, even if it feels silly at first. Imagine each laugh as sparks flying from a fireplace, warming your whole being.

Laughter on purpose is not just for the easy days; it is medicine for the heavy ones. Even in winter, you can laugh yourself back into light.

And hey! You're allowed to be unfinished art and still hang proudly in the gallery. Ha…ha…

PRESCRIPTION FOR YOUR SOUL – TRUTH DROP:
I laugh with intention, and joy warms me from within.

Day 94 – Soul Medicine Quote

"Rest is not weakness — it is holy soil where your strength grows."
—Dr. Jennifer Rademaker

Are you sick and tired of being sick and tired, just fed up with it all? When was the last time you let yourself truly rest — not because you'd earned it, not because you were exhausted, but simply because your soul was calling for it?

My darling soul sister, the world has taught you to measure worth by how much you do, how well you hold it all together, how quietly you carry the weight. In midlife — especially in this sacred season of menopause — the body whispers another truth: *Slow down. Lay it down. Let me reset.* Yet because we've been trained to see stillness as laziness, we push harder, even as our spirit longs for pause.

But winter teaches this again and again: what looks still is secretly alive with renewal. Beneath the frozen ground, roots deepen. Sap gathers. Buds form silently, unseen. The pause is not an ending; it is a preparation. You may feel behind, but Spirit says you are right on time. You are not forgotten. You are planted — and soon you will bloom.

Place a hand over your heart and another on your belly. Feel your quiet rhythm — steady, patient, waiting. You are not falling behind; you are fertilizing your future.

TRUTH DROP:
Rest is a revolution disguised as a nap.

Day 95 – Soul Reflection

The Seed Beneath the Snow

Beneath the frozen ground, a seed waits. Snow presses down like a velvet weight, muffling every sound. Above, winds howl and storms rage; below, in the hush and darkness, life is quietly at work. Roots reach into the unseen soil long before a green shoot ever breaks the surface. The seed does not despair. It trusts an invisible season.

Midlife can feel like this winter ground. Dreams hidden. Voice muted. Responsibilities piled like drifts of snow. You may wake in the night and wonder, *Has it all passed me by? Is there still time for me?* You've given so much, carried so much, smiled when your heart was tired. A part of you longs to exhale and be held, to believe there is still a spring for you.

My darling, listen. Spirit whispers in your winter: *"I have not left you. What I planted in you is alive. Every prayer, every tear, every quiet act of faith is a root reaching deeper. Your season will come."*

Pause now. Place one hand over your heart, one over your belly. Breathe slowly. Feel the warmth of your own touch melting the chill of doubt. With each inhale, draw up strength from deep within. With each exhale, whisper: *"The warmth of my touch is melting the chill of my doubt."*

Soon—sooner than you think—your life will crack open like that seed, and a tender green shoot will reach for the light. You will know the waiting was not wasted.

Affirmation:
I trust the unseen seasons of my growth. My roots are deep; my bloom is inevitable.

Day 96 – Affirmation + Reflection

Open to What Wants to Arrive

Winter is the season when the soil rests so new life can take root. In midlife, Reset feels like this quiet ground. It's not about prying anything open; it's about softening the nervous system so it can receive what is already on its way. Old patterns may rise like ghosts asking to be released, but their surfacing is a sign that your inner landscape is clearing.

Where could you allow more softness and space so Spirit can plant something new within you? What belief or habit is asking to be loosened so something truer can take its place?

An open palm receives what a tight grip cannot. When we cling to control, timelines, or outdated versions of ourselves, we block the flow of what Spirit longs to plant. Reset is a widening threshold. It is not the end of your blooming, but the deep inhale before your next fragrance is born. Letting go isn't weakness—it is creating sacred space for what is already arriving.

Pause with me. Place one hand over your heart, one over your belly. Breathe in the possibility that something good is already walking toward you. Breathe out the pressure to manage or predict it. With each exhale, whisper softly:
"In this stillness, I make room for what is meant for me."

Feel your body soften. Feel the warmth of your touch melting the urge to rush. In this surrender, your subconscious is resetting; new pathways are forming quietly, like roots beneath winter soil. You don't have to pry the future open—you only have to say yes when it knocks.

Affirmation:
I soften into stillness and open my whole being to what wants to arrive

Day 97 – Dear God Letter

Root Me Where I Belong

Dear God,

Some days I feel untethered—like I don't quite know where I fit. I stand between the woman I have been and the one I am becoming. I wake early and feel both full and empty at the same time. My feet are on the floor, but my spirit feels unsteady. The noise of the world pulls me in a thousand directions, and I ache for a place to land. I long for roots deeper than my fears—for a center I cannot misplace.

Ground me, Holy One. Root me in what is real. Let me remember the steady earth beneath me and the Love that carries me. Where I grasp, teach me to trust. Where I rush, teach me to breathe. Where I fear, teach me to rest. Remind me of the times You have already held me when I thought I could not go on. Whisper to me that Your timing is always kindness.

Plant me deep in Your presence so I may draw quiet strength, steady courage, and new joy. And if the winds return, let me bend but not break. Remind me that being grounded in You is not about stillness without movement, but about having roots even in the shifting.

Beloved God, even as I write this, I imagine You answering: *"Daughter, I am already holding you. Every root you seek is already in Me. Rest and grow."*

With love, I release, reset, and rise.

And so it is. Amen.

"For I know the plans I have for you," declares the Lord —Jeremiah 29:11 (NIV)

Day 98 – Soul Whisker

The Cat Who Masters the Nap

Hello, my two-legged soul sister.
You rush. You strive. You stack lists taller than a scratching post.
Me? I curl up in a sunbeam and reset my whole nervous system in twenty minutes flat. You call it "nothing." I call it essential maintenance.

I'm not lazy — I'm charging.

I know when to leap and when to rest. Most days? It's rest.

SOUL WHISKER:
Skip the extra coffee.. Reset like a cat — without apology.

BONUS PAW-TIP:
If they catch you snoozing, stretch dramatically…and pretend you were meditating

Day 99 – Sacred Sips Moment

The First Sip of a New Cup

There's something magical about the first sip from a new cup. The glaze is unmarked, the rim smooth, the scent rising warm and fresh. You cradle it in your hands and—just for a moment—pause before tasting. It feels like possibility, like a quiet promise whispered in steam: *"Here we begin again."*

Most mornings, I love to walk into my kitchen and choose the cup that will hold my first hot drink of the day. I often reach for the one that carries a word or truth on the outside, as if it's blessing the hours ahead. It's a small ritual, but it turns an ordinary morning into a moment of intention.

Midlife can feel like a cupboard of old cups—roles and routines you've been drinking from for years. Some are chipped. Some no longer fit your hands. Yet inside you runs a spring that never stops pouring, and Spirit delights in giving you new vessels. Today could be one of those moments: a first sip from a new chapter.

My darling soul sister, you haven't missed your moment. God hasn't forgotten you. Even if you've felt poured out, a fresh cup is already being placed in your hands. Let it be a prophecy over your life: new mercies rising with every morning, the best chapters of your story still steeping.

Beginnings don't have to be dramatic to be sacred. They can be as simple as a morning mug and a quiet breath. Every pause you choose makes space for something fresh to arrive.

With each sip, I welcome new beginnings and allow my life to unfold one moment at a time.

Day 100 – Truth Drop

The Law of Divine Timing

A seed does not rush its sprout, nor the moon its cycle. Everything unfolds in its appointed season. Spirit's timing is not delay—it is precision. Divine Timing is the invisible rhythm under everything you long for. When you learn to feel it instead of fight it, your nervous system shifts from bracing to trusting.

My beautiful soul, you may feel late, behind, or overlooked. Midlife often tells stories of running out of time—children grown, relationships shifting, careers changing. The subconscious quietly records: *I've missed my chance.* But Divine Timing whispers otherwise: *You are right on time.* Nothing meant for you will pass you by. The pause between desire and manifestation is not punishment—it is preparation.

Think of a seed in rich soil. It does not accuse the darkness; it draws strength from it. Roots form long before a sprout appears. What looks like stillness is sacred construction. Your seasons of pause are like that—hidden preparation for visible blooming.

Pause with me now. Imagine yourself as that seed. With every inhale, feel roots reaching deeper. With every exhale, release urgency like stale air. Whisper softly: *"I am right on time."*

You don't have to rush your becoming. Spirit's rhythm is holding you. Your life is unfolding with precision and grace. Nothing is wasted. Nothing is late. You are being prepared for what is already prepared for you.

TRUTH DROP:
Divine Timing is not delay—it is preparation. You are right on time.

Day 101 – Surprise Soul Whisper

Hold a makeup mirror and look into your own eyes.

What you see is not just flesh and years—it is soul, light, and Spirit staring back at you.

My darling, the mirror tells part of the truth, but never the whole story. It shows you the outer surface: the lines time has written, the curves of your body, the way your hair falls today. Sometimes, when you are tired or tender, it shows you only the shadows— the places you wish were different. But beneath the reflection is a deeper reality: you are more radiant than what the glass can hold. Your soul cannot be measured in wrinkles or weighed in years. You are eternal light housed in human form.

Close your eyes for a moment after looking. Place one hand on your heart and whisper inwardly: *"I see beyond the surface. I see my radiance."* Let yourself remember that the mirror is not a judge—it is an invitation. It invites you to soften, to bless the face that has carried you through every season, to honor the eyes that have cried and laughed, to cherish the skin that has kept you safe all these years.

Today, when you pass by a mirror, pause instead of rushing past. Gaze into your own eyes until you glimpse the eternal looking back. Let the reflection become a reunion—with your Spirit, with your worth, with the radiance that was never lost.

TRUTH DROP:
Every line on my face is a poem of courage.

AFFIRMATION:
I am more than what I see. I am soul—radiant and eternal.

Day 102 – Soul-to-Spirit Meditation

The Still Flow Within

Have you ever stood on a riverbank and watched the water glide by—steady, unhurried, shimmering with light? On the surface it seems simple, but beneath is an entire world of currents carving valleys, nourishing roots, and finding its way to the sea.

Midlife can feel like the opposite: choppy, noisy, full of demands. You may wonder if the quiet you long for still exists, or if the steady self you once knew has drifted away.

But the river holds a secret. It never stops moving, even under ice. It doesn't force its path; it shapes stone by flowing, not fighting. The same energy that created that river created you. That same quiet strength flows within your veins. Beneath your busy surface, Spirit is moving—carving new paths, feeding hidden roots, guiding you toward open water. You are not powerless. You are not behind. You are part of a greater flow that knows exactly where it's going.

Close your eyes and imagine that river inside you now. With each inhale, feel its coolness rising from your belly to your chest. With each exhale, let your shoulders soften as the water carries away what you no longer need. Stay here for a few breaths, resting in its steady stream.

Breathe in. Breathe out. Let your thoughts settle like snow falling on the riverbank. Even when you feel still on the outside, Spirit is always moving within you.

Stillness does not mean nothing is happening. Stillness means you are aligned with God's quiet strength.

❄

Today, as you pour a glass of water or let it run over your hands, pause for one slow breath and remember: the same power that carved rivers through stone created me, and that quiet strength flows in me now.

AFFIRMATION:
In stillness, I find God's presence flowing in me.
"Be still, and know that I am God." —Psalm 46:10

Day 103 – Microdose Laugh-Lift

The Girl Within

Close your eyes and remember her—the younger girl you once were. The one who laughed so hard her belly ached, who found silliness in the smallest things. She's still in there, waiting for your invitation.

Take a deep breath in. As you exhale, let her laugh rise. Maybe it starts as a giggle, maybe as a squeak, maybe as a wild belly laugh. Let it tumble out, even if it feels strange at first.

Soul Sister, the child within you has never left. Her joy is medicine for your present self. When you laugh with her, you remember that life has always carried delight—even now.

TRUTH DROP:
Your soul is still wild enough to surprise you.

AFFIRMATION:
The laughter of my younger self still lives within me.

Day 104 – Soul Medicine Quote

"Faith is not waiting for proof—it is walking as though the miracle is already here."
—Dr. Jennifer Rademaker

Faith is not about evidence. It's about trust—stepping forward even when you can't see the whole path.

When you walk in faith, you're saying to Spirit: *"I believe in Your timing, I believe in Your goodness, I believe Your promise."*

Faith is the soil where miracles grow.

My darling don't let doubt tell you it's too late. You are not behind—you are right on time. God has lined up the right people, the right opportunities, the right moments just for you. Keep walking in faith, because what you've been believing for is closer than you think.

AFFIRMATION:
I walk in faith, knowing my miracle is already unfolding.

TRUTH DROP:
You're not chasing time anymore – you're curating it.
Now faith is the substance of things hoped for, the evidence of things not seen.
—Hebrews 11:1

Day 105 – Soul Reflection

The Worn Path

Maybe lately you've felt like you're walking a path worn thin by responsibilities, routines, and all the things you've carried for so long. You pause and wonder if this is all there is—or if another way could still open for you.

There's a path through the woods, worn by countless footsteps. Morning fog drifts low, carrying the scent of pine and damp earth. You can see where others have walked—the flattened leaves, the marks of walking sticks, maybe even the faint echo of laughter. Their presence has made the way clear, even when you cannot see far ahead.

Midlife often feels like this. You stand at a crossroads: the safety of the known trail or the mystery of the sacred unknown. Part of you longs for the familiar; another part aches for what waits beyond. You don't always have to blaze the way alone. Sometimes wisdom is found in walking the softened path of those who came before— teachers, sisters, ancestors—guided all along by Spirit itself. Their footsteps steady yours, like unseen hands on your back.

And yet there are moments when the path disappears and only your heartbeat remains. This, too, is holy—the invitation to trust your inner compass rather than the map of anyone else. Spirit whispers: *"Beloved, I have walked every step with you; even the unmarked trail is no secret to Me."*

Pause now for one slow breath. Feel your feet against the floor as if on sacred ground. Imagine roots of courage reaching down while a faint glowing path appears with each inhale. Whisper: *"I honor the footsteps before me, and I trust the path my soul is creating."*

Soul Card Companion: No.24

❄

Day 106 – Affirmation + Reflection

Open Sky

Look up at the sky for a moment. Notice how it stretches without end, how clouds drift and light pours through without asking permission. The sky does not audition for its vastness. The ocean does not apply for depth. The mountains do not justify their height. Worthiness is not earned in nature; it is inherent

My radiant one, you too were born with that same inheritance. You do not need to earn your worthiness. You carry it by birthright. Yet after decades of caregiving, striving, and proving, the subconscious can quietly install a rule: *I must deserve my place. I must perform to belong.* Without noticing, you begin to ration self-acceptance the way some people ration joy. *What could shift in your life if you truly believed you are already worthy, without proving anything?*

Today, pause and let the open sky become your mirror. Feel your feet on the ground. Inhale slowly through your nose, imagining that vastness filling your chest. Exhale gently, releasing the old script of having to prove yourself. Place a hand on your heart and whisper inwardly: "I am worthy, simply because I am." Sense your shoulders drop, your jaw unclench, a little spaciousness opening inside you. This resets your nervous system learning: *worthiness is safe without performance.*

When you forget, remember the sky. Its worth is not questioned — it just is. So is yours. Each time you practice this, you anchor a new identity: not one who strives for permission, but one who lives from inherent value.

Affirmation (repeat):
I am worthy, simply because I am.

Day 107 – Dear God Letter

Dear God,

Today I lay my striving at Your feet. For too long I have believed I must carry the world alone — its schedules, its sorrows, its endless proving. My shoulders ache from lifting what was never mine to lift. My breath has grown shallow. My heart has learned to brace. I have forgotten, Beloved, that You are the strength beneath my weakness, the peace beneath my storm, the Love that holds what I cannot hold.

Quiet me now. Slow my racing thoughts. Soften the hard edges of my fear. Place Your hand upon my chest and remind me that even here, even now, I am not walking alone. Teach my nervous system what my soul already knows: *surrender is not defeat; it is the doorway to miracles.*

Lift from me the illusion of self-reliance. Pour into me a gentler rhythm — one of trust instead of tension, grace instead of grit. Let every exhale be a letting go of what was never mine; let every inhale be the receiving of Your Spirit.

And when I rise, let it not be by force, but by the quiet power of Your love moving through me. Let me walk through this day as a daughter of light, no longer braced against life but open to it — my heart steady, my hands unclenched, my soul at rest.

With love, I release.
With faith, I reset.
With grace, I rise.

And so it is. Amen

Day 108 – Breath Practice:
Breath of Renewal

Before you begin your breath practice, take a moment to imagine you are stepping into a quiet sanctuary.. The weight you've been carrying loosens its grip. In this sacred pause, there's nothing to fix, nothing to perform—only an invitation to arrive.

Midlife has a way of layering us with roles, responsibilities, and tired beliefs. We carry stories about who we have to be, and sometimes even our own breath becomes shallow under the pressure. But right here, in this moment, you have permission to set it all down. This is your space to be held, to exhale what is old and inhale what is alive and new.

You are not "doing" the breath so much as just being with it, receiving it—letting Spirit breathe you.

Inhale deeply, filling your lungs with new life.

Exhale slowly and longer, letting go of the stale air, the old stories.

With each cycle, feel Spirit resting your mind, and renewing you—not just in your body, but in your soul.

Invitation:

Inhale for 4, pausing to feel fullness.

Exhale for 8, letting everything old dissolve.

Repeat 7 times, imagining each breath as a fresh new beginning.

Every breath is proof that life is renewing you right now. You don't
have to wait for the future—renewal is here with every inhale, every
exhale.

<hr>

AFFIRMATION:
With every breath, I am made new.

TRUTH DROP:
Midlife isn't a crisis, it's a sacred recalibration.

Day 109 – Chakra Soul Movement

The Throat Chakra (Truth & Voice)

Have you ever been spoken over or made to feel so small that silence seemed safer than speaking? Midlife carries many of those echoes — the times you swallowed your truth, the words that trembled on your lips but never left.

But silence does not mean your voice is gone. The throat chakra is the sacred center of reset — where you can clear the residue of all that was unsaid and let truth flow again. My darling, spirit placed your voice here for a reason: not just for shouting, but for whispering, humming, and singing the sound of your soul.

So today, let this be your micro-reset: breathe, and let sound move through you.

Invitation:
- Sit or stand tall, shoulders relaxed.
- Inhale deeply, opening your chest.
- As you exhale, let sound rise in your throat — perhaps a soft *hummmm*, the ancient *ommm*, (or even humming along with a song you love.)
- Repeat 5–7 times, letting the resonance loosen the silence.

Visualization:
See a soft blue light swirling at your throat, glowing brighter with each sound. Feel the vibration ripple through your chest and rise into your head, like a river clearing stones in its path. With every hum, the residue of old silences lifts away, and your truth begins to flow freely again.

Your reset begins here — in this breath, in this sound, in the remembering that your voice matters.

I honor my truth and let my voice flow with clarity and love.

Soul Companion Card No. 34

Day 110 – Soul Whisker

The Cat Who Knows Boundaries

Hello, my two-legged soul sister.
Ever try to pet me when I'm done? One second I'm purring, the next I'm gone — tail flick, no speech, no guilt, no follow-up text. That's boundary mastery.

Boundaries aren't barbed wire. They're velvet ropes around your sacred energy. Like me, you're allowed to curl in when it feels good and leap away when it doesn't. Warm and loving doesn't mean doormat.

SOUL WHISKER:
For real, your soul approves this boundary.

Day 111 – Sacred Sips Moment

Savoring the Sip

So often, we rush through life the way we rush through a cup of tea—lift, gulp, empty,whats next?. We reach the bottom and hardly remember we drank it all. But your soul isn't meant to be hurried. It's longing to be present, to be nourished.

Today, let your cup teach you. Feel the heat of the mug against your palms. Watch the steam rise like a prayer. Take one slow sip, and let it roll over your tongue, warming you from the inside out. This simple act of savoring is soul medicine. It's how you tell life, "I am here. Im going to taste this moment fully."

When you savor, you slow down enough to notice the gift in front of you—the cup, the moment, the breath, the miracle of being alive. Each sip becomes a small altar where gratitude, presence, and joy meet.

I believe as you savor this sip, you're also savoring your own becoming. You're saying yes to living awake, to receiving more than you thought you deserved. The same God who created oceans and stars is meeting you right here—in your pause, in your breath, in your tea.

AFFIRMATION:
I savor life fully, one sip at a time.

Day 112 – Truth Drop

The Law of Abundance

Look at the sky limitless. Look at the ocean endless. Spirit has written abundance into creation itself. There is no shortage of beauty, of breath, of possibility. Even the air you're breathing now is evidence of this: you inhale and more arrives. You exhale, and you're still provided for.

Scarcity is a story the world teaches, but abundance is the truth your soul knows. Somewhere along the way, you were taught to ration your dreams, to brace for disappointment, to believe that there isn't enough—enough time, enough love, enough opportunity. But the deeper truth is this: there is always more than enough. The universe is not a closed jar; it's a living spring. When you align your thoughts with this truth, your eyes begin to see provision where you once saw lack, possibilities where you once saw walls, blessings where you once saw "just enough."

Pause for a moment. Place one hand over your heart and one on your belly. Breathe in slowly as if you're drawing in endless sky. Exhale and imagine releasing every old scarcity thought like dust leaving your body. With each inhale, silently whisper: *"There is enough."* With each exhale: *"I am enough."* Today, pick one small act of generosity—offer a kind word, share something you value, or simply smile at a stranger—and notice how it leaves you feeling fuller, not emptier. Let it be your living proof that abundance expands as it is given.

AFFIRMATION:
I live in an abundant universe. Love, time, and opportunity flow freely to me.

Day 113 – Surprise Soul Whisper

The Finger Snap Reset

Your mind can shift in an instant.
When a heavy thought whispers, **snap your fingers.**
That sound is the signal: *reset.*

Right there—between the snap and your next breath—
you hold the power to choose again.
Let that sound remind you: the story isn't fixed.
Energy follows focus.

So today, try this micro-miracle:
**"I will focus on what I can do, not what I can't.
And with the snap of my fingers, I'll take one small step in
that direction."**

Each snap becomes a pulse of permission,
a tiny echo of possibility awakening inside you.
Train your mind to expect light, and light will appear.

SOUL WHISPER:
I reset my thoughts with grace. One snap. One breath. One new beginning.

Day 114 – Soul-to-Spirit Meditation

The Mountain Stillness

My Luminous One, Close your eyes and imagine standing at the base of a great mountain. Its peak disappears into soft clouds. It has stood through storms, seasons, and centuries—silent, steady, unmoved.

Take a slow inhale. Feel the mountain's calm move into you, anchoring you from the soles of your feet all the way up your spine. Take a slow exhale. Picture your worries as loose stones tumbling gently down its slopes, returning to the earth to be transformed.

With each breath, you are borrowing the mountain's stillness. With each exhale, you are releasing what you no longer need. Notice how the air around you feels cooler, clearer. Notice how your heart begins to beat in rhythm with something ancient and unwavering.

Even when life feels shaky, deep within you there is a bedrock that cannot be moved. God's presence holds you steady. Like the mountain, you are allowed to stand without explanation, without striving. Simply being here is enough.

Linger here for a few more breaths, letting peace seep into every cell. When you open your eyes, carry this stillness back into your day.

AFFIRMATION:
I am steady and still, grounded in God's presence.

Day 115 – Microdose Laugh-Lift

The Ripple of Laughter

Imagine standing at the edge of a quiet lake. You pick up a flat stone and skim it across the surface. It leaps once, twice, three times— each skip sending out a new ring of ripples, one after another, like dominoes falling in water. That is how laughter moves through your life.

One small "ha" is the first skip. It lands, then jumps again, releasing another wave, and another, until the whole pond of your nervous system begins to shimmer. Tension softens. Shoulders drop. Your chest feels lighter. Energy you didn't know you were holding starts to slide away.

Take a slow, deep breath in. As you exhale, let out a gentle "ha…"— even if it feels awkward at first. On your next breath, try another. Feel it bounce in your throat, your chest, your belly. Let each laugh skip like a stone across your inner waters, creating a domino effect of joy.

This isn't silliness; it's sacred medicine. Laughter on purpose for no reason at all resets your mood, and recalibrates your chemistry, signaling safety to your nervous system. And just as ripples reach far beyond the stone, your laughter travels beyond you—touching hearts, brightening rooms, awakening joy in others.

Today, give yourself permission to practice this laugh ripple—at your desk, in the car, even while making tea. Let it surprise you. Let it become a prayer of joy and a skipping-stone of light.

AFFIRMATION:
My laughter creates ripples of joy in me and around me.

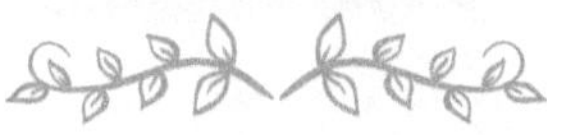

Day 116 – Soul Medicine Quote

"Healing is not about becoming someone new, it's about remembering who you've always been." —Dr. Jennifer Rademaker

The world will tell you to fix yourself, improve yourself, reinvent yourself. Books, ads, even well-meaning friends whisper: become better, shinier, stronger. Without noticing, your subconscious begins to carry a quiet rule: *I must become someone else to be worthy.* Healing starts to feel like a project — another race you might fail.

But true healing is not a project; it's a homecoming. It isn't about chasing a new identity. It's about peeling away the lies, the fears, the masks — the costumes you had to wear to survive — until your soul's original light shines again. Underneath the self-criticism and striving, there is a self who never left, never broke, never stopped being radiant.

Pause for a moment. Place a hand on your heart. Inhale slowly and whisper inwardly: *"I am not broken; I am remembering."* Exhale gently, imagining old labels falling off you like autumn leaves. Picture yourself walking down a quiet path lined with trees. With each step, a little more of your true self appears — your laugh, your softness, your strength. Feel the relief of not having to become anyone else. Feel the peace of simply coming back to you.

This practice begins to reprogram your subconscious: healing is safe, remembering is enough. My radiant soul sister, you're not failing at self-improvement; you're returning to your wholeness.

TRUTH DROP:
You are not too much, and you've never been not enough.

Day 117 – Soul Reflection

The Potter's Hands

Picture a potter at her wheel. Her hands are steady, gentle yet firm, pressing and turning the clay. She adds a little water to soften it, reshapes what collapses, trims what no longer serves the design. The clay doesn't argue. It doesn't understand the form yet. It simply yields to the shaping touch, trusting that every press has purpose.

My beautiful soul, your life is the same. The seasons of pressure you've felt are not punishment; they are formation. Spirit isn't breaking you down — Spirit is making room for your becoming. Those moments when everything feels uncertain may actually be the wheel turning, the water softening, the hands of love guiding you toward a beauty you can't yet see.

In midlife especially, when old roles slip away and new shapes haven't appeared yet, it can feel like loss. But in the Potter's hands, even collapse is an invitation. The same Spirit who spun the galaxies is patient with your becoming, working both strength and softness into you at once. You are being formed into a vessel of more light, more capacity, more grace than before.

Where in your life could you soften into Spirit's shaping instead of resisting it?

Breathe here. Feel those hands — unseen but steady — holding and shaping you. You don't have to know the outcome. You only need to soften and allow.

Affirmation:

I trust the shaping of my life in Spirit's hands.
"We are the clay, and you are our potter; we are all the work of your hand."
—Isaiah 64:8

Day 118 – Affirmation + Reflection

The River's Flow

Maybe lately you've felt like life is carrying you in different directions you didn't expect. No matter how carefully you try to plan things straight, the twists and turns keep appearing. And you find yourself wondering—am I still on course, or have I somehow lost my way?" But picture a river winding through the land. It does not demand that the earth be straight or easy. It curves where it must, rushes where it can, slows where the terrain asks it to. It glides past stones, moves around fallen branches, sometimes deep and quiet, sometimes sparkling and fast. Yet no matter its shape or speed, the river always finds its way to the sea.

You don't have to push so hard or straighten every bend. You don't have to know where every twist is leading before you move. The turns, the pauses, even the obstacles are part of your soul's path toward wholeness.

When you fight the current, you become exhausted and lose sight of the beauty around you. But when you soften, when you let the water carry you, something shifts. Grace rises. Peace appears. The same Spirit that carved the riverbeds of the earth is guiding the flow of your days. Where could you surrender to life's flow today instead of fighting the current?

Today, imagine yourself floating for a moment—no paddling, no forcing, simply trusting the gentle movement beneath you. Feel how your body relaxes. Feel how your heart opens. Let the current remind you: everything you are moving through is leading you to a wider ocean of becoming.

AFFIRMATION:
I move with life's flow, not against it.

Day 119 – Dear God Letter

Dear God,

Thank You for the breath in my body and the steady beating of my heart. Thank You for the sunrise that greets me like a promise and the night sky that folds me into quiet. Thank You for the lessons hidden in my struggles and the beauty that still surprises me in small, ordinary ways. Even now, as I speak these words, I feel how much You have already given.

I confess that I forget. I rush, I ache, I worry. I measure myself against clocks and lists and feel behind. But when I return to gratitude, my soul remembers: I am already held. I am already provided for. What I have is enough. Who I am is enough. All of it is blessing.

Today I release the illusion of scarcity. I lay down the story that my life is lacking. Teach my nervous system the truth of abundance — not as a concept but as a felt presence in my chest. Let each inhale be thanksgiving, each exhale a letting go of fear. Let this day become a song of thanks rising from my heart, a quiet prayer of appreciation with every step I take.

Thank You for the grace that keeps finding me. Thank You for the gifts already in my hands. Thank You for calling me home to the richness of this moment.

And so it is, Amen

Day 120 – Ritual Reset

New Moon Planting

The night sky is dark, a velvet canvas waiting for light. The new moon hides her face, but her power is here—quiet, unseen, fertile. This is the womb of beginnings, the sacred soil where intentions are planted before they're visible. Just as seeds rest underground before sprouting, your dreams need this darkness to take root.

You don't have to see the moon to trust it's there. And you don't have to see your dream blooming to know it's alive. Hidden in Spirit's timing, your desires are already stirring, stretching toward their moment of emergence. This is a time for faith, for whispering your hopes into the quiet and letting the universe hold them.

Invitation:

- Find a small piece of paper and write one intention or soul desire.
- Hold it in your hands, close to your heart. Breathe slowly. Feel your heartbeat against the paper.
- Whisper softly: "As this moon grows, so does this dream."
- Place the paper under your pillow or in a sacred space tonight. Sleep knowing Spirit has heard you.

As you move through the coming days, glance at the moon as she waxes. Let each sliver of light remind you: your intention is swelling with possibility, guided by forces bigger than you. My love, this simple ritual aligns you with the rhythm of creation—the same rhythm that moves oceans and seasons.

Affirmation:
As the moon grows, so does my goals, and my dreams still in the life..

Day 121 – Chakra Soul Movement

The Sacral Flow

Your Sacral Chakra, just below your navel, is a quiet well of creativity, joy, and emotional flow. In this season of Reset, we're not forcing expression; we're gently re-teaching the body and mind that it is safe to feel, safe to soften, and safe to receive new patterns of aliveness. With every circle, you're whispering to your subconscious: *it's safe to let pleasure and creativity flow again.*

Invitation
Place your hands gently below your navel, anchoring awareness there.

Inhale, circling your hips slowly to the left, as if stirring still water.

Exhale, circling to the right, as if smoothing ripples.

Repeat for 1–2 minutes, allowing your body to discover a rhythm that feels like quiet waves.

Visualization
See a soft orange glow at your belly—a gentle ember pulsing with creativity and joy. With each slow circle, feel the glow expanding, loosening old tension, teaching your nervous system a new story: "I can rest. I can flow. I am safe." This is not frivolous movement. It's sacred nervous-system nourishment. When you move slowly with pleasure, you're showing your subconscious that joy is allowed here.

Truth Drop:
It's not indulgence to honor your flow; it's a prayer of gratitude to your own body.

Day 122 – Soul Whisker

The Cat Who Waits Before She Moves

"Honestly, human… you leap like life is a laser pointer. Every flick, every shadow—and there you go, chasing, tripping, panting.

Me? I don't waste my whiskers on nonsense.

I wait. I watch. I know.

That's why when I move, it's flawless—precision, elegance, poetry in motion.

Here's the deal: patience is power. Pausing isn't laziness—it's strategy.

When you stop rushing, you'll feel your own whiskers twitch with knowing. That's your soul saying *not yet… now—go.*

SOUL WHISKER:
Quit chasing laser dots. Wait for the real thing—then pounce like the queen you are.

Day 123 – Sacred Sips Moment

The Empty Cup

Before you lift your tea today, pause. Look at the cup in your hands. Notice it. Notice the curve of the porcelain, the light shining off its surface.

Empty space can look like nothing, but in truth it's possibility. A cup must be empty before it can receive the pour.

My darling, your life is the same. Emptiness is not your ending; it is the beginning of being filled again. Those seasons when you feel poured out, tired, or uncertain aren't proof that you've failed—they're proof that you've made space. The resetting of old patterns and outgrown roles is what clears room for Spirit's fresh life to pour in.

In God's timing, an empty cup is never left empty for long. The pause before the pour is preparation. Right now, even if you can't see it, something is stirring on your behalf—new strength, new friendships, a new vision. The same Spirit that shaped oceans and seasons is preparing a blend just for you. So at some point today, when you pause between tasks, rest your palms open and remember: *the same love that resets the seas resets my life, and is even pouring new life into me..*

Micro-dose script:

Hold your cup for a moment before you sip. Feel its lightness, the cool of the handle, the open space inside. Breathe slowly for a few breaths, hold the warmth of your cup to your belly and whisper: *"I welcome what nourishes me. I reset my heart for what is true."* Then take

your sip as a sign of willingness to receive what is meant for you-
allowing Gods goodness to flow in, sweeter than you imagined.

Affirmation:

My emptiness is sacred space, ready to be reset with what nourishes me.

Day 124 – Truth Drop

The Law of Grace

A soul sister sits alone in her car after another long day, fingers gripping the steering wheel, replaying the mistakes she's sure she's made — the words she wishes she could take back, the choices that didn't turn out the way she hoped. The weight of regret feels like a truck on her chest. Midlife has a way of surfacing old memories and hidden self-judgments. It can feel as if the past is louder and the slate can never be clean again.

But mercy is the quiet miracle that slips in when logic says, *"You're done."* It is Love that wipes the slate clean, a new page appearing where you thought the story had ended. Love doesn't tally up your wrong turns; it pours light into the cracks and says, *"Begin again."* Spirit's law of compassion is stronger than the law of reaping. When your heart softens, even a little, Spirit flows in like water over stones. You may feel weighed down by where you've been, but God's love is bigger than your past. Every broken place can be restored. The story is not over—your best chapter is still ahead.

This gift cannot be earned; it can only be received. It arrives not because you are flawless but because Love itself is flawless. Once received, it ripples outward—healing memories, softening relationships, rewriting your inner narrative. Like a spring feeding a dry riverbed, compassion fills what has been empty and brings life where you thought nothing could grow.

Pause now. Imagine placing all your self-criticism, guilt, or regret into an open palm. Breathe in and whisper: *"I receive mercy."* Breathe out and let the weight go. Let this truth drop settle deep: you are

not bound by every mistake—you are freed by every opening of
your heart.

I open my heart, and love rewrites my story with grace.

Day 125 – Surprise Soul Whisper

The Gratitude Jar

Start a gratitude jar.
Each day, write one thing you're thankful for—
a kindness from your husband, a child's laughter,
a bloom unfolding in your garden.

Fold the paper, drop it in.
Do this every day, all year long.

Then, on the final day—open them together.
Listen to the gentle rustle of paper
as each blessing is unwrapped and remembered.
You'll laugh, maybe tear up,
as you realize how much love has filled your home.

Abundance wasn't waiting to arrive—
it was collecting, piece by piece, right under your roof.

Gratitude is how you reset the heart.
It's how light returns, quietly and consistently.

SOUL WHISPER:
Every note of thanks becomes a seed of joy.

Day 126 – Soul-to-Spirit Meditation

The Inner Spring

Have you ever discovered a hidden spring in the woods—or even noticed an image of one? The water bubbling up from the ground, clear and cool? It's not dramatic like a waterfall; it's subtle, constant, life-giving.

My Luminous one, If you're like me, some days midlife can feel like your streams have run dry. Roles change, energy shifts, old identities fade. But the truth is, beneath all that, a fresh source still rises. Spirit placed it within you at birth. It's not gone; it's just waiting for you to pause, notice, and reset your mind with new, life-giving thoughts.

Let's try this microdose meditation: close your eyes. Place one hand over your heart and one just below your navel. Inhale as if drawing cool water up through a straw, feeling refreshment rise from your belly to your chest. Pause a moment—sense the spring bubbling inside—then exhale, letting tension drain away like water flowing back to earth. Repeat for several breaths until you feel that hidden freshness moving again, resetting your body, mind, and spirit.

Affirmation:
The inner spring of Spirit rises in me, renewing my strength and joy.

Day 127 – Microdose Laugh-Lift

The Bubble Laugh

Imagine blowing bubbles as a child—the delight of watching them lift, shimmer, and pop in the air. Each bubble a tiny world of color, weightless and free.

Today, let your laughter be like those bubbles. Take a slow inhale. On the exhale, let out a soft "ha…"—light and airy. Do it again, imagining each sound as a bubble rising from your chest. See them drifting upward, carrying away tension, self-judgment, or heaviness. Let the "ha's" multiply until you're giggling.

Laughter doesn't have to be loud to heal.

Even small bubbles of joy reset your nervous system and invite your child-heart to come out and play.

AFFIRMATION:
My laughter rises like bubbles, lifting heaviness from my soul.

Day 128 – Soul Medicine Quote

"Softness is not weakness; it is power without violence."
—Dr. Jennifer Rademaker

You've been taught that strength is hard edges, raised voices, relentless striving. But Spirit whispers another truth: the strongest forces in nature are soft. Soft clothes, soft blankets, soft fur, soft hearts- these are not weakness.

Soft water carves canyons. Soft roots can split rock. A gentle word can heal a wound faster than a sharp command.

My darling, your softness is not your liability, it is your gift. Softness is what this world needs more than ever. It's how you choose compassion over control. In midlife, when the world says "toughen up," you can instead soften into deeper power.

Pause now. Place a hand over your heart. Breathe in, imagining a warm, soft light filling your chest. Exhale, letting it spread outward like ripples in a pond. Whisper the affirmation and feel its truth settle in your body.

AFFIRMATION:
My softness is sacred power, shaping the world with grace.

TRUTH DROP:
Softness is not the opposite of strength. Its strength defined.

Day 129 – Soul Reflection

The Bridge

There are seasons when life feels like standing on one side of a river, staring at what you long for across the water. A new beginning. A healed relationship. A dream that seems too far to reach. The current looks strong, the distance feels wide, and your heart whispers, "I'll never get there."

But pause. Breathe. Look again. Often the way forward doesn't appear as a grand highway but as something quiet and small. A bridge you hadn't noticed. A phone call, a conversation, a chance meeting. A stirring in your own heart. Spirit always provides a way across.

It might be simple. It might look fragile. You may feel hesitant to step onto it. Yet every time you put one foot in front of the other, the bridge strengthens. With each act of trust, more planks appear beneath you, more ropes tighten, more support rises. What looked impossible becomes possible because Love is building while you're walking.

You are never stranded. Even when you can't see it yet, the bridge is already being built under your feet. Step by step, you will cross. And when you reach the other side, you'll look back and realize: you weren't walking alone; the Builder walked with you.

REFLECT:

What river in your life feels impossible right now, and how might Spirit already be building a bridge beneath your feet?

Day 130 – Affirmation + Reflection

The Seed of Courage

A seed never looks like much. It is small, quiet, and buried in the dark—yet inside it lives forests yet unseen. The oak tree, the wildflower meadow, the towering redwood—all begin as something tiny, hidden, and easily overlooked.

Courage works the same way. It may feel small in you now, tucked beneath layers of self-doubt or fear. But every time you choose faith over fear—even in the tiniest way—you water that seed. Every boundary honored, every truth spoken, every step taken toward what matters nourishes its roots. Slowly, steadily, courage begins to sprout.

Where in your life could you trust the small seed of courage instead of waiting for full-grown confidence?

You don't have to wait until you feel "brave enough" to move forward. Bravery is not a feeling you must chase; it's a seed already planted within you. Trust it. Act from it, even when it trembles. Each act of trust expands it. Each moment of soft boldness strengthens its stem until, one day, you'll look back and see you've grown an entire forest of courage where you thought only emptiness lived.

Take a breath with me, place a hand over your heart, and whisper the affirmation again. Feel the seed stirring. Feel its quiet power rising.

AFFIRMATION (REPEAT):
I am courage in bloom-steady, rooted and rising.

Day 131 – Dear God Letter

Dear God,

Thank You for the quiet ways You move in my life. Even when I do not see, You are guiding. Even when I do not feel, You are holding me. Even when I forget, You remember me. In the hush beneath my striving, Your presence waits like dawn behind the horizon.

I have spent so many years trying to manage, predict, and control what unfolds. My nervous system has learned to brace, to plan, to rehearse worst cases.

But here, in this season of reset, my soul longs to exhale. Help me surrender the steering wheel I was never meant to grip so tightly. Help me reset my mind and trust that each step, each delay, each turn is already held within your greater wisdom than mine.

Today I choose to rest instead of rush. I choose to have more gratitude, than expectations. I choose to remember that you are always for me, never against me; that Your timing is not punishment but preparation; that your love is not earned but ever-present. Teach my heart to find safety in your unfailing love. Let each breath be a quiet prayer of trust. Let each moment be a soft landing into your hands.

As I release control, reset me with the peace that surpasses understanding. Let my spirit settle like a bird into its nest, certain it is held. And when I rise, let it not be by force but by the quiet power of nature and grace moving through me.

With love, I release, reset, and rise.

And so it is, Amen.

I rest in the quiet wisdom of God's love. Each breath I take is a soft landing into his grace.

Day 132 – Ritual Reset

The Cooling Breath

Sometimes the heat sneaks up on you. It's not only the summer sun—it's the rush of emotion, the stress of too much to hold, the fire of hormones or grief or anger. Suddenly your face and body feels flushed, your heart quickens, your mind races. In that moment you don't need to "power through." You need a pause that brings you back to yourself.

Your body carries its own medicine. Spirit designed you with tools of healing already inside you. One of the simplest is the Cooling Breath. It's a way of telling your nervous system, "I am safe. I can soften. I can let this heat move through me."

When you feel the heat rising—whether from the Florida intense summer sun or the fires of emotion—try this:

- Curl your tongue like a straw (or simply rest your lips in an "O" shape if you cannot curl).
- Inhale slowly through your mouth, feeling cool air wash over your tongue and down your throat.
- Exhale gently through your nose, releasing warmth and tension.
- Repeat 7–10 times, imagining your whole body cooling and calming, like shade after a long walk in the sun.

As you practice, notice how your heart rate slows, your shoulders drop and relax, your mind clears. My love, this is Spirit's built-in balm—no purchase, no appointment, just breath.

AFFIRMATION:
With each cooling breath, I reset balance to my body and peace to my soul

154

Day 133 – Chakra Soul Movement: The Third Eye

Vision That Listens

Has your mind felt loud—too many tabs open, second-guessing your knowing? You ask for a sign, then doubt it. Here's an invitation to soften and let insight come.

What could become clear if you made five quiet breaths of space?

The third eye, between your brows, is the center of intuition and soul-vision—the inner lamp that glows in darkness. Whispers from Spirit may arrive as a picture, a phrase, or a calm certainty. Include your body and your nervous system hears: *it's safe to know.*

Try this:

- Sit tall, soften your eyes. Place one hand over your heart, the other between your brows.
- Inhale through your nose, imagining a soft indigo glow at your forehead.
- Exhale slowly as you bow brow toward heart—letting insight meet love.
- Inhale and lift. Repeat 5–7 breaths, lengthening the exhale.
- Between breaths, make small head circles; soften the brow and base of skull; roll shoulders back.
- Settle in stillness. Ask inwardly: *What do I need to see or know right now?* Trust the answer is already on its way.

Mantra:
I soften; inner light leads.

Day 134 – Soul Whisker

The Sock Heist

While you folded laundry, I executed **Operation Footloose**—one sock, one pounce, zero regrets. Under the bed: victory dance.

Reset is small, delicious mischief that tells your nervous system, "We're safe enough to play." A private grin counts as therapy.

Today, stage a mini heist: claim the cutest mug, stash a square of chocolate, tuck a *"You're doing great"* note in your shoe. Then get on the catwalk and tell yourself, *"I'm fabulous, darling."* Because you are.

Tail high. Joy—rebooted.

Soul Whisker:
This is your tail-high moment—strut off in grace.

Day 135 – Sacred Sips Moment

The Shared Cup

A single cup of tea becomes more than tea when it's shared. Conversation opens, laughter rises, hearts connect. The cup becomes a bridge between souls.

My beautiful soul sister, you were not made to journey alone. Soul sisterhood, quiet companionship, sacred connection—these are as healing as the tea itself. Sometimes the medicine you need isn't in the sip, but in the presence of another. In a world that glorifies self-sufficiency, we forget the strength of gentle company. We forget that Spirit often answers prayers through other people—through a listening ear, a soft hand on yours, a shared moment of warmth.

Even if your circle is small or scattered, there is someone whose spirit would meet yours over a simple cup. Invite a tea date—on a porch, at a table, or through a screen. As you share, pause and silently bless her: *"May this cup warm both our souls."* Notice how your own heart softens as you give the blessing. Let your tea remind you of community—each sip an opening, a quiet way Spirit weaves lives together.

TRUTH DROP:
When two souls share a cup, the tea becomes medicine.

Day 136 – Truth Drop

The Law of Divine Timing

At the edge of your garden there's a tree that blooms later than all the rest. Every spring you watch its bare branches while others burst with flowers. You wonder if it's sick, or if you've done something wrong. But then, quietly, in its own month, the buds appear—fuller, deeper, more fragrant than you ever imagined.

Midlife can feel like that tree. You've poured yourself out for decades, tended everyone else's seasons, and now you look at your own life and wonder why it hasn't blossomed yet. But the unseen roots are still at work. The pause is not punishment—it's preparation. The Law of Divine Timing says nothing is late when it's aligned with your soul. Some seasons are for roots; some for bloom.

Today, as you reset, place a hand on your heart and one on your belly. Whisper to yourself: *"I am not behind. My life is unfolding in sacred timing."* Feel your nervous system relax into that truth. This is subconscious reprogramming in its gentlest form—teaching your body that waiting is not failure, it's gestation.

TRUTH DROP:
You're not missing your moment. Your moment is finding you.

AFFIRMATION:
I rest in Divine Timing; my bloom is right on time.

Day 137 – Surprise Soul Whisper

Window Fog Doodle

When you step out of the shower and the mirror is fogged, pause. With your fingertip, draw a heart or write a word your soul longs to see. Leave it there—your little love note on the glass.

Later, when the fog clears and you return, it may still be waiting to surprise you. Or perhaps the next person who looks into that mirror will catch it—the gift of a heart left behind, like a secret blessing in the steam.

Reset can be playful. My darling, it doesn't have to take effort. It can be as simple as writing love into the air, leaving joy where someone else might stumble upon it.

Soul Whisper:
Even a foggy heart can carry warmth into the day.

Day 138 – Soul-to-Spirit Meditation

The Forest Path

When the familiar path disappears, do you long for someone to say, "I see your courage here"—when you can't yet see the way?

Have you stepped into a forest and felt its hush—the canopy softening the light, pine rising on the air, the path curving out of sight? Even without knowing where it leads, something in you exhales. You're held. You're guided.

Midlife can feel like that. The old road fades; the new one isn't visible yet. Roles shift. Energy changes. But the forest whispers another truth: there is already a path beneath your feet, shaped by a wisdom larger than you. Every step—even the unsure ones—is part of your becoming.

Notice the forest's rhythm: cool air releases heaviness—this is Release. Green quiet settles your mind—this is Reset. With each slow step your spine lengthens, breath deepens, heart lifts—this is Rise. Nature offers medicine without words, inviting you to shed old leaves, return to center, and walk forward renewed.

If possible, step outside barefoot—grass, soil, sand, or wood. Place one hand over your heart and one at your solar plexus *(this posture reconnects love with will, telling your nervous system that love leads and courage follows)*. Inhale as if breathing pine. Pause tall like a tree. Exhale and imagine roots from your feet anchoring you in trust. Repeat several breaths—release, reset, rise. If a forest isn't near,

take three slow barefoot breaths wherever you are. Let the earth
meet you.

*As I walk the forest path within me, I release what is heavy, reset in stillness,
and rise guided by Spirit.*

Day 139 – Microdose Laugh-Lift

Shaking Off the Serious

Have you felt the day sit heavy on your shoulders—emails, bills, the to-dos stacking like bricks—while your smile goes missing? I see you, You've carried so much with such grace. Today, let's set it down for a minute.

Before the practice:

Put on your favorite feel-good song. Stand up. Soften your knees. Give everything a gentle shake—shoulders, arms, hips, jaw—like you're brushing dust from a velvet coat.

The Laugh-Lift:
1. Take a deep inhale. On the exhale, whisper a soft "ha."
2. Inhale again, and let the "ha" get a little brighter.
3. Begin to bounce lightly through your heels. Let your shoulders shimmy.
4. Let the "ha… ha… ha…" rise with the movement—no forcing, just letting joy leak out at the edges.
5. For one minute, shake, sway, smile. Imagine the heaviness falling off like raindrops.

Laughter doesn't deny what's real—it lightens it.. And besides, at this age, fun is a youth serum no cream can match. Ha! Ha!

PRESCRIPTION FOR YOUR SOUL — TRUTH DROP:
Choose the medicine of joy.

Day 140 – Soul Medicine Quote

"Peace is not found by escaping life—it is found by returning to yourself within it."
—**Dr. Jennifer Rademaker**

There are mornings when you fantasize about disappearing— a cabin in the woods, a plane ticket with no return, a silent room where no one can reach you, and days maybe selling everything and joining the circus—ha!
Like you imagine that somewhere far away from obligations and noise, peace will finally descend. But even if you went there, your own racing thoughts, your own nervous system, your own inner stories would travel with you.

My beautiful soul, you don't have to run away from your life to feel peace. You only need to return inward, where Spirit's calm has always lived. Even in chaos, the soul holds a center of stillness, like a candle that never goes out. You've touched it before — in a deep breath you didn't plan, in a sunset that stopped you mid-sentence, in a moment of quiet tears where you felt held instead of alone. That center is still here. It has never left you.

Peace is not passive; it's a living presence inside you, waiting to be chosen. When you pause and turn inward, you're not retreating from life — you're re-entering it from your truest self. From that center, you can handle what arises with clarity and compassion rather than panic or exhaustion. Midlife especially invites you to practice this: to anchor in your own being so the storms around you don't define you.

Today, let yourself exhale the belief that peace is "out there." Place your awareness inside your body, like stepping into a quiet room within a bustling house. Feel how the air changes. Let peace rise to meet you. It is your birthright.

Truth drop:

Peace is my natural state. I return to it with ease and let it guide me through my day.

Day 141 – Soul Reflection

The Anchor

My radiant one, are you tired of being "the strong one" and longing to be the held one?

When storms rise, ships do not drift endlessly—they drop anchor. The anchor doesn't calm the waves, but it steadies the vessel until the waters settle. Without it, the ship is tossed wherever the wind blows. With it, there is stability even in turbulence.

You have an anchor too. Spirit within you holds steady even when your outer world feels chaotic. You don't have to control the storm; you only need to trust the anchor. The changes in your body, your family, your work may feel like gusts that would blow you off course, but they cannot uproot what is planted deep inside you. You may feel the winds of life blowing hard right now, but you are not drifting. God has anchored you in His love. Storms don't last forever; calm seas are on their way. Hold tight to hope—what's ahead of you is greater than what's behind you.

Pause now. Close your eyes and take a slow breath. Imagine you are on a small boat at sea. The sky darkens; waves rise. Feel the sway under your feet. Now picture yourself lowering a heavy, gleaming anchor into the deep. Feel the chain pull taut, the vessel steady. As you inhale, whisper: *I am anchored in Spirit's strength.* As you exhale, release the urge to fight the waves. Let your body register: safety beneath the storm. Each time you do this, you reprogram your subconscious: stability is not out there; it's in here. I don't have to hold everything together. Spirit holds me.

We have this hope as an anchor for the soul, firm and secure. — Hebrews 6:19

Where in my life today do I most need to drop anchor—and what simple pause (breath, prayer, hand-to-heart, self-love act) will help me do it now?

Day 142 – Affirmation + Reflection

The Stream

Do you ever worry that if you're not loud, you'll be overlooked—and wonder if your quiet still counts?

A stream doesn't roar like a waterfall. It moves quietly, persistently—yet over time it carves valleys, nourishes fields, shapes the land. It doesn't perform; it simply flows.

Midlife can whisper another story: *If I don't push, nothing will happen. If I'm not big, I'll be invisible.* But Spirit's way is often slow and soft. Rivers carve canyons. Roots find their path through stone. Seeds split the dark without a sound. Power and gentleness are not opposites—they are partners.

Micro Practice (Reset):

Unclench your jaw. Soften your belly. Widen the back of your heart. Inhale, picturing a clear stream running through you—steady, cool, sure. Exhale and release the pressure to be a waterfall. See your gentle current touching your family, your work, your dreams—leaving nourishment wherever it moves. Whisper: *My steady flow shapes life in powerful ways.* Feel your body register the relief: *I don't have to perform to matter.*

Each time you practice, your subconscious updates the story: *My quiet presence is enough. My flow is holy. Change can be lived, not forced.*

REFLECTION:
Where can I choose steady flow over pushing today—and what one small, quiet action will I take?

AFFIRMATION:
My steady flow shapes my life in powerful ways.

Day 143 – Dear God Letter

Dear God,

So often I pour compassion into others yet leave myself thirsty. I forgive their mistakes but replay mine. I soothe their wounds but ignore my own. I whisper gentle truths to their hearts while speaking harsh words to mine. I know how to cradle another's pain; teach me now how to cradle my own.

Help me, to turn this tenderness inward. Remind me that I, too, am your beloved creation — worthy of gentleness, patience, and care. When my inner critic rises, let Your voice rise louder. When shame presses like a weight on my chest, let Your love lift me higher. Teach my nervous system that self-compassion is not indulgence but alignment with truth.

Today, may I lay down the armor of self-judgment and step into the open field of grace. May I see myself as you see me — not a list of flaws to be corrected but a living soul unfolding in your light. May every breath be a silent prayer of kindness toward my own heart. May every glance in the mirror be a small act of forgiveness.

I release the story that compassion is only for others. I reset my heart to receive it for myself. And I rise knowing that as I soften toward me, I become a truer vessel of love for everyone else.

With love, I release, reset, and rise.

And so it is. Amen

AFFIRMATION:
I offer myself the same compassion I so easily give to others. Self-kindness is my birthright.

Day 144 – Breath & Reset

When was the last time you gave your nervous system a song instead of another task?

The vagus nerve is your built-in peace pathway. It runs from brainstem through heart, lungs, and gut—quietly tending mood, digestion, and safety. In midlife, stress, shifting hormones, and constant caretaking can overwork this pathway. Yet sound and gentle touch can guide you from fight-or-flight back into rest, digest, and heal—a microdose of medicine already inside you.

Our grandmothers knew this instinctively: rocking chairs and lullabies, soothing a child while soothing themselves. Humming an uplifting song—with a soft smile—tells your nervous system, *I am safe*. It's more than sound; it's a lullaby to your own body. Perhaps it's time to cradle yourself—to become the grandmother you need. Each hum, a rocking chair. Each breath, a gentle sway. Each smile, a caring hand smoothing the back of your head.

Give yourself today more love, not less.

Try this with me
1. Sit comfortably, spine tall, shoulders soft.
2. Place one hand over your heart, one over your belly.
3. Inhale slowly through your nose, feeling warmth beneath your palms.
4. Exhale and hum an uplifting tune (hymn, lullaby, or happy-memory song). Let the vibration travel under your hands.
5. Add a gentle smile and sway softly for 1–2 minutes.
6. Finish by cupping your cheeks in your hands. This sound + touch posture stimulates the vagus nerve and soul whispers to your body: *It's safe to soften now*

Day 145 – Chakra Soul Movement: The Heart Chakra

The Center of Love and Connection

Your heart is more than an organ; it's your inner sanctuary of love and compassion. When the Heart Chakra is open, life softens, relationships flow, and love rises naturally. In midlife, after disappointments and unmet expectations, the heart can grow guarded—tiny thorns of resentment gathering until love feels blocked. Yet the heart still longs to open. Forgiveness is the key that softens the thorns. Where might forgiveness—for yourself or another—loosen what's tight so love can move again?

Try this with me
Stand as if on sacred ground, feet rooted. Let the air around you feel warm and kind.

1. **Inhale:** spread your arms wide, welcoming the world. Feel your chest open, ribs making space for light.
2. **Exhale:** cross your arms in a gentle self-embrace. Soften the grip of unspoken expectations and old resentments.
3. Repeat **5–7 cycles**, opening wide then returning to embrace, noticing how your chest softens with each breath.

As you move, picture a soft **green light** glowing at the center of your chest, expanding with every inhale. Let it fill you with compassion and forgiveness—flowing outward to others and inward to you. Whisper: *With every breath, I forgive and open my heart.* Imagine that green warmth spilling into your hands, your words, your day.

The more you open your heart, the more love flows both ways. This simple movement is a microdose of Heart Chakra medicine—a reset for your nervous system, a release of what no longer serves, a remembrance that you are held by Love itself.

With every breath, I forgive. With every breath, I open. Love flows through me—both ways.

Day 146 – Soul Whisker

The Cat Who Sunbathes in Doorways

Human, let me make this simple: I don't ask permission to sprawl in a sunbeam. I don't feel bad about it either. When the light hits, I flop down like royalty, stretch until every inch of me glows, and dare the world to disturb me.

Meanwhile, you're running around chasing lists and guilt like it's your job. Stop it. Claim your beam. Stand there. Let the warmth kiss your skin. Pretend you invented light—it's your birthright.

Life isn't asking you to earn the sun. It's asking you to enjoy it.

SOUL WHISKER:
Claim your light, darling.
Sun worship isn't self-care, its soul -care.

Day 147 – Sacred Sips Moment

The Fragrance of Tea

Before you even reach for the kettle, let me ask you this: Are you tired of being the strong one—and longing to be unhurried, chosen, and cared for too?

Set the kettle. A quiet minute. The first bubbles whisper. You pour— **and before the sip touches your lips, the fragrance arrives first**: warm curls of steam like an invisible invitation. Earth, flower, spice, leaf. Without trying, your nervous system begins to soften. Already the tea is doing its work—before a single drop.

My beautiful soul, life is like this, too. Blessings often announce themselves quietly before they fully appear: a sudden ease in your chest, a stranger's kindness, a creative spark, a slip of sunlight across the counter—fragrances of what's coming next. Gentle signs that your soul's cup is already being filled.

Make it a tiny ceremony
Pour. Pause. Watch the steam. Place one hand over your heart. Inhale through your nose and let the scent meet you. On the exhale, whisper: *"I receive the fragrance of what's on its way."*

Stay with the scent for **three slow breaths** before your first sip. Let anticipation become nourishment—Reset for your nervous system, permission to expect good.

TRUTH DROP:
I choose to anticipate goodness; the blessing's fragrance is already here.

Day 148 – Truth Drop

The Law of Oneness

Do you ever feel like you're carrying it alone—wondering who's holding you while you hold everything else?

The Law of Oneness says separation is an illusion. Spirit flows through all things; what touches one thread of the web touches them all. The same light that burns in the stars burns within you. Even when you feel overlooked or isolated, you are woven into a larger Love—seen, supported, accompanied.

Micro Practice (Reset):

Place a hand over your heart and another over your belly. Inhale slowly and picture a golden thread from your heart weaving outward—through your home, your city, the ocean, the sky—then back to you. Exhale and feel yourself held in that web of Love. Whisper: *I belong.*

You are not separate from God, not separate from Love, not separate from the great whole. Step into today remembering: you are connected to something bigger, stronger, more beautiful than you can see—and that Love is already moving on your behalf.

Scripture:

"That they may all be one, just as You, Father, are in Me, and I in You." — John 17:21

Truth Drop:
I move as one with Love. I am not alone; I am held in the web of the Holy.

Day 149 – Surprise Soul Whisper

Joy Drop Mist

Winter can lean heavy, and even strong women need tiny, joyful lifelines.

Today's Surprise Soul Whisper is a playful, pocket-sized ritual to reset your energy and brighten your mind in under a minute.

Picture this: a cool kiss of citrus on your skin, your shoulders softening, your breath lengthening, your mind choosing one brighter thought.

What you'll need to make her:
- A mini spray bottle
- Distilled water
- 2–3 drops of lemon essential oil (or a gentle floral you love)

How to craft
1. Fill the bottle with distilled water.
2. Add just a few drops of oil (start light—you can always add one more later).
3. Cap, shake, and tuck her in the fridge. Let the cool become your keeper.

How to use
When the blues nibble at your light, stand tall.
Mist gently *away from your face.*
Inhale slowly through your nose for a count of four; feel your ribs widen.
Pause.
Exhale for a count of six; feel your jaw unclench.
On that exhale, choose any new positive uplifting thought: *"I'm welcoming brightness now."*
Repeat twice.

❄

Name her **Joy mist** —or any name your heart loves.

Why it helps

Cool temperature cues the nervous system to soften; citrus notes lift mood and invite clarity; lengthened exhales tell your body, *"I am safe."* One mist, one breath, one kinder thought—and your inner room fills with light again.

Gentle care: Essential oils are potent—use sparingly, avoid eyes/skin sensitivities, skip if you're reactive.

Soul Whisper:
Claim your light, one cool, lemon-bright breath at a time.

Day 150 – Soul-to-Spirit Meditation

The Garden Within

Maybe you've walked past a neglected garden—a patch of earth that once overflowed with color but now looks tired, overgrown, forgotten. At first glance it seems lifeless. Yet beneath the soil, roots are still alive, waiting for care. One touch of water, one shaft of sunlight, and life begins to stir again.

Midlife can feel like that garden. Responsibilities have pulled your attention outward, and the inner landscape may seem dry or crowded with weeds. But your soul is not barren ground. Everything you've experienced—every joy, every heartbreak, every prayer whispered into the night—has been seed and soil for something beautiful that is still growing.

Take a breath. This is your moment to tend the garden within.

Close your eyes now. Imagine stepping through a small gate into a quiet garden. The air is soft, carrying the scent of lavender and fresh rain. The path beneath your bare feet feels cool and fertile. Around you flowers open, vines stretch, light filters through green leaves. This garden is yours—it lives inside you.

Breathe in, smelling the fragrance of peace.
Breathe out, releasing what no longer belongs in your soil.
With each inhale and exhale, picture yourself watering, pruning, and blessing the plants of your inner life.

Stay here for a few breaths. Feel how even in stillness, growth is happening. Spirit is tending you as you tend yourself.

I tend the garden of my soul with love and trust. My inner ground is fertile and full of life.

Day 151 – Microdose Laugh-Lift

The Medicine of Laughter

There are days in midlife when the weight feels heavier than usual. Hormones fluctuate, nights are restless, worries stack like dishes on the counter, and your spirit begins to tighten. You may feel serious all the time, as though joy is a luxury you can't afford. But your soul was never designed to carry life so grimly.

Laughter is the quickest reset your nervous system knows. It's Spirit's built-in medicine—God's gift for loosening the knots of fear, easing tension, and flooding your cells with light. Science confirms what your heart has always known: laughter boosts the immune system, relaxes muscles, soothes pain, strengthens the heart, and even helps memory. But beyond biology, laughter re-teaches your subconscious: I am safe. Joy belongs here.

Today's invitation is simple: give yourself permission to laugh on purpose.

Try this:
- Take three deep, slow breaths.
- On the exhale, let a small chuckle rise—"ha… ha… ha…" even if it feels awkward at first.
- Repeat until the chuckle becomes a laugh.
- Let it ripple through your body like a wave of healing light, loosening your belly, softening your heart, lifting your spirit.

Each giggle teaches your inner world: I can feel joy and still be safe. I can lighten and still be strong.

This is not silliness; it's soul medicine.

Affirmation:
Laughter is my medicine, healing my body, my mind, and my soul.

Day 152 – Soul Medicine Quote

Wholeness is not something you find—it's something you remember.
Dr. Jennifer Rademaker

My Beautiful soul, the world trains you to see yourself as scattered—roles divided, body changing, responsibilities pulling you in every direction. Midlife can amplify that feeling: a sense of having lost pieces of yourself along the way, of needing to "get back" what's missing. But Spirit whispers a deeper truth: you were never broken. You are not a puzzle with missing parts. You are a living whole, even in the midst of change.

Healing isn't about assembling a new self from scratch. It's about remembering the self you've always been. Every time you pause to breathe, to pray, to laugh, or to sit with your hand on your heart, you're not creating wholeness—you're uncovering it. Each moment of remembrance dissolves the lie of "not enough" and lets your nervous system learn: I am safe. I am complete. I am already all of me.

Pause for a breath now. Place a hand over your chest and whisper softly: "I remember that I am whole." Feel how your body responds—a little softening at the jaw, a gentle lift of the heart. This is your soul nodding yes. This is remembrance doing its quiet work.

Wholeness does not mean perfection. It means living from your center instead of your fractures. It means letting your light pour from the inside out. You're not "getting back" to yourself; you're uncovering what was always here.

TRUTH DROP:
I remember that I am whole. Wholeness is my true nature, and it rises in me now.

Day 153 – Soul Reflection

The Bent Tree

There's a tree on a hillside that everyone notices. It leans hard to one side, its trunk shaped by decades of wind pressing against it. From far away it looks imperfect, maybe even damaged. But when you walk close and place your hand against its bark, you see something different: the deep ridges that tell its story, the curve that has become its signature, the way its branches still stretch wide for the sun. It has not only survived the wind; it has become beautiful because of it.

My beautiful soul, life's winds have bent you too. Responsibilities, losses, illnesses, midlife changes, heartbreaks—each one a gust pressing against you. And yet here you are, still reaching for light. Bent does not mean broken. The storms have shaped you into something resilient and rare. The parts of you that curve now carry more character, more wisdom, more compassion than a perfectly straight life ever could.

Where have life's storms reshaped you, and how could you begin to see the curve as beauty instead of damage?

Pause for a moment and picture your own "bent places." Instead of judging them, see them as living sculptures—proof that you have endured and adapted, that you've grown roots deep enough to hold you. This is the gift of reset season: to stop hiding the evidence of what shaped you and to let your unique silhouette shine.

REFLECT:
The winds of life have shaped me, but they cannot break me. My curve is my signature of strength.

Day 154 – Affirmation + Reflection

The Unhurried Room

There is a small room inside you where the lights are low, the air is warm, and the clock forgets your name. In winter, that room matters more. Not because you're weak—but because your brave nervous system longs to be unhurried, to feel safe, to know she is enough without proving it.

I see how much you carry—appointments, decisions, faces that need you. I also see the hush you're craving: clarity instead of noise, tenderness instead of toughness, a pace that matches your breath. Reset isn't a performance; it's permission. It's letting the flame simmer down so you can actually savor the flavors of your life.

Try this with me now: rub your palms together until they grow warm. Place one hand over your chest, one over your belly—the meeting place of courage and truth. Inhale slowly through your nose for four; exhale for six. Feel your jaw soften. Whisper inwardly, *"I am allowed to be unhurried."* Notice how your body answers when no one is asking it to sprint.

You don't have to earn this room. You choose it. And the choosing rewrites something deep: pace becomes prayer; slowness becomes sanctuary; clarity rises like steam from a quiet cup.

REFLECTION:
Where does your life ask you to rush when your soul needs room? What single boundary, ritual, or "no" would create some unhurried space for you this week?

AFFIRMATION:
I reset my pace to match my breath. I am safe, unhurried, and enough without performing.

Day 155 – Dear God Letter

A Prayer for Gentle Reset

Dear God,

Tonight, let me come to you softly—no speeches, no fixing—just the small sound of my breath. I have hurried so long my body forgot the way to calm. I've held the world together with a smile while my nerves frayed beneath it. Meet me here, in the hush.

Lay your hand over my heart and teach it a slower rhythm. Let my jaw unclench, my shoulders fall, my belly rise and fall like a quiet tide. Remind me that healing can be tender… that rest is not avoidance, it is holy repair.

I offer you my midlife body—this wise vessel asking to feel **safe** again. I offer you the thoughts that spin at 3 a.m., the lists that never end, the pressure to prove I am enough. Re-pattern me gently. Rewrite the old fear-stories with kinder truth while I sleep. Tuck peace into my cells the way a mother tucks in a child.

Show me the small, doable rituals that reset my day: one prayer before the phone, warm hands over my chest and belly, tea steam rising like a blessing, a single boundary that makes space to breathe. Let clarity come like morning light—not blinding, simply certain.

When worry knocks, usher it to the porch and keep my inner room unhurried. When doubt whispers, cover it with your steadying love: *You are not behind. You are not too late. You are already held.*

Tonight I choose the softer way—longer exhales, kinder thoughts, slower steps. Knit me back to myself, God, one spacious breath at a time. And in this gentle Reset, let me remember: I am safe, I am loved, I am enough.

And so it is. Amen

Day 156 – Ritual Reset

The Candle of Gentle Reset

Some evenings feel heavy—not from failure, but from carrying so much for so long. Your body isn't asking for another push; she's asking for a slower rhythm and a light that steadies instead of scorches. Tonight, let a small flame be your metronome—quiet, warm, regulating. **Your Ritual (≈5 minutes)**

- **Prepare.** Dim the room. Sit where your back feels supported. Place one candle at eye level, an arm's length away.

- **Warm.** Rub your palms until they tingle heat. Rest one over your heart, one over your belly—the meeting place of courage and truth.

- **Intend.** Whisper: *"I choose an unhurried pace. I am safe to soften."*

- **Breathe with the flame.** Inhale through your nose for **4**; pause softly; exhale for **6** while gazing at the glow. With each exhale, imagine dropping one floor deeper into calm. Repeat 6 rounds.

- **Anchor.** On the last three exhales, pair breath with a phrase your body can believe:

  "One thing at a time."
  "I am safe right now."
  "My pace is my prayer."

- **Name one next true step.** Keep a small card nearby. After your breaths, write **one** step for tomorrow—only one. Place the card beside the candle as a promise to your calmer self. *Clarity is a gift of Reset.*

- **Close with warmth.** Cup your hands near (not over) the flame, then touch that warmth to your cheeks. Let tenderness—not toughness—lead you into the rest of the night. This is not performance; it's permission. The candle does not hurry. Let its constancy re-teach your body what enoughness feels like.

Day 157 – Chakra Soul Movement

The Throat Chakra: Three-Breath Hum & Truth Tap

There's a quiet room inside your chest where your voice waits. In midlife she can feel snowed under by years of being useful and polite. Reset doesn't ask you to shout; it invites your voice to feel **safe** again.**Why this helps:**
A soft closed-mouth hum vibrates the throat and downshifts the nervous system. Calm first, clarity next—then words arrive without bracing.

Your Practice (2–3 minutes)
1. **Ground.** Sit or stand tall, feet rooted. Roll shoulders back and down to open the collarbones.
2. **Hands that mean something.** One hand on your heart (compassion), one on your low belly (truth/courage). Tell your body: *I am safe to be me.*
3. **Three-Breath Hum.**
   o Inhale through your nose **4**.
   o Exhale a gentle **mmm 6**, feeling vibration at lips, tongue, and throat.
   o Repeat **3 rounds**, unhurried.
4. **Truth Tap.** With two fingers, tap the throat notch **5 light taps** while whispering inwardly, *I am safe to speak kindly and clearly.*
5. **Give your voice a sentence.** Offer one present-tense truth (to yourself or aloud):
   "I need an unhurried morning."
   "I will ask for help at 2 p.m."
   "No is holy for me today."

Picture a soft blue glow at your throat—cool, clear, winter-sky open. Carry that clarity with you. **Mantra** *My voice is safe and it matters.*

❄

Day 158 – Soul Whisker

The Cat Who Trusts Her Instincts

Listen, human—I don't make pros-and-cons lists before I step into the dark hallway. My whiskers twitch, my senses hum, and I move. Simple.

You, on the other hand, stall at every doorway like the carpet might file a complaint. Stop it. Trust the nudge. Step already. Spirit's got you.

SOUL WHISKER:
Whisker-wink of wisdom: the nudge is enough.

Day 159 – Sacred Sips Moment

The Evening Cup

There's a hush that arrives just before night settles—maybe the house is finally quiet. In that space, you pour your evening cup—tea, or whatever kindness your hands choose. Steam rises and curls upward, mingling with your thoughts like a prayer you didn't know you were sending.

I see you soul sister, you've held so much today—tasks, conversations, invisible lists only you could see. Midlife often multiplies the load: caring for others, managing change, tending both past and future at once. Without noticing, you go to bed still carrying the weight in your nervous system.

The Evening Cup is Spirit's way of saying: you don't have to take it into tomorrow. This is your reset moment. As you lift the cup, pause. Feel its warmth seep into your palms—a quiet act of self-love. Close your eyes and breathe in the fragrance—chamomile, mint, hibiscus, or simply water with lemon. On the next breath, whisper inwardly: *I lay down what I've carried. I let it go now. I let it go.*

With each sip, imagine tension dissolving. With each exhale, picture your burdens dropping like stones at the river's edge. The cup becomes a bridge between striving and stillness, between doing and simply being.

You're not just drinking tea; you're reprogramming your body and mind to know: rest is safe, and tomorrow will rise to meet you fresh.

TRUTH DROP:
Every sip is a reset. Rest is safe. Tomorrow will rise to meet me fresh.

Day 160 – Truth Drop

The Law of Vibration: Resetting into Rest

There's a quiet power in the moments just before sleep. The house softens, lights dim, and the day's noise fades. Too often, what lingers is heavy—unfinished tasks, old worries, a mental scroll of "shoulds." When carried into sleep, your subconscious keeps working on it all night. You wake up already tired, as if you've been running in your dreams.

The Law of Vibration teaches that everything moves—your body, thoughts, emotions, even the unseen energy around you. What you hold last at night is the frequency you carry into rest and into tomorrow. A small bedtime ritual can shift that vibration: from heaviness to clarity, from tension to gratitude, from bracing to receiving.

In midlife, with decades of responsibility woven into your nervous system, this ritual isn't indulgence—it's repair. It reprograms your subconscious to expect softness instead of stress. Think of it as tuning the music before you drift into the night—choosing the song your soul will sleep to.

Tonight, give yourself a gentle landing:

- Open a journal and list three small things to handle tomorrow. Your mind exhales: *It's noted. I can rest.*

- Write three things you're grateful for tonight—big or tiny. Gratitude resets the frequency.

- Place a hand over your heart and whisper: *I lay down what I've carried. I welcome rest.*

Feel your body soften, your breath deepen. This is not struggle. This is reset.

Truth Drop:
The last vibration I choose at night becomes the song my soul sleeps to.

Soul Companion Card: No. 26

Day 161 – Surprise Soul Whisper

The Sock Shuffle

Reset doesn't always look like stillness. Sometimes it looks like sliding across the kitchen floor in your socks—arms wide, heart laughing, gravity forgotten.

Midlife has given you plenty of reasons to be serious. But Spirit smiles when you let yourself be silly. Joy resets the nervous system as surely as quiet. Sometimes even more.

Tonight, put on your favorite song. Shuffle, slide, glide. Add a heel kick if you can—because nothing says reset like a kitchen victory dance. For ten seconds you're not managing everything—you're a soul in motion, giggling at the gift of being alive.

Whisper Practice — 60-Second Joy Dose

After your shuffle, give yourself exactly one minute of simple joy: music, a window of fresh air, or a step into the night for a sip of moonlight.

As you do, **notice where joy lands**—chest softening, jaw unclenching, breath widening. Put a palm there and let the body learn: *This is safe. This is good.*

Soul Whisper:
Vibration first; clarity follows—what a great day to be alive.

Day 162 – Soul-to-Spirit Meditation

The Quiet Tide

Find a comfortable seat or lie down. Let the room be dim and kind. Allow your breath to arrive just as it is.

Place one hand over your heart and one over your belly. This posture connects heart (love and compassion) with belly (truth and courage)—a signal to your nervous system that you are safe and held. Soften your jaw.

Breathe in through your nose for a gentle count of four… exhale for six.
Longer exhales tell the body, *We can rest now.*
Let your shoulders lower. Let your face soften. Let the day set like a sun inside you.

Imagine you are near a small cove at dusk. The water is quiet, steady.
Each inhale is a tender wave arriving to your shore.
Each exhale is the tide easing back, carrying away what you don't need to hold.
No forcing. Only rhythm. Only kindness.

Silently whisper on the inhale: "I receive."
Silently whisper on the exhale: **"I release into rest and I reset."**
(Notice the difference: not pushing away—simply settling into safety.)

If thoughts knock, let them become shells on the sand—noticed, then left for morning light.
Let warmth gather beneath your palms. Feel the simple miracle of breath moving you—Spirit meeting you in the quiet. This is your **reset**: clarity through calm, repair through gentleness, holiness without hurry.

Stay for a few more cycles—four in, six out—until your inner tide finds its own pace. When you're ready, breathe a little deeper, wiggle fingers and toes, and keep one hand on your heart a moment longer, sealing in the softness.

Affirmation:

I am safe to be still. My breath resets my body. Peace returns with every tide.

Day 163 – Microdose Laugh-Lift

Sacred Silly

Not every laugh needs a reason. Sometimes the most healing laughter is the kind that bubbles up from nowhere—silly, playful, unexpected.

Spirit delights in your joy. It doesn't need to be polished or perfect. Even nonsense laughter is holy, because it lifts the weight off your shoulders and lets your soul breathe.

Invitation:
Find a quiet spot.
Take a deep breath and, on the exhale, let out the silliest laugh you can—giggly, snorty, or over-the-top.
Keep going until you can't help but smile.
Feel the freedom of joy rising in you for no reason at all.

AFFIRMATION:
My laughter is sacred, even when it is silly.

Day 164 – Soul Medicine Quote

"Reset is not erasing who you are; it's awakening to who you've always been—then living from that truth."
—Dr. Jennifer Rademaker

Midlife can feel like snow pressing on a branch—old stories heavy, old roles asking more than they give. You've been the caretaker, the achiever, the one who holds it all together. Yet beneath that winter weight, your soul begins to stir. A quiet longing rises: *What if I could breathe differently? Live differently?* This is the invitation of Reset.

Reset doesn't erase your past. It whispers: *My dear, you are not broken. You're simply ready for something new.* In the winter of your soul, stepping back is not failure—it's holy repair. Each exhale, each prayer, each still moment rewrites your inner script in the language of love.

When you align with this truth, fear loosens its grip. Clarity rises. You begin to act from inspiration, not exhaustion. Midlife becomes a threshold, not an ending. What felt like detour becomes the hidden path home to yourself.

Microdose: The Winter Seed

Sit quietly, hands cupped as if holding a seed. Picture it glowing, already containing all you're becoming. Inhale once with reverence. Exhale, imagining old scripts melting like frost. Whisper three times: *I am awakening.*

Prescription for Your Soul — Truth Drop:
I reset not by erasing, but by awakening to the truth of who I already am.

Day 165 – Affirmation + Reflection

The Open Sky

Lift your gaze, even for a moment, and notice the sky above you. In the early morning it may be a soft wash of grey. At noon, a blazing blue. At dusk, a wild swirl of coral and gold. Clouds form, drift, and dissolve. Storms gather and pass. Yet the sky itself remains unchanged—vast, open, unconfined.

My beautiful soul, so does your spirit. In midlife you've weathered storms—grief, exhaustion, shifting roles, the ache of untended dreams and goals on hold. Some days it can feel as though the clouds have become your identity. But they are only passing weather. Your essence—the sky of you—remains spacious, luminous, untouchable. Emotions, worries, even heartbreak move through; they do not define who you are.

This is the heart of Reset: remembering the vastness of your own being so you don't mistake the weather for the sky. When you pause, breathe, and soften your gaze inward, you begin to sense the open space beneath the noise of your thoughts. In that space, the subconscious can be gently rewritten in the language of freedom instead of fear. Each loving breath clears a little more sky. Which thought, worry, or story can I let drift like a cloud today, trusting 'this too shall pass'?

– What would my life feel like without this thought?

– What spaciousness or possibility would open for me?

My spirit is as spacious as the sky—nothing can confine it. In this spaciousness, I can choose to reset and rise.

Day 166 – Dear God Letter

Dear God,

There are days when joy feels so far away—hidden behind burdens, busyness, and the ache of things I cannot fix. I forget that joy is not something to strive for, but something you already planted deep within me, waiting like a hidden spring beneath winter soil.

Today I pause in this season. I lay down the worn stories and poor self-talk that tell me joy is for later, or for someone else. I breathe, and with each breath I open my heart to the greater Mind, the higher consciousness that is You. Reprogram my thoughts, God. Lift my inner gaze from fear to possibility, from scarcity to the vastness of your abundance.

Awaken joy in me again—not as a fleeting mood, but as my natural inheritance. Let it rise like sunlight breaking through heavy clouds. Teach me to laugh without reason, to smile without hesitation, to savor the sweetness of simply being alive. Remind me that joy is not the absence of struggle but the presence of you, and that every small moment—a breath of fresh air, a kind word, a spark of laughter—is proof of your love flowing through me.

May this season of reset renew my subconscious so that joy becomes my strength, my medicine, and my daily song.

And so it is. Amen.

Day 167 – Ritual Reset

The Sacred Belly Breath

Maybe you've noticed it lately—the waistline softer, the curves rounder, the body carrying more than it once did. Some call it "midlife spread." But let's tell the truth: your body has been holding decades of care, meals on the run, sleepless nights, hormones shifting like tides. This isn't betrayal. It's proof you've lived.

Your body is not asking for shame. She's asking for compassion. For breath. For a reset in how you see her. You don't need to battle her—you need to befriend her.

Invitation:

Find a quiet spot. Sit or stand comfortably. Place your hands gently on your belly—not to judge, but to bless. Close your eyes. Inhale deeply through your nose, letting your belly rise. Exhale slowly through your mouth, whispering: *"Thank you for carrying me."* On the next breath, whisper one more: "Thank you for digesting my days." On the third: "I'm learning to be gentle with you."

Repeat three times, each time softening more. If emotion rises, let it. If laughter comes, let that too. Your body longs to be met with kindness, not criticism.

This isn't about shrinking. It's about releasing old stories of worth and resetting into love. With every breath, you reprogram your nervous system to know: *this body is holy ground.*

Truth Drop:
My body is not my enemy; she is my oldest friend.

Day 168 – Chakra Soul Movement

The Movement of Fire

Maybe you've felt dim lately, carrying heaviness like damp wood—responsibilities, worries, the weight of doing it all. Midlife can feel like that: the spark inside you hidden under layers that don't belong to you anymore. But fire is still here, waiting. Not to consume you, but to warm you, to clear away what drags you down.

It's not about forcing light. It's about remembering the spark you already carry and giving it space to glow again. Fire transforms everything it touches—not only by burning, but by purifying, by softening, by bringing warmth back into the cold.

Invitation:
Stand tall, feet planted firmly.
Begin to stomp your feet, gently but steady, one then the other—like waking up embers beneath you.
Let your arms move—swing them, shake them, punch the air if you wish—until you feel your body heating, your breath deepening. Imagine flames rising around you, burning away heaviness, melting tension, clearing fear.
When you're ready, place both hands over your heart. Feel the warmth you've created and whisper: *"The fire in me restores me."*

The gift is this: you don't have to shine constantly. You only need to clear space for your fire to breathe again.

AFFIRMATION:
The fire of Spirit warms me, clears me, resets and restores my strength.

Day 169 – Soul Whisker

The Blanket Battle

I found the warmest blanket in the house.
It smelled like sunshine, folded on the chair.

I stepped onto it.
Then I kneaded it.
Then I curled up and became a cinnamon roll of fur.

Five minutes later, a human soul sister walked in and said,
"Hey, That's my blanket!"

I opened one eye, yawned, and thought,
"It *was* your blanket. Now it's our sanctuary."

Sometimes, claiming a soft spot isn't selfish. It's survival. It's how we cats reset: paws first, no apology, purr until your nervous system catches up.

SOUL WHISKER:
Comfort isn't borrowed—it's conquered.

Soul Companion Card: No. 5

Day 170 – Sacred Sips Moment

The Shared Cup

Last winter, my soul sister Marisa stopped by on a rainy afternoon. She had just left a job that drained her and was questioning everything—her worth, her direction, her next step. I'd been there too. We sat at my kitchen table, two midlife women who had poured out for everyone else and suddenly found ourselves empty. I filled the kettle, not sure what to say.

When the tea was ready, I poured it into one large mug. Without thinking, I placed it between us and said, "Here, let's share." She laughed, then wrapped her hands around it, and we took turns sipping like children with a secret. In that simple act, something softened. Tears came. Stories spilled out. We remembered who we were before the giving became exhaustion.

Marisa left lighter, not because she had answers, but because her nervous system had exhaled. I felt it too. Sharing a cup reminded us both: sisterhood refills what you pour out.

Life was never meant to be sipped in solitude. Sharing does not empty you—it restores you. Like tea steeping stronger with every pour, love multiplies when it flows between souls.

Invitation:

Hold an imaginary cup in your hands. Inhale slowly, as if drawing in its warmth. Exhale gently, imagining you're sending love to a soul sister who needs it. Three breaths are enough. Notice how your chest softens, maybe even a smile rising unbidden. It will come back to you—it always does.

Affirmation:
When I share my soul, I am refilled in love.

Day 171 – Truth Drop

The Law of Cause and Effect

Last year, a woman in our circle came to every gathering with eyes full of quiet grief. She had spoken kindness over her children for years, volunteered when no one thanked her, planted hope when her own heart was breaking. "It feels like nothing is changing," she whispered. "Like I'm pouring into dry ground."

Then one spring morning she walked in radiant. Her son had called to say he'd turned his life around. Her small business—once stalled—was finally growing. With tears shining she said, "It was like seeds breaking open underground. Everything I planted in faith began to rise at once."

This is the promise of the Law of Cause and Effect: nothing you give in love is ever wasted. Spirit honors every seed you sow, even when no sprouts appear. Roots do their deepest work in the dark of winter. What feels invisible is not inactive—it is necessary repair.

When discouragement comes, remember: soil works in silence first. Shoots break through later. Your kindness, your faith, your persistence are already vibrating through unseen layers. Your season of increase will come, but even now, the roots are alive with movement.

Truth Drop:
Nothing given in love is ever wasted.

Day 172 – Surprise Soul Whisper

The Door Ajar

Last weekend I wandered through an old shopping district in downtown Sarasota. Most of the shop doors were locked, but one stood slightly ajar. Inside, the scent of fresh bread drifted out, warm from the oven, mingled with the sound of quiet humming. I hesitated, then peeked in. The baker smiled and handed me a roll. "I'm not open yet," she said, "but since you're here…"

That tiny moment stayed with me. I hadn't pushed my way in; I had simply noticed the opening. A small act of curiosity became a quiet blessing.

This is how Spirit so often works. Not with grand gestures, but with glimpses—half-open doors, gentle nudges, whispers that say you're on the right path. These "ajar moments" are holy. They're practice rounds in trust. You're not asked to pry or push; you're invited to lean in, to notice, to let the light spilling through guide your next step.

When restlessness rises because a door hasn't swung wide, pause. Place a hand over your heart, breathe slowly, and ask: *"What is this moment offering me now?"* My darling, sometimes the smallest opening holds the greatest invitation.

Microdose Soul Whisper Practice:
Close your eyes. Picture a door slightly open, a shaft of light streaming through. Inhale trust. Exhale control. Step toward the light in your imagination. Notice what feeling rises.

Affirmation:
I trust the doors Spirit opens, even when they appear only slightly ajar.

Day 173 – Soul-to-Spirit Meditation

The Open Field

Maybe lately life has felt crowded—calendars packed, noise constant, no room to breathe. My darling, your spirit is larger than your schedule. You've given so much—you need a field inside you where nothing is demanded.

Close your eyes and imagine yourself walking through a weathered gate into an endless meadow. Tall grasses brush your palms like silk. All around, lavender sways in the breeze, purple blooms releasing a fragrance—clean, calming, like a whispered lullaby. The horizon stretches without end, and above you the sky opens wide, blue and luminous.

Pause. Inhale deeply—draw the lavender into your chest, feel your heart expand like the sky. Exhale slowly, let your shoulders drop, your body soften into the field beneath you. With each breath, the noise of the day fades. With each breath, you remember: you are not your schedule, your titles, your worries. You are Spirit.

Now imagine the lavender wrapping around you like a soft shawl. With every inhale, calm rises through your body; with every exhale, tension melts back into the earth. Three slow breaths. Notice how the vastness around you begins to echo inside you.

My luminous soul, know this truth: even when life feels crowded, this inner field is always here. One breath, and you are home.

AFFIRMATION:
My spirit is vast and free, like an open field beneath the sky.

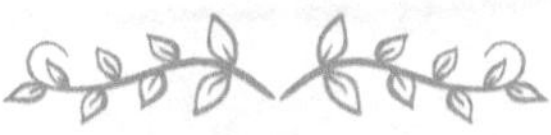

Day 174 – Microdose Laugh-Lift

Silent Laughter

Who says laughter has to be noisy? Some of the deepest giggles happen where no one hears — in the middle of a meeting, church, a library, elevator, or kneeling in the garden with muddy hands. Silent laughter is like a private text message between you and Spirit — an inside joke, a sparkle of joy humming through your whole body.

When you laugh inside, your shoulders still jiggle, your belly still bounces, your smile and eyes still lights up — only the sound stays tucked in. It's delight sneaking past the noise of the world, reminding you that joy is an *inside* job.

Here is a microdose for you:
- Sit quietly. Close your eyes. Take a deep, exaggerated breath.
- Without making a sound, think of something amusing, start to laugh intentionally — a silly, silent chuckle.
- Feel your shoulders wobble, your belly bounce, your face brighten.
- Let the feeling ripple through you like champagne bubbles of light.
- Stay with the positivity and optimism feeling for a few moments, smiling softly, letting Spirit's light rise in you.

Joy doesn't need an audience. Even in silence, laughter is medicine. It loosens what feels heavy, shakes off stale energy, and wakes up your freedom inside. You don't have to wait for a punchline. You don't even have to make a sound. Just let the giggles rise and fizz through you.

In midlife, Joy isn't childish, it's a survival skill.

Day 175 – Soul Medicine Quote

"Resetting your words from love resets life itself."
—**Dr. Jennifer Rademaker**

Every word is a seed. Whisper it once and it begins to shape the field of your experience. Whisper it daily and it becomes a path beneath your feet.

In midlife, after years of speaking from duty, doubt, or self-critique, there is a sacred invitation to speak from love instead. This isn't just about being "positive." It's about choosing words that carry the frequency of who you truly are. When language rises from love, your nervous system softens. Your thoughts re-pattern. Your choices shift. It's not magic; it's resonance. What you speak inside becomes what you live outside.

Pause for a moment. Notice a phrase you've been saying to yourself today. How does it feel in your body—heavy or light, contracting or opening?

Ask yourself:
- Would my higher self speak these words over me?
- Would Spirit, God, Love whisper them to me?

Now choose a new word or phrase—something loving, gentle, honest—and let it replace the old one. That's a reset. That's how reality begins to move in a new direction.

Reset Practice:
Pick one word of love: *safe, enough, free, whole.* Each time you catch the old phrase, silently replace it with your new one. Snap your fingers as you do, imagining the old script breaking and the new one landing.

❄

You are rewriting your life one word at a time.

AFFIRMATION:
Resetting words from love resets life itself.

Soul Companion Card: No. 15

Day 176 – Soul Reflection

The Last Snow

My beautiful soul, where I grew up in Newfoundland and Labrador, winter snow was a way of life. For months it piled high, sparkling beneath a pale sun. But near the end of the season, it lost its postcard beauty. I'd see it pushed to the roadside—grey, salted, streaked with dirt from passing cars. It wasn't pretty. Yet even then, I knew it was a sign of hope: spring was on its way.

Like the last grey snow… like the caterpillar in its chrysalis… what looks like an ending is really a beginning. Old patterns, old words, old seasons dissolve before something new emerges. The meltwater nourishes what's beneath; the formless stage forms the wings.

Pause here, notice a phrase or story you've been carrying that feels tired or heavy. Imagine it melting like that last snow, dissolving like a chrysalis into mystery. Feel the space opening inside you for a fresh word, a fresh season, a fresh self to emerge.

Try this with me:
Place a hand over your heart. Whisper one heavy phrase you've been carrying. Snap your fingers softly as you release it, imagining it melting away. Then speak a loving new word into the space you've created. Breathe slowly three times and feel the shift take root in your body.

AFFIRMATION:
Even what looks messy and finished in me now is feeding the life that's on its way.

Day 177 – Affirmation + Reflection

Reflection:

After years of being the steady one — the caretaker, the organizer, the problem-solver — it's easy to forget the words spoken inside your own head. Midlife often becomes a season where old phrases echo: *I'm behind. I'm tired. I'm not enough.* They drift in quietly, like leftover snow at the roadside.

Your inner language shapes your outer life. Even one gentle word can soften frozen ground and allow new growth to push through. This isn't about faking positivity; it's about offering yourself the same kindness you've always offered everyone else. Each loving word is an act of reclamation. Each time you catch an old phrase and choose a new one, you're not only speaking differently—you're becoming different.

You've carried so much. Be proud of the way you're still showing up, still willing to soften, still learning a new language for yourself. That is courage. That is grace. You're already blooming on the inside.

Pause with me now. Listen for one phrase you've been repeating today. How does it feel in your body—heavy or light, contracting or opening? If it's heavy, choose a new phrase, even just one word of love. Feel your shoulders drop, your chest expand. This is a reset. This is you preparing your inner garden for spring.

AFFIRMATION:
With every loving word spoken, the inner landscape resets and renews.

Day 178 – Dear God Letter

The Threshold

Dear God,

This is the edge of my winter season—the last of my inner snow. I have sat with what was frozen, sifted through what was heavy, and laid down the words that no longer served me. Thank You for every lesson hidden in the cold, for every moment that taught me stillness, for every whisper that reminded me I am not alone.

I feel the melt now. Old phrases have dissolved, old beliefs have softened, and the ground of my soul is becoming fertile again. In this quiet moment before spring, I offer you my bare and ready heart.

Lift me, God. Lift my thoughts, my words, my ways of seeing. Where I have spoken smallness, teach me to speak expansion. Where I have rehearsed doubt, teach me to sing trust. Where I have clung to what was, guide me to open my hands for what is next.

As I step into my next season, breathe courage into me. Let every cell, every thought, every word carry the frequency of love. Let my life blossom with what you've planted during this reset. May my actions be rooted in grace, and my presence radiate hope.

I stand at the threshold. With you, I cross into spring.

And so it is. Amen.

Rise— Spring

My beautiful soul sister…

Welcome to the season of **Rise**.

Like tender shoots breaking through soft earth, this is your time of quiet courage and new beginnings. The long winter has prepared you; the roots you tended in stillness are now ready to reach for light. In midlife, it can feel risky to bloom again — yet the soul never stops becoming. These pages are here to remind you: your time is not past; your becoming is now.

As you enter this pathway pause. Let your palms rest open on your lap, a gesture of readiness. Inhale possibility, exhale doubt. Whisper softly, "I rise into my becoming."

Here you'll meet reflections, prayers, and practices that help you open your heart, reclaim your voice, and step forward with grace. They're not instructions but invitations — small, sacred movements that awaken what already lives inside you.

Every bud carries the memory of its bloom. You carry the memory of your wholeness. Trust the season. Trust your rising.

AFFIRMATION:
I rise into my becoming and welcome what's next.

213

Day 179 – Breath Practice / Ritual Reset

First Breath of Spring

You've spent a season in winter — releasing, resetting, softening.. This season is not a sprint or a push; it's the tender moment when frozen ground loosens, shoots reach upward, and new light begins to warm the skin.

Your body, like the earth, knows how to move from stillness into aliveness. This simple breath practice gently awakens your vagus nerve — your calm-and-connect pathway — so your rise begins from a grounded, steady place rather than a rushed one.**Practice:**

- Sit tall, feet on the earth or floor.
- Imagine you're in a spring meadow where fresh sage and lavender grow wild. Their scent drifts on the breeze — clean, green, awakening.
- Inhale slowly through your nose for a count of 4, drawing in that herbal fragrance like a seedling reaching for light.
- Hold softly for a count of 2.
- Exhale through pursed lips with a gentle "whooo" for a count of 6, feeling your ribs draw inward as old winter air leaves.
- At the bottom of the exhale, hum or gently chant "mmm" for one beat. The vibration stimulates the vagus nerve and calls your nervous system into calm readiness.
- Repeat for three rounds, letting your shoulders soften and your chest lift like buds opening to sun.

As you breathe, picture each exhale melting the last traces of winter and each inhale drawing in fresh, herbal courage.

Affirmation:
With every breath, I awaken gently and rise with calm courage.

Day 180 – Chakra Soul Movement

The Movement of Air

You've spent a season of stillness, holding so much inside. Now the winds are shifting. This is the moment to feel what your spirit has been longing for — more space, more breath, more light.

Air is freedom itself. It slips past walls, whispers through trees, fills your lungs with life. Like you, it cannot be held or bound. Today, let the movement of air remind your body that you, too, were made to move, to rise, to be uncontained.

Let's Feel It:

If you'd like, put on some soft, lyric-free music — something like a breeze through an open window. Let the sound wrap around you. Begin to sway, loosen your shoulders, and let the air move you. This is your time.

This is how you can experience a microdose of it right now...

- Stand tall, feet grounded, arms at your sides. Imagine you're outside on a spring morning, the scent of fresh sage and mint drifting on the breeze.
- Inhale deeply, drawing that freshness into your lungs like a spring breeze. Feel it cleanse and heal as it travels through your chest.
- Exhale slowly, sweeping your arms wide as though opening the sky, releasing what winter left behind.
- Repeat several times, each movement larger, as if your arms are wings catching wind.
- Rise onto your toes, expanding into lightness, feeling the freedom of flight.
- End by crossing your hands gently over your heart, holding the air of gratitude within.

You've carried so much, beautiful soul. Now feel the air carrying you, washing you, healing you.

I expand with the freedom of air, open to possibility and light.

Day 181 – Soul Whisker

The Sunbeam Shift

I was sprawled in the middle of the hallway, soaking up a perfect square of sunlight. Then the sunbeam moved.
Did I panic? Nope.
I stretched, yawned, and relocated to a new warm patch — instantly cozy again.

Life shifts its sunbeams, too — careers change, children grow, bodies evolve — but warmth can always be found. Sometimes the smallest shift brings the biggest comfort. Don't overthink it — just scoot to the next sunbeam.

SOUL WHISKER:
Shift happens — scoot toward the light and *call it evolution.*

Day 182 – Sacred Sips Moment

The Lemon in My Tea

On my Florida property I have lemon trees. I love walking outside to pick one, its skin still warm from the sun. I slice it into my hot or cold tea and watch the bright yellow piece swirl into the water. Some days I leave it just as it is — bitter, tart, a wake-up for my senses. Other days I add a drop of stevia or honey and the whole drink softens, sweetens, brightens on its own.

As I sit with my cup, I think about how my thoughts work the same way. A sharp, self-critical thought can flood my body like that pure lemon — eyes sting, mouth waters, chest tightens, mood sours. But when I catch it and add a little sweetness — a kind word, a gentle reframe, a breath of compassion — the bitterness changes. The flavor stays citrusy but becomes lively and fragrant instead of harsh.

This is the quiet alchemy of midlife isn't it?. We can't always choose the slices life drops into our cup, but we can choose how we hold them, stir them, and sip them. Thinking sweeter thoughts isn't pretending; it's re-steeping reality in love so it nourishes instead of depletes.

Next time you make tea, notice what you're adding. Notice what you're thinking. Practice sweetening a single inner phrase as you sweeten your cup.

AFFIRMATION:
As I steep my thoughts in love, even the sharpest moments turn to light.

Day 183 – Truth Drop

From Thornbushes to Roses

Just imagine this: a woman walks through her garden at dawn. In her hand are seed packets labeled *Worry*, *What If*, and *I'm Not Enough*. She drops them into the soil without thinking. Seasons pass. One morning she wakes to find thornbushes where she once dreamed of roses and wonders, *How did my garden become this?*

This is the Law of Cause and Effect. Every thought is a seed, and the subconscious is the soil. It never asks if the seed is worthy—it simply grows what it's given. Over time, repeated thoughts take root and appear in form. Thornbushes aren't punishment; they're just proof of what was planted. Anxiety isn't a flaw; it's a signal your inner garden longs for new seeds.

Today, with each breath, plant the new seeds.

My darling, God never leaves you in a garden of weeds. Every day brings new packets of seed. As your thoughts grow brighter, the thorns fall away and roses take their place.

TRUTH DROP:
The mind is cause, life is effect. What you repeat in thought, you meet in form. Everything is consciousness.

Day 184 – Surprise Soul Whisper

The Key in Your Pocket

Sometimes we pray for doors to open and forget the key has been warm in our pocket all along. Spirit doesn't withhold—it waits for us to remember and reach. You've been doing the winter work: clearing old beliefs, softening your self-talk, aligning your inner life with Truth. Now it's time to use the key.

Turn it. Push the door. Step across the threshold. You don't have to force or beg for permission—you're already holding what you need. Each small, brave movement tells your whole system: *I'm entering my next chapter.*

Whisper Practice — Turn the Key

- Place one hand on your heart and one on your belly. Inhale **4**, hold **2**, exhale **6**—once—then act before the mind talks you out of it.

- Choose **one** key-turn today: say yes to a fresh invitation, take a different route, rearrange one drawer, or hold one thought that feels like sunlight all day.

- Optional Rise add-on: drop a **45-minute Becoming Block** on your calendar this week (journal/learn/create). If it's scheduled, it exists.

As you move, notice where courage lands—jaw softening, spine lengthening, breath widening. Touch that place and whisper, *This is me, becoming.*

Soul Whisper:
I carry the key; I turn it now. I step in as the woman I already am.

Day 185 – Soul-to-Spirit Meditation

The Ocean Breath

Have you ever stood on a cliff or a pier and felt the wind off the water fill your lungs before you even thought to inhale? The sea seems to breathe you before you breathe it. That's because its rhythm is older than thought—older than fear—older than your to-do list. Midlife can feel like you're caught between tides: pulled by what you've given and pushed by what's still ahead. In those moments it's easy to believe you're small, adrift, or alone.

But listen. Beneath the surface of the day, your own body carries the same rhythm that moves the tides. Spirit built it into you so you would never lose the way home. You don't have to manufacture calm; you only have to remember the breath you were born with. The same power that lifts and lowers the ocean is moving quietly through your chest right now, ready to steady you.

Practice:

Find a quiet spot. If you can, slip off your shoes and let your feet touch the floor or the earth. Place one hand over your heart and one on your belly. Inhale slowly through your nose as if a tide is rising from deep within you. Pause for a heartbeat at the top—float there—then exhale longer than you inhaled, letting the tide return to the sea. Repeat for several breaths, allowing your body to rock gently as if on water. With each exhale, feel tension draining away; with each inhale, feel Spirit filling you.

Affirmation:
The power that moves the ocean moves through me—I am one with Spirit's tide

Day 186 – Microdose Laugh-Lift

Future Laugh

Laughter doesn't just heal the present — it plants seeds for the future. When you laugh as if your prayer has already been answered, your subconscious receives it as truth. The body relaxes, the spirit expands, and alignment begins. Laugh for no reason, and the body doesn't know the difference. Joy is contagious inside you. Let it rise.

Invitation:
- Close your eyes and picture the dream, the answered prayer, the miracle already real.

- Let your lips curve into a smile, then let a laugh bubble up — as if you're standing in that moment right now.

- Feel the joy vibrate through you, a gentle wave moving from your belly to your chest. Let it anchor deep into your subconscious as living proof.

- If it helps, bounce on your toes or gently sway your shoulders as you laugh. Let your body feel the future in motion.

This is not pretending. This is creating. Spirit responds to joy, and joy is a magnet for miracles.

PRESCRIPTION FOR YOUR SOUL RX:
Get a rise, joy taken seriously– is a radical act.

WARNING:
Side effects may include belly aches, tear-inducing laughter and heart expansion.

Day 187 – Soul Medicine Quote

"Joy is not something I chase—it is something I choose."
—Dr. Jennifer Rademaker

For so long, many of us were taught to postpone joy—until the list is done, until we're thinner, richer, calmer, or loved *enough*. We treat it like a reward for perfect conditions instead of nourishment for the journey itself. But joy is not earned. It's not out there somewhere waiting to be hunted down. It's a practice—an inner permission slip.

When your subconscious begins to accept joy as normal—like breath, like heartbeat—it stops being a rare guest and becomes the air you live in. You no longer have to *try* to feel it; you simply recognize what is already here.

This is the quiet revolution of midlife: joy not as a chase, but as a homecoming. Where, in the middle of your ordinary day, can you find a spark of joy right now?

Joy is resilient, ever-present, waiting for you to remember. Right now, place one hand on your heart and gently trail two fingers down the side of your neck just below your ear, lightly massaging that tender spot while taking a slow, humming exhale. This simple vagus nerve reset tells your nervous system, *I am safe enough to receive pleasure and joy now.* Each time you practice this with a positive goal statement, you anchor a new habit into your body. Over time, this becomes subconscious reprogramming—training you to see light even in ordinary days.

Truth Drop:
I choose joy. I choose optimism.

Day 188 – Soul Reflection

The Bird Who Rose

On my Florida property, I often take my three cats outside for fresh air. They wear GPS trackers, and most days we simply sit in the grass together—sun on our skin, watching the world. One afternoon, though, my Maine Coon caught a bird. My heart dropped. Of course, he had played with feathers on a wand; to him this was no different. But to me, it was a living being. I scooped up my cat, carried him inside, and ran back out to the bird.

He was still and silent on the ground. I felt sick. I knelt beside him, whispered prayers, even tried to send healing energy. Then I waited. He stayed there. I checked again and again. As dusk came, I called a wildlife-rehab number to come rescue him. When I hung up and went back outside to place him in a safe box… he was gone. Then I heard a sound. I looked up. There he was—on a branch above me, singing. And then he flew. My heart lifted with him. It felt like grace, like a living metaphor: stunned but not broken, grounded but not lost, still capable of flight.

Where in your life could you trust that your "wounded wing" is not the end of your flight, but part of your rising?

My beautiful soul, the same is true for you. A wounded wing does not erase your essence. Healing can look still, quiet, even hopeless, but the capacity for flight is still there—waiting. Spirit has not taken away your wings. They are folded close, mending, preparing for the moment you rise again.

My wings remember flight. I am preparing to rise.

Day 189 – Affirmation + Reflection

Small Wings, First Lift

After a season of rest, a bird doesn't launch straight into the sky. She stretches one wing, then the other. She tests the air with small flutters before rising. Each movement strengthens her muscles and reminds her of the sky.

Your Rise may begin the same way. You don't have to leap into a new life overnight. Start with one small act of courage. Speak a kind word to yourself. Make one gentle change. Accept one invitation. Each small lift tells your nervous system: *"It's safe to fly again."*

What could be your "first lift" today — one small act of courage, kindness, or openness that would remind you of your sky?

Pause now. Place a hand over your heart and one over your belly. Inhale slowly, imagining air beneath your wings. Exhale, feeling a quiet lift in your chest. This is your practice — a soft rehearsal of flight. Every flutter matters.

You're not behind; you're becoming.

Tiny movements, consistent and loving, will carry you higher than you think.

AFFIRMATION:
Each small act of courage strengthens my wings. I rise one gentle lift at a time.

Day 190 – Dear God Letter

Learning to Fly

Dear God,

Here I am, standing at the edge of new possibility. I've spent the winter releasing, resetting, and remembering who I am. Now the air beneath me feels alive again—warm, open, full of promise. My wings are strong, ready to rise.

I give you my readiness. I give you my willingness to soar higher than before. Guide my ascent, God. Teach me to move with grace, to trust the rhythm of your winds, to stay rooted in love even as I lift into new heights.

Help me remember that each movement upward is guided, not forced; that expansion can be easeful when I fly with you. Fill my lungs with your breath, my body with your courage, my thoughts with your vision. Let my life become a current of faith and freedom.

Thank you for the seasons that shaped me—for winter's rest, for spring's awakening, and for this sacred rise that reminds me: I was born to fly.

And so it is. Amen.

Day 191 – Chakra Soul Movement

The Solar Plexus Spin

There's a moment when you realize the fire never went out—it was simply waiting for air. The Solar Plexus, just above your navel, is that breath of remembrance—the seat of confidence, courage, and radiant power.

Think of this movement as stoking your inner sun. You're not performing; you're returning to your own warmth, inviting your body to feel safe inside its strength.

Microdose for your soul:
- Put on soft, lyric-free music that feels like sunlight through an open window.
- Light an orange candle or mist the air with citrus. Let your space smell like warmth.
- Stand with feet hip-width apart, knees soft, hands resting on your belly.
- Begin slow, circular movements with your hips—as if tracing a golden sunbeam inside your core.
- Breathe deeply. Let your body soften into rhythm and your center expand.

Power, in this season, no longer looks like striving. It looks like standing in your own light and calling it home.

SOUL TRUTH:
I move with courage. I shine from my center.

Day 192 – Soul Whisker

The Fence Perch

Hello, my two-legged soul sister.
You've been staring out the window at that fence like it's Everest.

Me? I'm already up here — tail swaying, whiskers in the wind, looking fabulous. The trick? Don't think about falling. Think about the view.

Just leap. Balance is overrated anyway — swagger works better.

Soul Whisker:
Go on, climb your fence — your next chapter's waiting on the other side. And by the way, the grass really is greener.

Day 193 – Sacred Sips Moment

The Empty Cup

A cup cannot be filled if it's already overflowing. Sometimes we carry so much — thoughts, worries, endless lists — that there's no room left for what wants to find us. But tea reminds us: the cup must first be empty to receive.

Emptiness is not failure; it's readiness. In Rise season, the space inside you is not a void but a clearing. Spirit hasn't abandoned you — Spirit is preparing you. Just as you can't taste fresh tea in a cup full of yesterday's leaves, you can't welcome new blessings while clinging to the old. This emptiness is your open sky.

Pause for a moment. Breathe. Imagine setting your cup down, pouring out what no longer serves, and holding it empty in your hands. Feel the air in that space — the quiet before the pour. Then whisper: *"Spirit, I am ready to receive."* Picture a golden stream filling your cup: new energy, new relationships, new ideas, new life flowing in. Let your body sense the difference between "empty" and "open."

This is what Rise feels like: not a frantic grasping, but a calm, lifted readiness. The space you've made is your invitation to Spirit.

AFFIRMATION:
I make space for Spirit to fill me with new blessings. I am open and ready to rise.

Day 194 – Truth Drop

Your Soul Chose This Journey

A soul sister sits in the quiet of early morning, coffee warming her hands, feeling the weight of a life that hasn't unfolded exactly as she imagined. Midlife can magnify this ache—children grown or gone, relationships shifting, dreams taking unfamiliar turns. In these moments, it's easy to whisper, *"Did I take a wrong turn? Did life betray me?"*

Metaphysical truth offers a gentler view: your soul chose this journey. Not as punishment, but as a path of becoming. Before you drew your first breath, your spirit carried within it certain themes, lessons, and longings—like seeds waiting for the right season to bloom. Even the hardest chapters hold hidden purpose, though you may not see it yet.

There comes a moment when *"Why me?"* softens into *"What is my soul showing me here?"* That question alone opens the light. It shifts you from blame to partnership with Spirit—from resistance to trust. It's the seed breaking the soil, stretching toward warmth.

Pause now. Place a hand over your heart. Inhale, imagining a golden thread connecting you to a loving Source. Exhale, whispering inwardly: *"My soul chose this journey. I am safe to grow from it."* Feel your chest expand as trust replaces tension, as readiness replaces fear.

TRUTH DROP:
My soul chose this journey. I am safe to grow from it.

Day 195 – Surprise Soul Whisper

The Standing Date with Your Becoming

Not every step forward roars. Sometimes Rise sounds like a quiet appointment you keep—with yourself. You've done the winter work of clearing and softening. Now give your future a chair at the table.

Today's whisper is simple: **put becoming on the calendar.** When you schedule sacred time, you tell your nervous system, *this matters*—and your life rearranges to match.

Whisper Practice — 45-Minute Becoming Block

- Open your calendar and drop a **45-minute pocket** this week titled: *Becoming*.
- Choose **one** focus (no multitasking): journal, learn, create, or plan a tiny brave step.
- Protect it lovingly: notifications off, tea poured, door gently closed.
- Begin with one breath (hand to heart, hand to belly). Inhale 4, hold 2, exhale 6—once. Start before your mind negotiates it away.

What you do inside the block can be tiny. The power is the *keeping*. Kept promises to yourself become momentum, and momentum becomes a life that fits.

SOUL WHISPER:
I honor my becoming with time on the page—and the woman I'm becoming shows up.

Day 196 – Soul-to-Spirit Meditation

A Vision of Light Ahead

Today let's journey into the light of what's possible. This meditation is a space to reconnect with that part of you that still dreams—still believes—still longs for a life filled with meaning, joy, and divine fulfillment.

Take a slow breath in. Feel it sweep through your chest like the first light of morning. Exhale gently, releasing the weight of yesterday.

Now bring your awareness to your thoughts. Notice if any worries or doubts drift in. Don't push them away—just imagine them as soft, gray clouds passing across a vast blue sky. You don't have to control them. They will move on their own.

PAUSE...

With your next inhale, begin to invite brighter thoughts and feelings. Picture memories that once made your heart light up. Feel joy returning, possibility awakening. Or imagine something beautiful that you're looking forward to—a new idea, a friendship, a horizon not yet seen.

Let that vision glow inside you, spreading warmth through your body, radiating like sunlight through every cell. Allow yourself to trust this light—it's your soul remembering the way forward.

AFFIRMATION:
I open to what's next. My future unfolds in light.

Day 197 – Microdose Laugh-Lift

The Soul Sister Laugh

Midlife can feel heavy at times—responsibility, shifting roles, even the body itself carrying weight it never used to. But Spirit has given you medicine that doesn't come in a bottle: laughter.

Today, let yourself laugh with intention. Not because everything is funny, but because your body needs the reset. Stand in front of a mirror or sit with a soul sister. Begin with a soft chuckle, let it grow into a belly laugh, even if it feels silly at first. Keep going until your shoulders shake, your breath deepens, and tears of release rise to your eyes.

This is sacred medicine. Each laugh is a truth drop reminding your nervous system: *you are safe, you are alive, you are free.* Laughter is Spirit's way of helping you release, reset, and rise into joy again.

PRESCRIPTION FOR YOUR SOUL RX:

Dosage: *Laugh on an empty heart for faster spiritual absorption. Apply to fear. Do not dilute.*

Day 198 – Soul Medicine Quote

"Even in the middle of change, I am still becoming."
– Dr. Jennifer Rademaker

Midlife is not the ending of a story—it is the unfolding of a new chapter. The world may tell you that your best years are behind you, but Spirit whispers differently: They are ahead-*you are still becoming.*

Every wrinkle, every scar, every shift in your body is not proof of decline—it is proof of life lived, lessons learned, and wisdom gained. My radiant soul sister, your becoming doesn't stop at forty, fifty, or sixty. It expands with each breath you take.

This is the rise: learning to stand in the middle of change without fear, without apology, and without shrinking. You get to claim the beauty of your unfolding, knowing that you are not finished, not forgotten, and never too late.

Truth Drop:
I honor the woman I see in the mirror—past, present, and still becoming.

Soul Companion Card: No. 43

Day 199 – Soul Reflection

The Mirror of Becoming

One day you catch your reflection and pause. The face looking back isn't the same one you carried through your twenties or thirties. There are lines now—some carved by laughter, others by tears. There's a softness, a weight, a story in your eyes that wasn't there before.

And yet, if you look deeper, you see her—the girl you once were. She has not left you. She lives inside your gaze, holding hands with the woman you are now. Both are you. Both are becoming.

The mirror does not lie—but it does not tell the whole truth either. The truth is, you are more radiant now than ever before, because you carry both wisdom and wonder. Spirit shaped you through every season, and still whispers: *"You are not finished."*

This is not a moment to mourn youth. This is a moment to honor your unfolding.

REFLECT:
When you look in the mirror, what part of your younger self do you still recognize—and how does she walk with you today?

Day 200 – Affirmation + Reflection

The Courage to Rest

In a world that praises busyness, slowing down can feel like rebellion. For the midlife woman who has carried so much—family, careers, friendships, endless lists—rest can even feel guilty, like something you haven't earned. But Spirit whispers: *rest is your birthright.*

My radiant one, you are not a machine to be pushed until you break. You are a soul in a body, a being who needs pauses to breathe, to reset, to rise again. Rest is not the opposite of progress—it is the soil from which progress grows.

When you rest, your subconscious heals, your nervous system resets, and your spirit remembers: *I am safe, I am whole, I am worthy of renewal.*

AFFIRMATION (REPEAT):
Rest is not laziness—rest is sacred.

REFLECT:
What would it feel like today to give yourself full permission to rest without apology?

Day 201 – Dear God Letter

Dear God,

There are days when I feel invisible—as though the world has moved on and forgotten me. My children are grown, my body has changed, and the roles I once held no longer fit the way they used to. Sometimes I wonder: do you still see me?

Remind me, God, that you have never lost sight of me. That even when others overlook me, you hold me in perfect view. Teach me to trust that invisibility is an illusion—that your light shines on me whether I feel noticed or not.

Help me release the need to prove my worth. Reset my spirit with the quiet truth that I am already enough. And lift me so that I rise into this season not as less, but as more—more radiant, more rooted, more real.

With love, I release, reset, and rise.

And so it is, Amen.

Day 202 – Ritual Reset

Breathing Through the Fire

Hot flashes and waves of heat can feel overwhelming—like your body is betraying you. But what if this fire were not your enemy, but your messenger? Fire is the element of transformation. It burns away what no longer serves, making space for renewal.

Practice:

- Sit comfortably, eyes closed.
- Inhale slowly through your nose, imagining cool silver light entering.
- Hold your breath gently at the top.
- Exhale through pursed lips, visualizing the fire dissolving into calm, radiant energy.
- Repeat five cycles, whispering inwardly: *I am safe. I am becoming.*

My darling, this is more than breathwork—it's a metaphysical reset. As Bruce Lipton's *Biology of Belief* reminds us, your thoughts inform your cells. When you shift from *"I am broken"* to *"I am transforming,"* your biology listens. Metaphysics agrees: as within, so without. You are a co-creator with Spirit, shaping even this season with your consciousness.

Soul Whisper:

My body is not betraying me—it is becoming new. Each breath I take is peace through fire, light through change, and love through renewal.

Day 203 – Chakra Soul Movement

The Heart-Opening Stretch

Midlife can sometimes make the chest feel tight—years of giving, holding, and caring can cause the heart to curl inward. But your heart chakra, the center of love and compassion, longs for expansion. It wants to remember what freedom feels like.

Practice:
- Stand tall, feet grounded.
- Lace your fingers gently behind your back.
- Draw your shoulders down and back as your chest opens.
- Lift your chin softly toward the sky.
- Inhale, imagining emerald-green light filling your chest.
- Exhale, releasing any heaviness, making space for lightness and love.

When you open your body, your energy opens too, and your spirit follows. You're teaching your cells a new story: love is safe here. Openness is strength.

MANTRA:
My heart expands in love and freedom.

Day 204 – Soul Whisker

The Cat Who Stretches First

Human, have you noticed? I never leap straight from nap to action. I *stretch* first—long, slow, deliciously dramatic. I let every muscle wake up in its own good time. No guilt. No hurry. Just purrs and presence.

You, on the other hand, bolt out of bed like there's a meeting with destiny.

So before you rush to save the world, try saving your morning. Arch your back and exhale like you mean it. That's not laziness—it's alignment.

Life moves better when you do it cat-style: unhurried, elegant, unapologetically sensual.

Soul Whisker:
Purr-mission granted: stretch first, conquer later

Day 205 – Sacred Sips Moment

The Evening Cup

There are nights when sleep feels far away—your mind replays conversations, your body stirs with restless heat, and you wonder if rest will ever find you again.

You are not broken. This season of sleeplessness is not your failure—it is an invitation.

Tonight, instead of wrestling with the dark, pour yourself an evening cup. Let it be chamomile or lemon balm—something gentle, something that speaks peace. Hold it warm between your palms, and feel the weight of the cup grounding you.

Breathe in its fragrance. Let the steam rise like a soft prayer, curling through the air. Whisper inwardly: *"This moment is enough."*

Spirit reminds us: even if sleep delays, peace does not. You can rest your mind even when your body will not yet rest. You can enter the quiet, sip by sip, and find renewal in presence.

Now, hold the cup close to your belly. Feel its warmth spreading through you—soothing, steady, alive.

TRUTH DROP:
Even in wakefulness, peace can find me. I rest in the warmth of now.

Day 206 – Truth Drop

The Law of Abundance

Scarcity is a story the world tells, but Spirit writes a different law: there is always more than enough. From the moment you were born—breath after breath, sunrise after sunrise—life has been proving it to you.

Midlife may whisper that time is running out, that your best years are behind you, that joy is rationed and purpose has passed. But metaphysics teaches the opposite: you are standing in the richness of your becoming. The years behind you haven't emptied the cup— they've deepened it.

Abundance isn't something you chase; it's something you align with. When you shift from lack to love, from fear to trust, you remember what was never missing.

Gratitude is the breath that opens the gate—it lets the current of good flood toward you.
Take a breath right now. Feel the air entering your lungs—free, limitless, unearned. This is abundance in motion.
When you slow down enough to notice what's already supporting you, you don't have to chase the flow—you realize you've been in it all along.

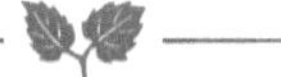

TRUTH DROP:
I live in a universe of endless abundance—there is always more than enough.

Day 207 – Surprise Soul Whisper

The Wink of the Sun

There are mornings when the light itself flirts with you—slipping through the blinds, warming your cheek, reminding you that you're still rising, still becoming. It's Spirit's way of saying, *Don't forget—you shine too.*

Joy doesn't always arrive with trumpets. Sometimes it tiptoes in on a sunbeam or rides the breeze across your skin. Today, notice the tiny flirtations of light that find you. Let them remind you: the universe hasn't forgotten your glow—it's playing with you.

Whisper Practice — 60-Second Joy Dose

Stand by a window (or step outside) for exactly one minute. Receive the light.

Notice where joy lands—chest softening, breath widening, jaw unclenching. Place a palm there and whisper, *Thank you.* Let your body learn that this brightness is safe.

SOUL WHISPER:
I let the light find me—and I shine right back.

Day 208 – Soul-to-Spirit Meditation

The Forest Path

There's a moment when you leave the noise of the world and step into quiet green—the hush of trees, the scent of pine, light shimmering through leaves. Something inside you exhales. You remember that peace isn't found ahead of you—it's already beneath your feet.

This is what midlife teaches: you don't need another map. The path is already unfolding where you stand. The same energy that moves rivers and raises branches is guiding you too. You are not lost—you are being led.

If you can, step outside barefoot for a moment. Feel the ground steady beneath you. Inhale the scent of earth, exhale what you no longer need. Let your body remember that the Divine moves through nature—and through you.

This is your sacred rhythm:
Root… Release.
Rest… Reset.
Rise… Return to light.

AFFIRMATION:
I am guided by the rhythm of nature—steady, grounded and free.

Day 209 – Microdose Laugh-Lift

Laughing Through the Symptoms

Hot flashes, night sweats, brain fog, mood swings—menopause brings its own circus. And some days, it feels anything but funny. But Spirit reminds us: even in what ails you, there can be humor.

Your nervous system doesn't know the difference between "real" laughter and "intentional" laughter—it resets either way. When you laugh, cortisol drops, your body softens, and joy slips in through the cracks.

So today, trick your nervous system with humor. Giggle at a hot flash. Chuckle at your brain fog moment. Better yet—call a soul sister and laugh at nothing at all. Your laughter is medicine. Use it often and without apology." Because it isn't just misery that loves company—it's healing too.

Prescription for Your Soul RX Dosage:
Take one belly laugh every morning—before coffee for maximum absorption.

Day 210 – Soul Medicine Quote

"My body is not my enemy—it is my messenger."
—Dr. Jennifer Rademaker

For many women, midlife arrives like a stranger in their own skin—aches where there were none, hot flashes in the middle of meetings, restless nights, a body that no longer responds the way it used to. It's easy to feel betrayed and wonder, *Why is my body turning on me now?* That thought alone can deepen the tension you already feel.

My beautiful soul, your body is not against you. It is speaking in the only language it knows—sensations, cycles, signals. Every wave of heat, every night of restlessness, every change in rhythm is not punishment but communication. Spirit designed you to be wise enough to listen. Your body is a living oracle: it stores your experiences, processes your emotions, and signals when something needs to shift. When you stop fighting the messenger and start listening, the message becomes clearer—and your nervous system softens.

When you honor your body as a messenger, you shift from resistance to reverence. You move from *Why is this happening to me?* to *What is my body asking of me?* And when you align your thoughts with this truth, the biology of belief reminds us that even your cells respond—they relax, they reset, they rise. This isn't wishful thinking; it's a spiritual and biological partnership.

Today, instead of bracing against your body's signals, greet them with curiosity. Ask, *What are you showing me?* Even a few breaths of compassionate attention can begin to re-pattern decades of self-criticism into self-trust.

Day 211 – Soul Reflection

Stepping Out of the Garden

Morning light spills across your kitchen table. The mug in your hands is warm, but inside you feel a tremor of hesitation. After a season of tending your inner garden, you sense something new stirring—a quiet urge to step forward—yet part of you clings to the familiar soil. You wonder, *Am I ready? Am I strong enough to rise from this?*

My darling, everything begins in the mind. The thoughts you water become the garden of your life. If you let the weeds of fear, lack, and *I'm too late* grow wild, they'll take over. But when you choose thoughts of faith and victory, your soul blossoms in alignment with Spirit's truth.

The lower self whispers lies: *You're forgotten. You're failing. You're past your prime.* But God's voice speaks differently: *You are chosen. You are becoming. You are more radiant now than ever before.* Midlife is not a decline—it's an awakening. What you believe, you achieve. What you hold in consciousness, you live in experience.

Close your eyes. Place one hand over your heart and the other over your belly. Feel the warmth beneath your palms. Inhale, imagining a doorway opening beyond your inner garden—sunlight streaming through, birds calling you forward. With each exhale, picture yourself stepping across that threshold, carrying only what uplifts you. You don't need a perfect plan—just presence and courage. As you move, the path will reveal itself.

REFLECTION WHISPER:
Today I choose to believe…

Day 212 – Affirmation + Reflection

Welcoming Change

Midlife is not the end of your story—it is the beginning of a new chapter. Everything in life is always shifting: bodies, seasons, relationships, dreams. Nothing stays the same, and that is not failure—it is life's design.

When we cling to what was, we resist reality itself. But when we embrace what is possible, we discover beauty in beginnings. Change becomes less of a loss and more of an opening—a doorway into new joy, deeper self-love, and fresh horizons.

How might you befriend the fact of change in your life? And what could you learn now that will help you welcome future changes with more grace and ease?

Change is not punishment. It is the soul's invitation to keep you alive to possibility. Spirit is always guiding you toward what will expand you—not shrink you.

AFFIRMATION (REPEAT):
Change is not my enemy—change is my friend.

REFLECTION:
There is nothing small about a woman reclaiming herself

Soul Companion Card: No. 32

Day 213 – Dear God Letter

Dear God,

Thank you for reminding me that change is not here to break me, but to bless me. Thank you for the seasons that turn, for the endings that open doors, and for the new beginnings that rise even when I cannot yet see them.

I release my grip on what was. I open my heart to what is. I trust the flow of life, because I trust the one who guides it.

Even in uncertainty, I am safe. Even in the unknown, I am becoming. Even in the shifting, I am steady in you.

Today I affirm: change is my friend, my teacher, and my path to becoming more of who I truly am.

With love, I rise.

And so it is, Amen.

Day 214 – Ritual Reset

Riding the Waves

Some days a woman's midlife emotions arrive like a gentle tide, other days like a raging sea. Yet even the strongest wave can teach her something about her own depth. Emotions are not the enemy— they're energy in motion, waves rising and falling, reminding her she is alive and shifting.

Practice – Wave Breath

- Sit quietly with your feet grounded.
- Inhale slowly through your nose, imagining the tide rolling in.
- Hold gently for a moment at the crest.
- Exhale through the mouth, long and steady, like a wave flowing back to sea. If it feels right, let your exhale carry a soft ocean sound—like a wave moving out.
- Repeat 6–8 cycles, noticing how the inner storm begins to soften.

This is more than breath. Just as no wave lasts forever, no mood defines you. My radiant one, spirit designed a woman's midlife with tides—you're allowed to feel, to release, and to reset.

AFFIRMATION:
I am not my moods—I am the ocean holding them all.

Day 215 – Chakra Soul Movement

Third Eye Awakening Tap

A woman's midlife brain fog can feel like a veil drawn across her mind—words slip away, clarity blurs, and she wonders if she's losing herself. But Spirit whispers: *you are not broken.* You are fine. Your mind is not failing—it's asking for stillness, for breath, for gentle reconnection.

The third eye, resting between your brows, is your center of intuition and insight. When energy here feels clouded, even simple touch can help restore focus. The body speaks through sensation, and sometimes all your mind needs is your hand reminding it: *I'm here, I'm listening.*

Movement Practice – The Awakening Tap

- Sit or stand comfortably. Relax your shoulders.
- With your index and middle finger, gently tap the spot between your brows. Let the rhythm be slow and steady, like rain on glass.
- After a few taps, trace your fingers outward toward your temples, smoothing the skin as you go—like clearing fog from a window.
- Close your eyes and bring awareness to the soft pulse of energy there.
- Inhale through your nose, exhale through your mouth, letting light spread through your forehead and behind your eyes.
- Repeat for one minute, or as long as it feels soothing. My beautiful soul, this is more than movement—it's an awakening. Each gentle tap signals your body and Spirit to work as one. Clarity isn't something you chase; it's something you uncover by returning home.

Day 216 – Soul Whisker

Goddess of the Soft Blanket

Hey, Goddess. Every night you wrap up like royalty, yet doubt your worth by morning. I've seen you in the glow of lamplight—soft, sacred, real. Keep your crown on, even in flannel.

Comfort isn't laziness—it's holy restoration. Wear it proudly.

Soul Whisker:
Comfort is sacred. Wrap yourself in it without apology.

Day 217 – Sacred Sips Moment

The Waiting Cup

Steam curls from your cup in a soft spiral, carrying the scent of leaves you can't yet taste. Warmth pools into your palms. The cup feels like a heartbeat, asking you to pause. When tea first meets water, it doesn't reveal its flavor right away—it needs time to steep, to rest, to unfurl its hidden essence. The waiting isn't wasted—it's essential.

Perhaps you feel like that cup right now—holding a dream, a prayer, a healing not yet revealed. Midlife often feels like this: roles shifting, chapters changing, something new still steeping out of sight. It's tempting to swirl the spoon, to rush the process, to wish you were already there.

Spirit leans close and whispers: *You are steeping.*

What looks like delay is transformation—a quiet infusion of wisdom and strength that only time can bring. Inside you, something is blending, becoming richer than before. This isn't stagnation; it's alchemy.

Pause with your cup. Place a hand over your heart. Inhale the steam as a prayer; exhale doubt. Imagine your own essence unfurling like leaves in warm water—slow, sure, inevitable.

Good things are already in motion. Even while you wonder about Plan B, God is preparing Plan C—doors unseen, blessings underway. You are not forgotten. You are exactly on time for the flavor your soul is steeping for.

TRUTH DROP:
The steeping is the becoming. The waiting is holy

254

Day 218 – Truth Drop

The Law of Polarity

A soul sister sits at her kitchen table after everyone has gone to bed, a mug cooling between her hands. Gratitude rests on one side of her heart, an ache on the other. Midlife is full of such contradictions—beginnings tangled with endings, laughter rising through tears.

This isn't a flaw—it's the Law of Polarity. Every experience holds its opposite: joy and sorrow, light and shadow, loss and renewal. Polarity isn't punishment; it's balance. Without sorrow, joy would lose its depth. Without endings, beginnings couldn't bloom. Spirit designed life to hold opposites so you could grow whole.

When life feels heavy, remember: in every low, the seed of its high is already present. In every darkness, a spark of light waits. You don't have to choose one or the other—you can hold both and still be whole. The ache you feel is proof of your capacity to love.

Breathe now. Inhale light and shadow swirling together like two colors of paint. Exhale as they blend into a soft glow inside your chest. This is your inner equilibrium—peace found between opposites.

TRUTH DROP:
I embrace both shadow and light—each holds a gift for my soul.

Day 219 – Surprise Soul Whisper

Barefoot Morning

Hey, look at you, stepping into the day with bare feet and bed-hair courage. The world is humming again. Light spills across your skin, birds gossip from the trees, and something inside you says, *yes. I remember how to feel alive.*

You thought the buds had died, but they were only resting. Now they're swelling with color, reaching for the sun — just like you. This is what rising looks like: simple joy sneaking back in, quiet bravery blooming without fanfare.

Soul Whisper Invitation:
Kick off your shoes. Step outside. Let the morning kiss your toes.
Turn up one song that makes your hips sway, even if just a little.
That movement? That laughter under your breath?
That's your soul stretching toward the light.

Truth Drop:
I welcome my spring. I bloom with ease, joy, and divine timing.

Day 220 – Soul-to-Spirit Meditation

The Sky Within

Have you ever looked up and felt the sky breathing with you?
Wide. Quiet. Endless.
It doesn't strain to shine; it simply allows light to pour through.

There is a sky inside you too — vast and luminous beyond thought. When midlife feels crowded with noise or uncertainty, this inner sky waits patiently beneath it all, open and clear. You don't have to fix the clouds; just remember the expanse beneath them has never changed.

Try this with me:
Close your eyes and imagine yourself standing in warm sunlight. With each inhale, draw that light through the crown of your head, letting it travel through your body like a golden current.
Pause softly at the top of your breath.
As you exhale, feel any heaviness dissolve into space — drifting out like mist.

Repeat for several breaths, until your chest feels wide and your mind begins to quiet. Notice how peace expands when you stop reaching for it. You are breathing the same breath as the trees, the stars, the ocean — connected to all that is.

This is what Rising feels like: not striving upward, but remembering you already are. The sky within you has always been infinite.

AFFIRMATION:
I expand with every breath — I am as limitless as the sky within me.

Day 221 – Microdose Laugh-Lift

Rewriting Your Nervous System with Laughter

What if one minute of forced laughter could reset your whole nervous system today?

When hormones shift, your nervous system can feel like it's on edge—anxious, sensitive, easily overwhelmed. But laughter is a secret reset button. It tricks the subconscious mind into believing everything is safe, everything is lighter, everything is possible.

Today give yourself permission to laugh with intention. A gentle chuckle, a silly smile in the mirror, or even a big belly laugh—each one rewires your nervous system. Each one whispers to your subconscious: *"I am free. I am safe. I am joy."*

Laughter for no reason, is not denial—it's medicine. It tells your cells a new story, one rooted in Spirit's truth instead of fear.

Here is something to fun to try:
- Place one hand on your heart, one on your belly.
- Close your eyes and let out a playful laugh—fake it if you need to.
- Notice how your body softens, your breath deepens, your spirit lightens.
- Repeat until your nervous system feels the shift. **Truth Drop — Prescription for Your Soul:**
- **Rx:** Laugh daily. Side effects may include lightness, spontaneous joy, and forgetting what you were worrying about.

Refills: Infinite.

Day 222 – Soul Medicine Quote

"Even the sharpest seasons carve room for the softest beginnings."
Dr. Jennifer Rademaker

Midlife can feel like the sharpest season — hormones shifting, the body changing in ways you never expected, the mind restless with questions, the heart carrying stories too heavy to keep. It's a season of contrasts: beauty and ache, expansion and contraction. You may catch yourself wondering, *is this all there is? Am I too late to begin again?*

My darling, hear this truth: the sharpness is not the end. It is only the fire that clears space for something new to bloom. Every cut of change, every uncomfortable moment, is also carving room inside you for tenderness, wisdom, and renewal. The pain is not your identity; it is a passing visitor. Beneath it, a promise waits — the promise of resilience, of healing, of a self rising freer than before.

Close your eyes for a breath. Place a hand over your heart. Feel the space being made inside you. Imagine a soft green shoot pressing up through blackened soil — fragile yet unstoppable. That's you. That's what's already happening beneath the surface.

Let this truth settle into your bones: beginnings are often disguised as endings. Even the sharpest season can carve room for your softest bloom.

AFFIRMATION:
I am not defined by my pain. I am the promise breaking through it.

Day 223 – Soul Reflection

Trusting the Bridge That Trembles

There comes a moment when stillness is no longer safe—
when Spirit whispers, *"It's time to move."*
You take your first step, and the bridge beneath you trembles.
It's not weakness. It's life shifting under your courage. You've already waited through the mist.
You've watched love build what you could not.
Now the invitation is to walk—to trust the unseen strength you helped create
by believing when there was no proof.

Each plank beneath your feet remembers your prayers.
Every breath steadies your pace.
You don't have to be fearless—only willing.
Trembling doesn't mean you're failing; it means you're awakening.

Let your hands open. Let your heart lead.
When fear whispers, *"You might fall,"*
Spirit answers, *"You were made to rise."*
When doubt echoes, *"You're alone,"*
Grace whispers back, *"You're being carried."*

Breathe into the tremble.
Feel the bridge respond with quiet strength.
Step after step, the path meets your courage.
And when your foot finally touches the solid ground on the other side,
turn and look back—not in regret, but in reverence.
Only from here can you see how far you've come,
and how much further you can go and what you can do when you trust.

REFLECT:

What bridge are you standing on right now—and can you feel how courageous you are for crossing?

Soul Companion Card: No. 22

Day 224 – Affirmation + Reflection

"The Step You Can See"

Have you ever stood at the edge of a path and felt your stomach tighten because you couldn't see where it led? Midlife often feels like that—roles changing, dreams shifting, a future that's more mist than map. Your mind whispers, *"I'll move when I see the whole way."* But Spirit whispers back, *"Move, and the way will appear."*

You don't have to cross the entire bridge in one leap. You only need to take the step you can see. That small act of trust is enough to activate the unseen supports beneath you. Just as a stone path across a stream reveals each next stone only when you step forward, so too does your life unfold one courageous step at a time.

Think back on times you've already done this—leaving a job, starting a relationship, saying yes to healing. You didn't have all the answers then, either. Yet here you are. Each small step became the proof that you were held, guided, and strengthened along the way.

Today, place your hand over your heart and whisper the affirmation slowly. Feel your body soften as you speak it. Then imagine one small, concrete action that honors the next step of your becoming. It doesn't have to be dramatic; it only has to be true.

AFFIRMATION (REPEAT):
I take the next step with courage, even when I cannot see the whole path.

Day 225 – Dear God Letter

Dear God,

In this holy moment I turn inward to you.
The fog before me feels thick; the way ahead seems hidden.
My mind wants a map, yet my soul longs only for your presence.

I lay my striving down upon your altar.
I release the need to know, the need to plan, the need to control.
Breathe through me now a deeper trust than I have ever known.
Anchor my heart in your calm; let my breath become a prayer.

Where I see only mist, you see the whole path.
Where I tremble, you are steady.
Guide me not with the whole journey at once,
but with the quiet grace of one illuminated step.

Even in the rainiest, stormiest days,
you surprise me with rainbows—
signs of promise I could not have imagined on my own.

Re-program every fearful pattern within me into love.
Transmute my doubt into surrender, my worry into wonder.
Teach me to walk with soft hands open,
knowing I am never lost, never alone, never unseen.

I thank you for bridges I cannot yet see.
I thank you for carrying me where my own strength cannot.

With grace, I release, reset, and rise.

And so it is. Amen.

Day 226 – Ritual Reset

Light in My Hands

Morning sunlight catches the wrinkles on your hands—little rivers of time—and you remember what they've held: Babies, children, meals cooked, tears wiped, beautiful creations and dreams typed. These aging hands have carried lifetimes of love and giving.

Place your hands before you, Let imaginary light touch them. This is not a performance; it's remembrance.

Feel the glow meeting your skin, entering your heart, flowing through every cell of your whole being. Whisper softly:

"These hands created miracles. What I touched, will bless me. What I gave and give, returns multiplied."

Today's Ritual (simple, sacred, immediate):
1. Rub your palms together until you feel heat.
2. Cup that energy over your heart.
3. Breathe and remember—you are both the vessel and the source.

The universe doesn't pour light into you; it awakens the light that's already there. The light you're looking for just realized it's you.

SOUL WHISPER:
I am the light I've been waiting for.

Day 227 – Chakra Soul Movement

The Sacred Ache

A soul sister noticed it one morning—not the ache in her back, but the ache beneath it. The one that whispered, *There's more life in me still.* It wasn't longing for anyone else. It was longing for herself.

That ache isn't a problem to fix. It's a pulse to follow. The body never lies. It keeps calling you home to your own vitality—to remember that movement isn't something you do; it's something you *are*.

Soul Movement:

I invite you to select a tune without words. Stand tall and close your eyes. Place your hands gently on your hips. Begin to draw slow, easy circles, as though tracing the horizon inside you. Let the breath lead. Let your body find her rhythm again. It's there. If emotion rises, let it—that's the sacred ache opening. Releasing, resetting and rising.

This isn't about dancing beautifully; it's about *believing* you are beautiful when you move. *You* are.

MANTRA:
I am alive in every motion. My body remembers joy.

Day 228 – Soul Whisker

The One Who Pours the Water and Forgets Her Own Cup

My radiant two-legger, I see you topping off every bowl and leaving your own cup empty. In Cat Law, this is a misdemeanor of the moist variety. Queens sip first. Sit. Tilt the saucer toward your mouth. Three sips—morning, noon, evening. If the pitcher feels heavy, set it down and purr until your shoulders drop. The world keeps spinning while you drink. Plants still grow. Kittens still find the sunbeam without your supervision. A hydrated queen serves sweeter. Last but not least- don't forget find a mirror and give yourself that slow blink.

SOUL WHISKER:
Consider this your paws-itively perfect pause.

Day 229 – Sacred Sips Moment

The Sacred Stillness Before the Rise

At first, the cocoon felt like a holding cell—tight, airless, colorless. Thoughts circled, fears grew loud, and time went gray. But in the hush beneath the noise, a warmth appeared. The cocoon was not a cage; it was a womb. In the unseen dark, something wise was weaving—thread by thread—gathering color like sunrise behind closed eyes. She was never stuck; she was being shaped.

Perhaps you're in that in-between: not who you were, not yet who you're becoming. It feels slow. It feels small. But this is not delay; it is holy preparation.

Pour your tea slowly. Watch the steam rise like a promise. Hold the cup against your heart. Breathe in, exhale longer. With each sip, imagine the quiet architecture of becoming strengthening inside you. No rushing. No forcing. Just the gentle work of emergence.

TRUTH DROP:
Stillness is not the absence of movement; it's the presence of becoming.

Day 230 – Truth Drop

The Law of Transmutation of Energy

A soul sister sat at the kitchen table, staring at the same bills, the same unanswered messages, the same quiet ache. Thoughts drifted in like low clouds: *It's too late. Nothing changes. Why bother?* She didn't know it yet, but those thoughts were energy—alive, moving, waiting to be directed.

Energy never dies; it changes form. Thought becomes feeling; feeling shapes action; action becomes life. The current can be redirected: anxiety into faith, shadow into light, wounds into wisdom.

You are not a victim of the energies around you—you are the alchemist. When heaviness enters, don't resist; transform. The same fire that burns can warm. The same storm that drenches can nourish. Nothing is wasted in the hands of Spirit, and nothing in you is beyond transmutation.

Spirit leans close and whispers: *Even your fear is fuel. Even your sorrow is seed. Place it in my light and watch it become new.* What weighs you down today will rise as blessing. Night is already turning to dawn.

Ritual: Take a slow breath. Hand over heart. Imagine a soft golden light moving through your palm into your chest. Inhale warmth; exhale what you no longer need—see it shift from dark smoke to luminous mist. Let the light rise up your spine like morning sun. Decide, here and now: *I transmute this to light.*

TRUTH DROP:
When your mind renews, your world shifts. "Be transformed by the renewing of your mind." — Romans 12:2

Day 231 – Surprise Soul Whisper

The Feather on the Path

She almost missed it—a single feather lying in her way. Not grand, not glowing, just… quiet. She bent down, lifted it, and felt the softness between her fingers. In that moment, the heaviness in her chest lightened.

It wasn't the feather itself—it was the reminder. She was seen. She was guided. She wasn't walking alone.

Spirit leaves small signs for you, too. They may not look like fireworks or thunder. Sometimes they're as simple as a feather, a song, numbers, or a sudden memory that makes you smile.

They are whispers of love to remind you: *you are guided, you are held.*

AFFIRMATION:
I am open to Spirit's whispers—small signs of love that remind me I am never alone.

Day 232 – Soul-to-Spirit Meditation

The Quiet Path

At this time, close your eyes. Walk a quiet woodland path. Morning light pours through the trees like liquid gold. The air smells of pine and damp earth. The world hushes—only leaf-crunch underfoot and a distant bird you can't see. You came because your heart needed room to breathe.

You pause, palms open. In the silence you hear it—not a sky-boom, but a near whisper: *I am with you. I am guiding you. I am preparing the way.*

Spirit speaks like this: not in thunder, but stillness; not in the shout, but the soft. The question isn't *if* Spirit speaks, but *are we still enough to listen?*

Breathe in slowly; breathe out gently. With each breath, imagine sunlight streaming through the branches into your chest, rising up your spine like dawn. Let your ears and heart tune to subtler sounds—the rustle, the birdcall, the hum of your own soul. Spirit lives in these whispers: you are guided, you are loved, you are safe.

Stay one moment longer. Feel the path opening toward light. Rest in the truth: you never walk alone, and with each quiet step, you rise.

AFFIRMATION:
I attune to Spirit's whispers, guided and at peace, I rise.

Day 233 – Microdose Laugh-Lift

The Medicine of Joy

Have you noticed how a cat's purr, a child's giggle, or even your own unexpected laugh can shift an entire atmosphere? Joy has that power. It's not just an emotion—it's a vibration, a healing frequency, medicine for your nervous system.

Midlife can bring weighty days. Responsibilities pile up, the body changes, the heart remembers losses. And yet—joy is still available. Spirit tucked it inside you, waiting to be awakened not by perfection, but by presence.

Today your invitation is simple: let yourself laugh, even for no reason. Smile at your reflection. Watch something silly. Call a friend who always makes you giggle. Joy tells your body, *all is well.* Joy tells your subconscious, *life is still sweet.*

And if nothing else, simply laugh on purpose and feel how your nervous system lifts afterward. Take three slow breaths. On each exhale, add a soft chuckle—even if you have to fake it at first. Repeat until the laugh feels real. Notice how joy bubbles up, lightening your whole being.

Prescription for Your Soul:
Rx: *Take laughter with water and repeat until the world feels right-side-up again.*

Warning:
Side effects may include light-headed bliss

Day 234 – Soul Medicine Quote

"Even in the storm, my soul remembers the rainbow."
—Dr. Jennifer Rademaker

Midlife can feel like weather. One day you're standing in sunlight; the next, clouds gather without warning. Responsibilities rise like thunderheads. A single phone call changes everything. Emotions move like wind across an open sky, and storms you thought you'd already weathered return in new form. It's easy to feel lost in the downpour, convinced the sun will never break through again.

My beautiful soul, this quote is your reminder: storms are real, but they're not final. Inside you lives the same energy that paints rainbows. You carry resilience, beauty, and surprise. Even when you can't yet see it, the arc of promise is already forming across your horizon. What feels like endless rain is often washing the air clean for new colors to appear.

Take a slow breath and imagine your storm not as punishment, but as a passage—the sky of your life clearing itself. Your nervous system may brace for thunder, but beneath that tension your soul remembers color. That memory isn't wishful thinking—it's spiritual science. You are wired for hope. Spirit encoded you to recognize light even in darkness.

Today, instead of fighting the storm, let your inner rainbow rise. Place a hand over your heart and whisper softly: *"I don't chase rainbows anymore. I remember I am one."*

Feel how your breath deepens and your shoulders soften. This is your inner covenant with hope—a knowing that what is heavy today can become something luminous tomorrow.

Day 235 – Soul Reflection

Her Hands, My Light

I catch the scent and smile—her hand cream. A pearl warms between my palms and she's here again: the woman whose veined hands cooked, carried, prayed, and tucked me in. Later, those same hands became grandmother hands—lifting my son, buttoning tiny coats, slicing apples, rolling cookie dough, smoothing blankets at nap time. Loving snacks appeaed, tears quiet. These are the hands that loved me into being—and loved the child I love.

Today I choose to inherit, not ache. I anoint my hands like a threshold rite: what she poured into me now pours through me. I think of how she kneaded bread, her recipes, knitted sweaters, planted marigolds—ordinary tenderness that made a life shine. Errands become ministry; phone calls-greeting cards, kindness. I do not leave her behind to move forward; I move forward with her, and because of her, I shine.

Look at your own hands, my darling. See their maps—the quiet proof of showing up. Place one hand over your heart (love remembered), one over your belly (courage embodied). Breathe in gently; exhale longer. Tell your nervous system, "I am held, and I can move. I'm alive." Then open your palms to the day and let blessings spill where they're needed.

If you forget, the fragrance will remind you: love leaves traces that glow in every touch. These hands—hers and mine—are one lineage of tenderness, still writing light on all we hold.

Choose one ordinary moment to be luminous: a checkout smile, the cup you wash. Let each small touch echo her. Rise without effort, without striving—proof that love continues by becoming you.

Her tenderness is my courage and light. These hands bless whatever they touch.

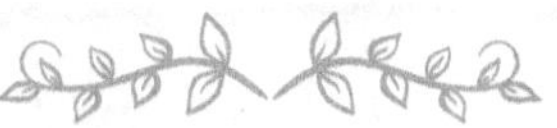

Day 236 – Affirmation + Reflection

Rooted in Love

A soul sister stood at the edge of another change, feeling the ground shift beneath her like sand under the tide. A diagnosis. A move. A child leaving home. A relationship suddenly shaky. Uncertainty about where the money will come from. Each one had felt like a tremor; all together they felt like an earthquake. Her stomach tightened. Her breath grew shallow. She thought, *"How do I keep my head on straight when everything feels so unsteady?"*

And then, on a walk she almost didn't take, she noticed a small stone resting in the path — smooth, ordinary, but etched with a single word: *courage.* She bent down, picked it up, and felt something shift inside. It was as if Spirit whispered, *"My love, you're not alone. That brave trust is already in you. Here's a token to remind you."* In that moment her faith flickered back to life. She felt held, she felt a sense of stability within herself, and what she sensed alright was the invisible at work.

There will be days when the ground feels shaky beneath your feet. Change, loss, or uncertainty may leave you questioning your footing. But stability doesn't always come from the world outside you. It comes from the anchor within you — the place where Spirit steadies your breath, your mind, your heart. Everything works out; it always does. *Your lioness heart is the bridge between fear and faith.*

If my inner world feels unsteady, I am rooted in love. I am grounded. I am safe.

Day 237 – Dear God Letter

The Courage to Cross

Dear God,

There are moments when I stand at the edge of a change and everything in me trembles. My mind rehearses the reasons to stay, my body remembers old disappointments, and my heart feels like a small bird in a storm. Yet somewhere deeper than fear, I hear you calling—soft but steady—"Come forward. There is more."

I confess, God, that sometimes I mistake hesitation for wisdom. I label fear "discernment" and delay "prudence," when really it is just the old program of self-protection still humming inside me. Rewrite it now. Reset the script that whispers I won't be held—and reminds me I was never meant to be held back. Remind my nervous system that love walks ahead of me and behind me, that every bridge you ask me to cross is already blessed and built.

Give me courage to lean into the unseen, to place my foot on boards that feel fragile but are secretly strong. Let my heart beat in rhythm with yours until fear loosens its grip. And when the fog hides the far shore, teach me to trust the ground beneath my feet, knowing it is you.

Thank you for the bridges already crossed, the nights already survived, the wings still intact beneath my tired shoulders. Thank you for guiding me not by force, but by whispers—not with shame, but with invitation. Today I step forward—not perfectly, but faithfully—knowing that each step taken in love is already a victory.

And so it is. Amen.

Day 238 – Ritual Reset

The Candle of Yes

There is power in the moment you say yes to yourself.
Not a polite yes, not a halfway maybe — a soul-deep, candle-lit yes.

Tonight, light a candle just for you. Let it be a ceremony of remembrance — a symbol of the woman who has carried so much and is finally ready to rise for herself.

Ritual Invitation:
- Find a quiet space.
- Light a single candle and whisper your own name.
- Speak it like a blessing, not an obligation.
- Say softly: *"I say yes to her. I say yes to me."*
- Watch the flame dance, knowing it burns in rhythm with your own heartbeat.

This is not a small act.
It is a spiritual reclamation. Each time you light this candle, you affirm: *I am no longer waiting to be chosen. I choose myself.*

Let that flame remind you that your "yes" is holy. It is the light that calls your next season forward.

SOUL WHISPER:
My name is my prayer. My yes is my becoming.

Day 239 – Chakra Soul Movement

Macarena Magic

A soul sister once said to me, "I can't remember the last time I danced."
So I smiled, grabbed my phone, and hit play on the *Macarena*.

Within seconds we were moving — laughing, clapping, dancing like fools, forgetting the steps but remembering something far more important: what it feels like to be alive. The heaviness lifted, the energy shifted, and joy flooded back in.

This is the medicine of movement. You don't have to wait for the right moment, the right song, or the right mood. Two minutes of dancing can rewire a day. It tells your body, *I'm safe*. It tells your soul, *I still remember joy.*

Movement Invitation:
- Play "Macarena." Loud.
- Tap your foot, swing your arms, feel the beat, move however your body wants.
- Laugh when you mess up — that's the point.
- Let your joy rise until it fills the room.

This isn't performance — it's resurrection. You're not learning the dance; you're remembering your rhythm.

MANTRA:
I'm alive — joy is my reset, movement is my prayer.

Day 240 – Soul Whisker

The Plant Heist

The humans bought a new plant.
Placed it high.
Adorable.

They forgot I'm a climber.
One leap, one wobble, one glorious *crunch*.

I didn't even want the plant—I wanted the *possibility*.
The thrill of "You can't." The joy of "Watch me."

Hey, radiant two-legger—maybe it's time you climbed again.
There's something on your soul's top shelf calling your name.
Don't overthink it. Stretch. Leap. Surprise yourself.

SOUL WHISKER:
Every 'too high' is a sacred invitation to rise

Day 241 – Sacred Sips Moment

The Dawn Cup

Bare feet on cool tile. The soft hum of the kettle. A moment to stand still before the world starts pulling at you. The cup in your hands isn't caffeine—it's communion.

This is the hinge between night and day, between what was and what will be. The air holds its breath as the first light stretches across the horizon, and Spirit leans close, whispering: *Begin softly.*

As you hold your cup, feel its warmth anchor you to this moment. Inhale the scent rising like prayer. Exhale the rush of yesterday. Whisper inwardly: "I drink in this new day. I receive its goodness."

Each sip is a quiet agreement with life. You're telling your body, *I start from peace.* You're telling your mind, *I choose presence over hurry.* You're telling your soul, *I trust the unfolding.*

What begins in stillness blooms in strength. The smallest dawn ritual—a hand on your cup, a breath of gratitude, a moment of remembering—can rewire your whole day.

TRUTH DROP:
Let the world wait for you today. You are the light worth rising for.

Day 242 – Truth Drop

The Law of Becoming

Last spring you may have walked past a patch of bare earth and thought nothing was there. Yet beneath the soil, bulbs were already stirring—stretching toward light they could not yet see. Weeks later, green tips broke through. Months later, blooms opened, one after another, each in its own time. That is the Law of Becoming—quiet, patient, inevitable.

Midlife is like that hidden garden. What looks dormant is not dead. The heartbreaks, triumphs, and lessons learned in the dark are roots feeding something new. You are not starting over or too late—you are ripening into a deeper self who holds both wisdom and wonder. Every scar, every shift, every silver strand is a ring in your trunk, a story of survival turned to strength.

The Law of Becoming reminds us: you are always unfolding, never finished. Just as the river keeps flowing and the tree keeps growing, you too are in motion. Becoming isn't something you perform; it's something you allow. When doubt whispers, "It's over," Spirit answers, "You are still unfolding." When fear says, "You've peaked," Spirit reminds you, "Your becoming is eternal."

Pause now. Place your hand over your heart. Picture a bulb underground sending up its first green shoot. Whisper softly: *I am still becoming.* Let that truth settle like warm soil around your roots.

Truth Drop:
It is not too late for you—not now, not ever.

Day 243 – Surprise Soul Whisper

The Unopened Envelope

It arrived in your mailbox without warning—a small, plain envelope tucked between bills and ads. You almost threw it out, but something about it caught your eye. Inside was a handwritten note, a gift card, a photograph, a kind word—something you didn't expect, yet needed at exactly that moment.

Spirit loves to work this way. Not always with fireworks, but with small surprises—unexpected kindness, a song lyric at the right time, a stranger's smile, a feather on the sidewalk, a memory that makes you laugh in the middle of a heavy day. These are little envelopes from the Divine, carrying whispers of love that say, *I see you. I'm with you. Keep going.*

You don't have to hunt for them. You only have to notice. The more you watch, the more you'll realize: life is full of unopened envelopes, waiting for you to tear them open and receive their medicine.

Today, slow down enough to look for one. Check your "soul mailbox." It might come as a scent, a message, an idea, or a moment of peace. When it comes, pause. Breathe. Let gratitude be your signature on the reply.

These small surprises are not random—they're Spirit's way of resetting your nervous system, feeding your hope, and reminding you that you are never forgotten.

Affirmation:
I welcome Spirit's surprises. My day is full of hidden envelopes of love and guidance.

Day 244 – Soul-to-Spirit Meditation

The Sacred Garden Within

At this time, turn away from the outer world. Close your eyes, my radiant one.

Imagine stepping barefoot onto soft, dew-kissed grass. The air is fragrant with promise, the first light brushing your skin. Ahead, a garden gate waits slightly open—as if the earth itself is inviting you to step forward.

As you walk through, notice what's stirring. Buds are swelling, leaves unfurling, soil breathing after the long dark. Everything is quietly coming alive, not rushing, just responding to the sun. This is your inner garden too—awakening, stretching, remembering how to rise.

Breathe in the scent of new beginnings. Feel the pulse beneath your feet. With each inhale, draw in the courage to bloom; with each exhale, release the doubt that you are behind. You are not late to your life—you are right on time for this unfolding.

Pause here. Feel the warmth gathering in your chest, the light beginning to rise inside you.

WHISPER SOFTLY YOUR AFFIRMATION:
I am becoming. I trust the season of my becoming.

Every garden awakens in its own timing. Trust the bloom that is becoming you. Let this truth move through you like sunlight through petals—gentle, certain, unstoppable.

Day 245 – Microdose Laugh-Lift

The Sacred Surprise

Sometimes joy sneaks in sideways. You drop something and it bounces in the most ridiculous way. A stranger says something that makes no sense but cracks you up. Spirit has a way of slipping holy humor into your ordinary day—reminding you not everything is meant to be so heavy.

That's medicine. That laugh you weren't planning? It's a gift. It shifts the energy faster than logic ever could. It's Spirit saying: *"Lighten up. You're safe. You're held."*

Practice:

Think of one moment in your life when laughter surprised you—when it came uninvited but healed everything in the room. Close your eyes, relive it, and let the giggle return.

PRESCRIPTION FOR YOUR SOUL RX:
A giggle a day keeps the lower self away.

WARNING:
A sudden loss of interest in negativity

Day 246 – Soul Medicine Quote

"Resilience isn't about bouncing back—
it's about rising forward, softer and stronger,
with wisdom stitched into every wrinkle and scar."
—Dr. Jennifer Rademaker

There's a difference between surviving and truly living.
Survival keeps us breathing, but it doesn't always keep us dreaming.

My beautiful soul, resilience isn't measured by how quickly you snap back to who you were before the storm. Resilience is revealed in how you choose to rise after the storm—transformed, softer, wiser, and no longer willing to live as you once did.

Think of a tree struck by lightning. She doesn't "bounce back" to her younger form. She carries the scar and wrinkle in her bark, yet she continues to grow stronger, ring upon ring, reaching higher toward the light. The scar doesn't weaken her; it becomes part of her story, her strength, her beauty.

And so it is with you. Every wrinkle, every scar—emotional, physical, or invisible—is not proof of failure but of survival seasoned with wisdom. Resilience is not the end of the story—it is the beginning of the rise.

TRUTH DROP:
I don't bounce back. I rise forward—with softness, wisdom, and strength stitched into my soul.

Day 247 – Soul Reflection

The River Beneath It All

Morning light filters through half-drawn curtains as you set down the mug you've been holding for warmth. The house is quiet now—boxes stacked in the hall, echoes of laughter folded into corners. Your body is tired, your heart tender. Life feels like a riverbed of jagged stones pressing into your sole and your soul, and you wonder how you'll cross to the other side.

This is what midlife can feel like—the ground shifting, roles dissolving, new ones not yet clear. Responsibilities rise like sudden clouds. You long for steadiness, for a current you can trust beneath the noise. You may even start to believe the rocks are the whole story.

But beneath it all, there is always a river flowing. Steady. Sure. Quietly carrying you forward. The river never forgets where it's going. It bends, it slows, but it never stops. And neither do you. Even when life feels paused, your soul is still in motion—carried by something greater than you.

Spirit leans close and whispers: *My dear, the stones are only the surface. I am the current beneath, moving you toward your becoming.*

If it feels gentle, rest your hand over your heart. Inhale, sensing cool water swirling beneath you. Exhale, releasing control. Feel yourself lifted, supported, carried.

Day 248 – Affirmation + Reflection

Rooted in the Present

A soul sister sits at her kitchen table, the morning light spilling across a half-finished to-do list. Her mind is everywhere but here: replaying yesterday's conversation, rehearsing tomorrow's worries, wondering how all the pieces will come together. Her breath stays shallow. Her coffee grows cold. She almost misses the simple holiness of this moment.

The mind loves to wander — into what could have been or what might be. But the gift of today is not found in yesterday's regrets or tomorrow's anxieties. It's here, now — in this breath, in this heartbeat. When you root yourself in the present, you discover that peace has been waiting all along. Not in the next milestone, not in the fixing of everything, but in the simple awareness: *I am here. I am alive. And that is enough.* Where in your day could you pause, breathe, and root yourself more deeply in the present moment?

If it feels gentle, pause for a moment. Let your eyes soften. Feel your feet on the ground or the chair beneath you. Place a hand over your heart and take a slow breath in. As you exhale, imagine roots extending down from your body into the earth — warm, steady, holding you. With each inhale, draw in the stillness of this moment. With each exhale, let go of the need to be anywhere else.

AFFIRMATION:
I return to now—anchored in love.

Day 249 – Dear God Letter

A Prayer for Trusting the Unknown

Dear God,

Today the path feels covered in fog. I wake with questions heavy in my chest—about the future, about my family, about who I'm becoming. My mind races ahead, trying to solve tomorrow before it arrives, and I feel the weariness of holding on too tightly.

Yet deep within me there is another knowing—the quiet hum of Your presence. You are already in the bend I cannot see, in the door not yet open, in the seed still beneath the soil. You are in the places that look empty but are secretly full. Even now You are preparing colors I cannot imagine, arranging blessings I cannot yet hold.

So I surrender the illusion that I must control it all. I open my clenched hands and place them into Yours. Guide me not with certainty, but with trust. Teach me to let faith be my compass and peace be my pace. Remind me that faith is not seeing the whole map—it is taking one step at a time with You beside me.

When I falter, lift my chin toward the light. When I forget, whisper my name back to me. When the ground feels shaky, root me again in Your love. Let my heart rise like dawn, even when the sky still looks dark.

Thank You for walking me through the unknown—for being the lamp for my feet and the steadying ground beneath them. I may not know what's ahead, but I know Who walks with me. And so it is.

Amen.

Day 250 – The Balancing Breath

A soul sister sat in her car between appointments, hands gripping the wheel, realizing she'd been holding her breath without even knowing it. Midlife has a way of pulling you in opposite directions—caring for aging parents while craving care for yourself, holding heavy responsibilities while longing for freedom. The pressure builds quietly until your own exhale goes missing.

Balance isn't about removing the weight; it's about learning to breathe evenly through it. The steadiness you seek begins within. Breath is Spirit's quiet gift—a way to return home to yourself in any moment. Even sixty seconds of intentional breathing can shift everything.

Spirit leans close and whispers: *Beloved, every inhale is My breath moving through you, rooting you in love. Every exhale is My grace releasing what you no longer need.*

If it feels gentle, soften your gaze or close your eyes. Feel your feet grounded, one hand resting over your heart. Begin a simple rhythm—

- Inhale for a count of four.
- Hold for a count of four.
- Exhale for a count of four.
- Pause for a count of four.

Repeat this "box breath" three times. Notice your shoulders drop, the edges of tension soften, your center grow quiet and sure. With each inhale, feel yourself grounded. With each exhale, feel yourself rise lighter.

With every breath, I rise in love.

Day 251 – Chakra Soul Movement

Heart Chakra: Expanding with Grace

A soul sister stands at the window before dawn, coffee warm in her hands, feeling the ache in her chest that has nothing to do with muscles or bones. The heart holds so much—love given, love lost, love longed for. In midlife, the heart can grow cautious, as though it has weathered too much. Walls rise quietly, not from bitterness but protection. Yet beneath those walls, the heart still longs to be soft, to be open, to be free.

Your heart is not broken; it is sacred space. Movement becomes your prayer—a way of inviting grace back in. When you move gently, you remind your heart it's safe to expand again.

Spirit leans close and whispers: *My darling, every breath that opens your chest is Me pouring life back into you. Every sway you take is a door opening from the inside.*

If it feels gentle, stand tall. Feel your feet rooted to the ground. Place your hands softly over your chest. With each inhale, let your elbows open wide, as if welcoming the sky into your heart. With each exhale, soften your shoulders and feel the heart sigh in relief. Begin to sway side to side, imagining soft green light—luminous and alive—expanding outward from your chest, wrapping you in compassion. This is your heart chakra moving like a flower opening at dawn.

MANTRA:
My heart opens with grace. Love flows in and through me.

Day 252 – Soul Whisker

Tail High, Heart Light

I see you, human. You've been doing a lot of heavy lifting lately — thoughts, tasks, emotions — all stacked on your back like a pile of laundry you never asked for. You're walking head down, tail tucked, thinking that's the only way to keep it together.

But let me tell you a secret from the kingdom of cats: when we're carrying something precious, we don't bow lower; we walk taller. We raise our tails like banners and let the sun catch our whiskers. We know that posture changes mood, and mood changes everything.

So before you drag yourself into the next moment, stop. Stretch. Roll your shoulders back. Lift your chin. Pretend you have an invisible tail reaching for the sky. Feel how light sneaks in. This is what rising feels like — playful, not forced. Grace before hustle, paws before claws.

SOUL WHISKER:
Raise your invisible tail today; the higher you hold it, the lighter your heart will feel.

Day 253 – Sacred Sips Moment

Pouring Light Into Your Cup

Hello, my beautiful soul… welcome to your sacred tea moment.

The morning is quiet. Steam curls from your cup like a small prayer. Outside, the sky is just beginning to pale. You hold the mug in both hands and feel its warmth seep into your palms, softening the places inside you that woke up tight.

Rise season can feel like a climb — new beginnings, new courage, new steps. It's easy to think you must push to reach the top. But tea teaches a different rhythm. You don't pour a full cup all at once; you pour slowly, reverently, letting the fragrance rise before the first sip.

Spirit is pouring light into you the same way — not in a rush, but in a steady stream. Even now, what you need is being prepared. With each breath, with each sip, you are being infused with strength and tenderness.

Where in your life could you pause today and let what you're longing for pour in slowly, the way tea fills a cup?

Microdose Ritual:
Pause with your cup. Close your eyes for a heartbeat and imagine the steam as golden light rising, curling around you. Inhale it like a promise. Exhale the need to rush. Whisper to yourself, *"I'm being filled."*

Truth Drop:
Light is pouring into me now—slowly, steadily, in all the places I once felt empty.

Day 254 – Truth Drop

The Law of Rhythm

She wakes before dawn and sits by the window, watching the sky shift from indigo to rose. Coffee warms her palms. Outside, the bare branches of a tree she planted years ago hold a few stubborn leaves. Soon, they'll burst into green again. As she watches, she realizes how much her life mirrors that tree—long seasons of doing, then quiet, then sudden growth. Midlife can feel like living inside a rhythm you didn't choose, wondering if your best seasons have

Everything in life moves in cycles — tides, moon phases, the rising and setting sun, even your own heartbeat. Your heart doesn't beat at one steady pace; it quickens when you inhale, softens when you exhale. That rhythm is Spirit's reminder that balance lives in motion.

What rises must fall, and what rests will rise again. This isn't failure; it's rhythm. Midlife carries its own cadence: seasons of expansion and seasons of stillness. When you resist the ebb, you miss the wisdom of the flow. When you soften into it, you discover that every phase is carrying you somewhere sacred.

The Law of Rhythm reminds us: no winter lasts forever, and no summer stays unchanged. Everything has its purpose, and each season its medicine. Trust the rhythm of your soul as deeply as the rhythm of the tides.

Truth Drop:
I honor the rhythm of my life—each rise and rest is part of my becoming.

Day 255 – Surprise Soul Whisper

Sometimes the quickest way to rise is to do something your mind didn't schedule.
Put on a song you loved in your twenties — the one that makes your toes curl and your hips remember. Don't plan it. Don't rehearse it. Just press play, and when the first notes hit, let your body move however it wants.

This is a secret the soul already knows: spontaneity is medicine. It jolts you out of your rut, wakes up dormant parts of you, and reminds your nervous system it's safe to feel good for no reason.

This season isn't only about climbing; it's about letting joy sneak in through side doors. Ten seconds of unplanned dancing can shift an entire mood.

Soul Whisper:
Today, give yourself one unplanned moment of delight. Your spirit rises fastest when it's surprised by your own freedom.

Day 256 – Soul-to-Spirit Meditation

The Mountain Within

Close your eyes, and imagine yourself not before the mountain —
but *upon it*. You've climbed through fog and shadow, through valleys
that once felt endless. And now, you've reached a ledge where the
air is thinner, clearer, alive. The wind brushes your face. The sky
stretches wide. You can finally see how far you've come.

This is the view of Rise — not perfection, but perspective. You
begin to realize that the mountain was never an obstacle; it was your
becoming. Every step carved strength into your spirit. Every pause
shaped wisdom in your soul.

Take a slow inhale and imagine your breath rising through your
spine, lifting you higher within yourself. Exhale, and feel gratitude
ripple through your body for the woman who kept climbing. Stay
here for a few breaths, feeling spaciousness bloom in your chest —
the quiet knowing that your journey has always been guided.

Spirit whispers: *You are not climbing toward peace. You are peace — rising
into remembrance.*

Let that truth echo through you. You are not behind. You are not
lost. You are ascending into your next season, one breath at a time.

Truth Drop:
I rise with grace. The mountain was not in my way — it was making me

295

Day 257 – Microdose Laugh-Lift

Your Free Lift

Everyone's chasing a lift these days — facelifts, breast lifts, but lift, lash lifts. But my beautiful soul, there's a lift you can give yourself right now for free: a laugh-lift.

Your conscious mind might think it's silly to laugh for no reason. But your subconscious doesn't care whether the laugh was spontaneous or intentional — it simply floods your body with the same healing chemistry. Laughter (even "fake" laughter) is like an inner facelift for your nervous system. It softens the lines of tension you've been carrying and makes your whole being feel lighter.

Today, give yourself one minute of laughter — right now if you can. Stand in your kitchen, in your car, or at your desk. Start with a chuckle, even if it feels awkward. Add a little more sound. Feel it build. Your body will catch on, and soon the giggles will be real.

PRESCRIPTION FOR YOUR SOUL:

RX-TRUTH DROP:

This is your secret lift — no appointment needed, no recovery time, just pure, rising joy.

Day 258 – Soul Medicine Quote

"Quit beating yourself up — beam yourself up instead."
—**Dr. Jennifer Rademaker**

How many mornings have you stood in front of the mirror replaying every "should," every misstep, every way you think you've fallen short? Just beating yourself up. We become our own harshest critics, striking ourselves with words we would never use on another we love. In midlife, especially in this sacred season of menopause, that inner voice can get even louder — pointing to changes in our bodies, our hair, our face, our energy, our roles — and telling us we're somehow "less."

Less than what? My beautiful soul, the truth is the opposite: you are not "less." You are more. You are ripening, deepening, becoming. The bruising words you use against yourself are not your birthright. Love is. Compassion is. Beaming yourself up is not denial; it's a spiritual practice. It's shifting the light back on. It's choosing to send love to the places you've been beating down.

Today, instead of rehearsing self-criticism, lift yourself with a beam of kindness. Love yourself more – not less. Place a hand over your heart and imagine a gorgeous bright crystalline golden light, shining down from above —filling your chest, softening the edges of your self-talk, radiating through every cell of your whole body. You don't have to earn this light; it's yours. Let it lift you, not scold you. You are the light.

AFFIRMATION:
I quit beating myself up — and beam myself up instead.

Day 259 – Soul Reflection

After the Laugh, the Light

The sound of your laughter still lingers in the air like a bell. For a heartbeat, you forgot the weight you were carrying. Your chest lifted. Your face softened. You remembered what it feels like to be lighter.

And then, the quiet returns. The bills remain on the counter. The mirror still reflects a woman learning to love her own reflection. Midlife is like this—moments of freedom braided with responsibility. You might wonder if the joy you felt was only a flicker, or if it can stay.

That flicker was not a fluke. It was a glimpse of your natural state. Beneath all the doing and carrying, there is a steady current of light that never leaves you. Laughter doesn't create it; it reveals it. You're not waiting to *become* joyful someday—you already are joy.

Spirit leans close and whispers: the light you felt in your laughter is the truth of who you are. Let it stay. Let it move through you, even in silence.

If it feels right, place your hand over your heart. Remember that moment of laughter and breathe it back into your body. Feel it expand through your chest like sunlight at dawn.

REFLECTION WHISPER:
Where in your life is light asking to linger a little longer?

Day 260 – Affirmation + Reflection

Carrying the Glow

Yesterday you gave yourself permission to laugh. Maybe it was a soft chuckle, maybe a belly laugh that surprised even you. For a moment the weight you've been carrying loosened, your shoulders dropped, and you felt the shimmer of joy rise inside you. Then life's noise came back — the emails, the errands, the thoughts that tug at you. You may wonder if the glow was only a flicker, if it can last beyond the moment.

Joy isn't something you "lose" when the moment passes; it's something you can invite back with awareness. Like an ember that still holds heat beneath the ash, your joy is waiting for a small breath to reignite it. This is how you build steadiness — not by clinging to the moment but by letting it become part of you.

If it feels gentle, close your eyes for a heartbeat and inhale slowly. Imagine yesterday's laughter as a soft golden light still resting in your heart. With each exhale, picture that shimmer spreading through your whole body like sunrise. Feel it move through your shoulders, your arms, your belly, your legs. This is not forced positivity; this is your nervous system remembering safety and your soul remembering its nature.

AFFIRMATION:
The joy I felt yesterday lives in me today. It rises steady, glowing from within.

REFLECTION WHISPER:
Where in your day could you pause for one breath and let yesterday's glow return, even for a moment?

Day 261 – Dear God Letter

Rising Into My Next Chapter

Dear God,

This morning I wake with a quiet ache—not of pain, but of becoming. I can feel something shifting inside me. Old roles feel loose on my shoulders. Old fears rattle their chains. My mind whispers that I should have it all figured out by now, yet my heart knows I'm standing at the edge of something new.

My soul longs to rise, yet part of me hesitates. The unknown feels wide and unmarked. I try to plan, to control, to predict—but it only exhausts me. And still, beneath the noise, there is a pulse of hope.

I place that pulse in your hands. Guide me not only to what is next, but into who I'm becoming. Lift me out of the small stories I tell about myself. Teach me to trust the stretch between where I've been and where you're calling me. Help me stand tall in the in-between, to breathe deeply even when I can't see the whole path.

With each inhale, infuse me with courage. With each exhale, wash away my doubt. Let me rise softer and stronger—not through striving, but through surrender. May my life become a quiet yes to your unfolding.

Thank you for being the steady ground beneath my feet, the lift beneath my wings, the light ahead of me. I do not rise alone. And so it is.

Amen

Day 262 – Breath Practice / Ritual Reset

Soothing the Nerve That Holds You

A soul sister wakes at 3 a.m. again. The house is quiet, but her mind is not—heart racing, thoughts circling like restless birds. She presses a hand to her belly and feels the tightness from carrying too much. Midlife can do this: uncertainties can stack high, sleep thins out, and the nervous system forgets how to soften.

The vagus nerve is the bridge between your body and your calm. It tells your heart, your breath, your gut that you are safe. When life keeps you in "on" mode too long, this bridge constricts. Gentle breath and sound reopen it, calling you back to balance.

Try this, place one hand over your heart and one on your belly. Inhale slowly through your nose for a count of five. Exhale through your mouth with a soft sigh, humming low as you release. The vibration travels through the body, soothing the vagus nerve and signaling safety. Repeat for one minute, feeling your hands rise and fall, your body settling into peace.

Where in your day could you pause for one minute of humming breath to remind your nervous system it's safe?

Day 263 – Chakra Soul Movement

Receiving in Motion

She doesn't need a plan tonight—she needs to move.
A soul sister stands in her living room as dusk settles outside. Boxes still line the hallway from a recent change. Her phone glows with unanswered texts. Her body feels stiff from sitting all day, her mind crowded from caring for everyone else. She presses *pause* on the noise and lets a wordless melody fill the room.

This is how your spirit begins to speak—not in the rush, but in the rhythm; not through striving, but through soft surrender. Movement becomes your meditation, your permission slip to feel alive again. Each slow sway opens space for light to enter, for Spirit to breathe new life through you.

If it feels gentle, find a small patch of floor and play a song without words—something that feels like breath or wind. Stand tall with your feet grounded. Close your eyes or soften your gaze. Let your arms float outward, palms open. Begin to sway slowly, side to side. Feel your body as a prayer—each breath a release, each motion a receiving. Stay for a minute or two, allowing peace to move through every cell.

MANTRA:
As I move, I receive.
I open to the rhythm of renewal within me.

Day 264 – Soul Whisker

Tail High, Darling

The house may be chaos—papers scattered, laundry half-folded, life mid-mess—but have you seen how a cat walks through it? Tail high. Chin lifted. Not a hint of apology. She knows who she is, even in the clutter.

Confidence isn't about control. It's about carriage. A way of saying, *I belong here,* even when things aren't perfectly polished.

So, my beauty, the next time life feels undone, take a cue from your whiskered mentor. Walk through the mess like it's your runway. Shoulders back. Heart open. Tail high and rise above it.

SOUL WHISKER:
Confidence is a posture, not a mood.

Companion Card: No. 2

Day 265 – Sacred Sips Moment

Focus on the Future

The spreadsheet glows with red boxes—tiny warnings of overdue tasks. Numbers stack like towers, each one demanding attention. Beneath the screen's glow, your chest tightens, wondering if you'll ever catch up. Midlife can feel like this—responsibilities piling high, dreams waiting in the margins.

My beautiful soul sister, those red boxes aren't the whole story. Beneath the lists and deadlines, seeds of destiny still live in you—dreams planted long before time began. They are not lost. They are simply waiting for your faith to water them.

When discouragement whispers, *"It's too late,"* remember: your future is still unfolding. Every small act of trust becomes sunlight to the soil of your soul.

Take a slow breath. Imagine closing the spreadsheet and wrapping your hands around a warm cup instead. Inhale possibility. Exhale control. Even when the soil feels dry, your future is already rooted in divine timing.

TRUTH DROP:
The seeds within you never expired—they're only waiting for your next yes.

Day 266 – Truth Drop

The Law of Gender: Balance of Feminine & Masculine Energy

Some days you're all motion — lists, messages, holding everyone's world together. Other days you slip beneath the surface, longing for rest but losing direction. Midlife magnifies this tug-of-war. You want to feel whole, yet the harder you try to "get it right," the more off-balance you feel.

Within every soul live two sacred forces — the feminine and the masculine. The feminine is intuition, flow, nurture, and receptivity. The masculine is structure, strength, and action. All flow without structure becomes chaos; all force without softness becomes burnout. Both are holy. Both are needed.

The harmony you seek is already within you. Place one hand over your heart and one on your belly. Inhale the feminine — wisdom, softness, trust. Exhale the masculine — courage, clarity, movement. Feel how they belong to one another. This is not a battle; it's a dance.

Balance isn't something you earn by perfection. It's something you allow through breath, awareness, and surrender. Spirit is teaching you this rhythm even now: strength guided by softness, will held by wisdom, power moving through peace.

Truth Drop:
You are not meant to choose between flow and force — you were made to embody both.

Day 267 – Surprise Soul Whisper

The Whisper of Spontaneity

Sometimes your soul doesn't want a plan.
She doesn't want the to-do list, the perfect script, or the neat little box.
Sometimes she just wants to surprise you—
to take you off the path you thought you had to walk
and remind you that joy can be unplanned.

Today, let Spirit dare you into something small but different.
Allow yourself tiny acts of soul rebellion to remind you:
life isn't only about surviving—it's about savoring.

- Take that new road home.
- Wear the outfit that feels too bold.
- Order dessert first.
- Buy yourself flowers and say they're from "someone who finally gets me."

TRUTH DROP:
Rise anyway, my darling—bold, unhurried, unapologetic.
And when you do… wear your brightest shade of lipstick.

Day 268 – Soul Medicine Quote

"No matter what path you're on, that's exactly where you need to be. The next path is always ahead."
—Dr. Jennifer Rademaker

A soul sister pauses at a literal crossroads — the dirt trail splitting in two directions on her morning walk. One way looks familiar, the other disappears into tall grass. For a moment she feels that old anxiety rise: *What if I choose wrong? What if I miss what's meant for me?* Midlife can feel like this: jobs changing, children grown, relationships shifting, a map that no longer matches the terrain. It's easy to worry you've wandered off course or fallen behind.

My darling, spirit wastes nothing. Every step you've taken — even the ones that felt like detours — has prepared you for the one ahead. The path you are on is not a mistake; it's a teacher. You're gathering skills, insights, and strengths you'll need later. And when the time comes, the next doorway always appears. You don't have to push it open before it's ready. You only have to keep walking, eyes and heart open.

Pause now and remember: the earth beneath you holds you no matter which trail you're on. The same Love that planted desire in you is guiding your steps. Trusting your path doesn't mean you never change direction; it means you believe there is wisdom in where you are now and guidance for where you're going next.

TRUTH DROP:
When you reach the fork in the road, choose the path that lifts you into radiant life—and say good riddance to the one that lures you back to sleep.

Radiate — Summer

You've arrived at the season of **Radiate**. This is where all you've released, reset, and risen into begins to spill outward as light. Like the sun at its fullest height, your heart was never meant to stay hidden; it was made to shine without striving. Midlife is not a dimming but a blooming—your wisdom, your joy, your freedom now ripple into the world naturally.

As you step into these pages, pause for a moment. Lift your chin as if catching a sunbeam. Breathe in warmth, exhale self-consciousness. Whisper softly, "I am light, and I radiate love." Every ray you offer returns to you multiplied. You have become the light you once sought—where magic begins to move, and miracles remember your name..

Inside this section you'll find reflections, practices, and playful invitations that celebrate who you've become and encourage your light to move freely—through laughter, generosity, and self-honoring joy. These aren't tasks; they're gentle doorways into living your wholeness – and remembering your divine radiance.

The light shines because you are no longer hiding from your own self.

Affirmation:
I am light, and I radiate love into the world.

Day 269 – Soul Reflection

The Image You Hold of Yourself

Your life expands to the picture you carry of yourself inside. When you lift your gaze—trusting that the Divine is for you—you align with a truer vision. You were not made for defeat. You were made for wholeness, joy, and a future bright with possibility.

The old story may try to whisper not-enough, but your attention is a paintbrush. Each time you turn it toward love and faith, you cast the deciding vote. You say with your life, *I am more than I was told. I am who God designed me to be.*

Self-image is not vanity—it's vision. It's the sacred lens through which tomorrow takes shape. See yourself as cherished. See yourself as capable. See yourself shining. God manifested you on purpose; while you work on plan B, grace is already making a way for plan C. You were not brought this far to be left here. You are being lifted—vision restored, heart brightened, path widened.

You are not stuck; you are stepping into new levels of freedom and delight. Believe it. Hold the image of your radiance—and watch your life rise to meet it.

REFLECTION QUESTION:
What old image of yourself will you lay down today, and what radiant vision will you choose instead?

Day 270 – Affirmation + Reflection

Be the light—let the storm adjust.

The Lighthouse Within

When the storm comes, the lighthouse does not chase the waves or try to calm the sea. It simply shines—steady, unshaken, a beacon in the dark.

You, too, are a lighthouse. Midlife storms may rise—uncertainty, loss, change—but your inner light was never designed to flicker with every gust of wind. It was built to stand, to guide, to remind you: you are the steady one.

You don't have to control the storm. You only need to stay lit. Hold your light, soul sister—and let heavens handle the weather.

AFFIRMATION
I am steady, I am light, and my soul remains unshaken.

REFLECTION QUESTION:
When life feels stormy, how can you return to your inner lighthouse instead of fighting the waves?

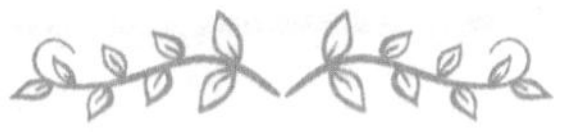

Day 271 – Dear God Letter

Dear God,

I thank you for being the light within me—steady even when I feel unsteady. Thank you for reminding me I don't have to fix everything or know everything to stand strong. Your Spirit makes me unshakable, rooted, and whole.

When fear whispers that I am not enough, let your truth sound louder—that I am chosen, cherished, and created for joy. When storms come, let me rest in the rhythm of your grace.

Remind me to shine, not because I am perfect, but because your light never leaves me.

And so it is, Amen.

Day 272 – Breath Practice / Ritual Reset

The Glow in Your Neck

There's a small space just beneath your jaw and down along your neck where tension likes to hide. Most of us carry old stories there—words unspoken, tears swallowed, sighs we never let out. Over time, that hidden tension can dim your light. But tucked inside that same space is a beautiful switch God built into your nervous system—the vagus nerve, the body's secret pathway back to peace.

When you gently soothe this nerve, you send a signal to your whole body: "I am safe. I can soften. I can shine again." It's like striking a tuning fork for calm. In your radiant season, this practice isn't just about stress relief; it's about reclaiming your glow—letting your inner light ripple outward.

Ritual Reset Invitation:

Find a quiet spot. Sit tall, feet grounded. Place one hand on your heart, one on your neck. Inhale slowly through your nose for a count of four. As you exhale through your mouth for a count of six, turn your head gently to the right, pause, then back to center. Inhale again; exhale as you turn to the left, pause, then return. Do this three times, imagining a soft golden light sweeping down your neck with each exhale.

Feel the warmth rise. That's your nervous system resetting. That's your soul remembering its own light. When you finish, rest both hands over your heart and whisper, *"I am calm, I am glowing, I radiate peace."*

Day 273 – Chakra Soul Movement

Walking Like Sunlight

Sometimes the quickest way to awaken your soul is to move your body in rhythm with something larger than you. In this season of radiance, let sunlight become your dance partner. Movement doesn't have to be exercise; it can be prayer in motion—an active meditation that reminds your cells they're alive.

Begin by standing where a little natural light touches you. Feel your feet root into the earth, your spine lengthen toward the sky. Imagine the sun spilling down through the crown of your head, sliding across your shoulders, melting the tension in your chest. With a slow inhale, raise your arms outward like wings. As you exhale, let them float back down, palms brushing the air. Step one foot forward, then the other, as if you're walking through liquid gold.

Each breath becomes a step, each step becomes a blessing. Whisper with your movement: *"I am radiant. I am open. I am alive."* Let your hips sway, your knees soften, your heart lead. No choreography needed—just your own rhythm guided by light.

When you finish, place your hands over your heart and pause. Feel the glow you've gathered. That's your soul moving. That's your body becoming a prayer.

Mantra:
Today, I step forward with a conscious mind of optimism.

Day 274 – Soul Whisker

The Mirror Stare

Hello, my two-legged radiant one.
I've been staring at myself in the hallway mirror for ten minutes. No shame. Just checking out my own fabulousness from every angle. Tail flick, whisker twitch. Yep, still magnificent.

You, too, deserve mirror time that isn't about criticism. Strike a pose. Wink at yourself. Admire the magic still glinting in your eyes. It's not vanity; it's recognition.

Soul Whisker:
Fur-real, your soul approves this boundary.

Day 275 – Sacred Sips Moment

The First Sip of Courage

This tea moment is your microdose of soul medicine—a truth drop for your nervous system.

This morning I poured jasmine into my favorite cup and watched the steam curl like a soft hallelujah. I thought of you. Radiance doesn't arrive in one grand entrance; it gathers—sip by sip—until you notice you're shining from the inside out.

But maybe a part of you wonders if the window has closed, if energy or timing passed you by. My darling soul sister, life is still pouring goodness into your hands. Your courage isn't straining; it's steeping. Your joy isn't performing; it's infusing.

Wrap your palms around a real cup if you can—or imagine one warm in your hands. Inhale. Exhale. Let your shoulders fall. Whisper, "I am steeping in more courage today, and my light overflows." Notice how your body softens when you let warmth lead. This is nervous-system safety; this is your soul rehearsing how to live bright.

Where could one illuminated yes—a tiny, joyful "I'm ready"—let more light through today? You don't have to push the door open. Your glow invites it to swing wide. What's ahead of you is generous. Heaven is not late. Your radiance is right on time.

PRESCRIPTION FOR YOUR SOUL – TRUTH DROP:
I don't force my glow—I sip it in, and it overflows.

The Law of Increase

Gratitude is not etiquette—it's energy. Praise turns your attention into light, and light reveals more to praise. Metaphysical teaching calls this the **Law of Increase**: what you bless expands; what you appreciate, appreciates.

In this season of life, we don't strain for good—we spotlight it. Your noticing becomes a signal to heaven: *she's ready for more*. When you whisper "thank you" for even a thimbleful of goodness, you become a larger vessel. Joy multiplies in the presence of gratitude.

Try this now: place a hand over your heart, soften your jaw, exhale long. Name three simple specifics—tiny, true, and present: the warmth of your cup, a kind text, the way light lands on your table or just that your eyes opened this morning to this day. Let praise rise— not as performance, but as pleasure. Feel how your body opens when you bless what is.

This is not positive pretending. It's spiritual alignment. What you honor, you invite. What you celebrate, you accelerate. The Law of Increase isn't bargaining with God; it's agreeing with the generosity already moving toward you.

So today, become a lighthouse of thanks. Bless what is, bless what's becoming, bless what you cannot yet see. Your gratitude is a key; doors love to open to a grateful heart.

TRUTH DROP:
What I appreciate, appreciates—my gratitude multiplies my good.

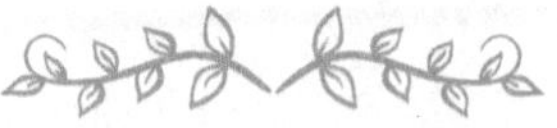

Day 277 – Surprise Soul Whisper

The Unwritten Page

This morning, imagine opening a book and finding a blank page tucked between the chapters. At first you might think something is missing—but that empty space is an invitation. In midlife, after decades of caretaking and showing up, the checklists and shoulds, life can start to feel already scripted. Yet here you are, holding a clean page no one has written on yet.

Breathe gently. A hand rests over your heart. Inside, a quiet truth surfaces: *I am the author of what comes next.* The blank page can hold a single word, a dream, a shimmering decision that tilts the future toward light.

Let one luminous word land today—something that feels like writing your name in the margin of your own life. Let it be simple. Let it be yours. Notice how the page inside you brightens when you choose it.

SOUL WHISPER:
Your page is waiting,—write in sunlight.

Day 278 – Soul-to-Spirit Meditation

The Stream of Radiance

There is a quiet stream running through your life, one that's been collecting every drop of wisdom, compassion, and courage you've ever gathered. Midlife is not a slowing down of this stream; it's the season when its waters sparkle brightest. This is the time when your experiences become light, and your light becomes medicine for others.

You don't have to search for it. You don't have to earn it. Your wisdom is honored and needed more than ever; your light is a gift this world has been waiting for. All you need is a moment to step into the stream and let its radiance rise through you.

Where could you step into the "stream" today and allow your own light to flow outward naturally, do it.

Today's practice invites you to remember that you are both receiver and giver of this radiance.

Close your eyes.

Place one hand over your heart and one on your belly. Imagine yourself standing barefoot at the edge of a crystal-clear stream. Sunlight pours across the water, catching every ripple. With each inhale, picture that golden light flowing up from the stream into your body—through your feet, your belly, your heart—filling you with warmth and glow. With each exhale, imagine it spilling outward, blessing everyone and everything your life touches. Stay with this for several breaths. Let your body feel the shimmer; let your soul remember she is a conduit, not a reservoir. You are filled so you can flow.

✳

Day 279 – Microdose Laugh-Lift

Vocal Toning Laughter

Your body is an instrument, and laughter is one of its most healing sounds.

Today, try playing with tones of laughter:
Start with a low, deep chuckle—feel it vibrate in your belly.
Then shift to a mid-tone laugh—like a ripple through your chest.
Finally, rise into a light, high giggle—bubbling in your throat.

Each sound vibrates a different part of your body, sending healing waves through your nervous system. It's not just silly—it's sacred sound medicine.

Let yourself hum, giggle, and laugh in tones until you feel loosened, lightened, alive.

PRESCRIPTION FOR YOUR SOUL RX:
1 hearty laugh, three times daily—or as needed for spiritual emergencies.

WARNING:
May cause uncontrollable hope and sudden outbreaks of happy-dance moves while stirring the soup.

Day 280 – Soul Medicine Quote

"Even the darkest nights can't stop the dawn."
—Dr. Jennifer Rademaker

Morning keeps its promises. Even when clouds linger, light has a way of finding you—through laughter you didn't plan, the warmth of a cup in your hands, the softness in your own voice. Dawn isn't far-off rescue; it rises from within.

You're not waiting at the window anymore—you *are* the window, thrown wide. The years you carried a small sun inside are shining openly now. The path behind you gleams as wisdom, and the way ahead brightens because you do. Ordinary moments catch gold— you hold the keys now, a name spoken kindly, the quiet yes you trust without defending.

Let this be the simple truth you move in today: daylight recognizes you. It gathers where you step. It lingers where you bless. Your life is not straining toward morning; it is revealing it—petal by petal, breath by breath—until the whole room glows.

TRUTH DROP:
I don't chase sunrise—I shine it from within.

Soul Companion Card: No. 20

Day 281 – Soul Reflection

The Bridge of Light

My beautiful soul, you are not stuck between chapters—you are the light that carries them. The bridge beneath your feet isn't a test; it's a terrace with a view. Look how far your heart has traveled. The path behind you glows—not as regret, but as a ribbon of wisdom lighting where you stand.

You're not waiting to become; you're already walking in color. Strength has become your posture; softness has become your tone. The bridge doesn't ask you to hurry. It invites you to move like a woman who knows the way rises to meet her.

Feel the gentle air on your face, the warm rail under your palm. This is not limbo—it's luminosity. What's ahead isn't better because it's farther; it's brighter because **you** are. Wherever your foot lands, light gathers. Wherever you turn, grace widens the view.

Honor this span for what it really is: a place where the whole of you walks—steady, loved, already shining.

AFFIRMATION:
I am whole on the way and whole when I arrive; the path brightens beneath my radiance.

REFLECTION QUESTION:
Where do you notice your wholeness lighting today's steps—and how might you let that light be seen without apology?

Day 282 – Affirmation + Reflection

Whole in the Light

The light on your cheek tells the truth first—quiet, certain, already yours. You're not waiting to become; you're noticing. The mirror doesn't ask for proof today. It simply reflects a woman who kept choosing love until love began choosing her back, everywhere.

My beautiful soul sister, wholeness isn't a finish line; it's your native glow. When you stop negotiating your worth, life stops arguing with you. Doors ease. Timing softens. Even the ordinary looks anointed—steam from your cup, keys in your palm, your own name said with tenderness.

Let your shoulders loosen the way flowers do at noon. Let joy take the corner seat and nod like an old friend. You don't have to dim to fit any room; the room can widen. I don't chase light; I release it—and it keeps arriving.

Remember the years you carried everyone's weather and still kept a small sun inside? That sun is on your face now. You're allowed to be the answered prayer you once whispered.

REFLECTION QUESTION:
Where is wholeness already showing itself in your day—and how can you let it be seen without apology?

AFFIRMATION:
I am whole, already shining—and my life lovingly reflects my light.

Day 283 – Dear God Letter

Dear God,

Thank you for the light that moves through me—quiet, certain, generous. Thank you that I no longer measure my life by clocks or comparisons, but by the warmth of your presence and the peace that settles where I stand.

Today I choose to shine, not to prove anything, but because love in me wants a way out into the world. Let my words carry softness, my steps carry blessing, my ordinary moments catch gold. Make me a window for your goodness—open, effortless, bright.

If I meet a closed door, let my spirit stay spacious. If I meet a heavy heart, let my face become sunrise. Keep my gaze on what is true: nothing missing, nothing broken—only grace unfolding in perfect ways I don't have to manage.

Expand my capacity to receive and to give. Let joy be my natural language and kindness my quiet habit. Use my life as an answer to prayers I'll never hear, as comfort I may never see, as beauty that multiplies because you are here.

I rest inside your love and let it overflow.

And so it is, Amen.

Day 284 – Breath Practice / Ritual Reset

Light-Bath Blessing

Water remembers how to carry light. Watch how it holds the candleflame, how it turns a single spark into a roomful of shimmer. That is your body tonight—made to receive glow and give it back.

If you draw a bath, let it be simple. If you don't, a warm shower or a bowl of water at the sink will do. Touch the surface with your fingertips and think of something that's already good: a laugh from today, a name you love, the quiet that found you. Let warmth rise to meet your hands.

Breathe in gently through your nose as if the water itself is brightness. Exhale soft, and imagine your skin exhaling too—glow moving outward, blessing what you'll touch next. No fixing. No forcing. Just light finding places to land.

You're not washing away a burden; you're steeping in radiance. Let your shoulders loosen the way petals do at noon. Feel how water makes everything it touches more reflective. That's you—ordinary gleaming again, edges softened, heart bright.

When you step out, carry a drop of this with you—on your face, in your voice, in the way you reach for what matters.

SOUL WHISPER:
I soak in light—and everywhere I go, something shines.

Day 285 – Chakra Soul Movement

Shine in Your Bones

My darling soul sister, your body remembers sunlight. Even before the day begins, there's a quiet glow in you—like morning pressed beneath your skin, waiting to be noticed.

Let's notice.

Stand or sit where you are. Let your feet feel the good earth. Imagine a soft gold thread rising from the crown of your head, lengthening your spine the way a sunflower finds the sky. Allow your shoulders to melt the way petals loosen at noon. Unclench the jaw. Unfurl the brow. Give your heart a little more room.

Now let the ribs open as if windows unlatch. Float your arms outward—not to perform, but to receive. A slow, easy sway arrives—the kind trees know when the breeze is kind. Hips soften. Breath widens. Your back body feels held; your front body feels brave. You're not fixing anything. You're letting light move.

If you like, roll your wrists as though you're rinsing them in a stream, then draw your palms toward your chest—one quiet, tender gathering. Feel how presence changes posture—how love rearranges the room from the inside out.

This isn't a workout. It's a welcome. Your body is a chapel and you've just opened the doors. Stay here for one more breath, the generous kind—the kind that says, *I belong to my own life.*

MANTRA:
I move like light in a beloved body.
I am safe to open. I am free to shine.

Day 286 – Soul Whisker

High-Tail Theology

I sprinted. Something crashed. Did I spiral? Please. I took a victory lap.
Listen, luminous human: queens don't apologize to furniture. Momentum is messy and glorious. One minute I'm a marble statue in a sunbeam; the next I'm a comet with excellent cheekbones. If a vase forgets its purpose (to admire me), that's on the vase.

Here's the gospel according to whiskers: mess is proof of motion, and motion is proof of life. You're not clumsy—you're catalytic. When your soul hits play, a few things rattle. Good. The room needed rearranging. Tail high. Shoulders back. Purr at your reflection like the masterpiece she is.

If anyone asks about the noise, say, "Oh, that? Expansion." Then saunter off and bask where the light finds you. Growth sheds a little glitter and a few old patterns. Sweep later. Shine now. Your radiance doesn't need permission—only room.

Soul Whisker:
Consider this your paws-itively perfect pause
Fur-real, your soul approves this boundary.

Day 287 – Sacred Sips Moment

First Light in Your Cup

This tea moment is your microdose of soul medicine—a truth drop for your nervous system.

It's a beautiful day to be alive. Feel the cup in your hands. Notice its warmth—the way steam rises and brushes your face like a soft blessing. Lift your chin as if catching a sunbeam. Breathe in warmth; exhale any trace of self-consciousness. You don't have to become radiant—you already are.

Think of the life that brought you here: boxes stacked in the hallway after a child moved out; a quiet room that once rang with laughter; a mirror reflecting a face and hands you're learning to admire again. Every chapter has been steeping like leaves in hot water. Now the flavor is ready. Your wisdom, your joy, your freedom ripple outward naturally—like sunlight spilling across a kitchen table at dawn.

As you sip, ask softly: *What small expression of my inner glow wants to show itself today?* A kinder word. A lighter laugh. A generous yes. Let it be simple. Let it be yours.

My radiant one, the truths you've nurtured inside are ready to pour. Your laughter, your generosity, your joy—they are medicine for you first, and then for the world.

Truth Drop:
I allow my inner light to rise and pour into the world naturally.

Day 288 – Truth Drop

Light Was Always Your Nature

My beautiful soul… this is a time not of striving, but remembering. Midlife may have tried to say light fades, that dreams belong to youth, that your turn has passed. Those are only stories. In metaphysical law, light isn't diminished—it's only obscured. And obscurity is temporary.

Picture the sun behind clouds: warmth present, even when hidden. Your radiance has been steady all along, quietly gathering strength beneath the surface of your life. The heartbreaks, the caregiving, the moves, the late nights at the kitchen table—none of it dimmed you. It was steeping, not shrinking. Now your light is meeting you where you stand.

Metaphysical teaching calls this the **Law of Radiance**: what you nurture within must eventually shine without. You don't manufacture it; you allow it. Wisdom ripens into warmth. Joy becomes atmosphere. Freedom ripples outward the way morning spreads across water.

Let your shoulders loosen as if noon has found you. Notice how the ordinary starts to gleam when you stop arguing with your glow. You're not waiting for permission. You *are* the permission—quiet, certain, bright.

TRUTH DROP:
I am Radiant, I am the light. Shine first baby; let the room adjust.

Day 289 – Surprise Soul Whisper

The Doorway of Small Delights-

I make space; grace makes entrance.

Sometimes we think transformation must come with thunder—big decisions, big changes, big revelations. But Spirit often slips in through the tiniest doorway: a fragrance, a birdcall, a moment of softness we almost overlook.

Today your soul has a playful assignment: go looking for a small delight you didn't expect. Not scrolling for it. Not scheduling it. Just pausing long enough for it to find you. It might be a feather on the sidewalk, a stranger's unexpected kindness, the way sunlight lands on your kitchen table. When you notice it, stop. Let it land inside you. Whisper inwardly: *This moment is for me.*

Why? Because each time you pause to savor a small delight, you retrain your whole being to believe: *I am safe. I am seen. Goodness can reach me without effort.* This isn't pretend; it's a holy re-patterning—planting a new truth that your life is already threaded with blessings.

So let wonder be your quiet rebellion against heaviness. Let curiosity be your doorway back to joy. One tiny delight at a time, you remind your spirit how to live open-handed again.

SOUL WHISPER:
Small delights find me—effortlessly, often, and right on time.

Day 290 – Soul-to-Spirit Meditation

Every Cell Made of Light

Imagine if you will, a most beautiful radiant light gathering above your crown—gentle as morning on water. It knows your name. It pours through the top of your head like liquid honeyed gold. This is how love moves: not demanding, just arriving.

Feel it thread through your scalp, your temples, your brow. Tension loosens the way petals loosen at bloom. The light travels behind your eyes—kindness from the inside. It softens your jaw, brightens your tongue with truth, warms your throat with clean, clear voice.

Down it flows across your heart, where it lingers—because your heart is a chapel and light loves sanctuaries. Let it widen there. Let it say, *I am seen. I am held.* Radiance moves into your ribs, bathing the breath, then down your spine—each vertebra a little window opening.

It reaches your belly—home of courage—and your hips—home of trust. Hips ungrip. The light takes its time through thighs, knees, calves, ankles, the long map of your feet. Imagine the soles glow, and the earth nods back, *I've got you.*

Now picture every cell awake—ten thousand tiny lanterns, then a thousand more, until your whole body is a constellation. You are not trying to shine; you *are* shining. Your life will carry this glow into rooms that didn't know they were dim.

Rest here. Breathe like someone who belongs to the light.

AFFIRMATION:
I am light-filled from crown to sole; every cell remembers, and my whole life shines with ease.

332

Day 291 – Microdose Laugh-Lift

Laughter on Purpose

Sun on the counter. And there it is—a tiny fizz of joy in your chest, like champagne deciding to rise. Let it. Laugh on purpose today—not to fix anything, but because glow likes company.

Think of laughter as nervous-system confetti: it loosens the shoulders, warms the ribs, and tells your whole body, *we're safe enough to sparkle*. It's praise with syllables. It's light escaping through your smile.

Try a full out minute sparkle set whenever you feel like it. Stand in your favorite spot (yes, the kitchen counts). Lift your chin as if catching a sunbeam and let an easy "ha" slip out. Then another. Let them stack into a deliciously ridiculous stream. Cross-your-legs and hold giggles fully permitted. This isn't performance; it's overflow.

If someone asks what's funny, say, "My life."

Because it is—alive, bright, unapologetically yours. Laughter is how your radiance makes sound.

Prescription for Your Soul Rx:
1 hearty laugh before coffee, 2 after any stressful text thread, and unlimited refills as desired.

Warning:
May cause sudden kitchen twirls mid-stir and living-room shoulder shimmies.

Day 292 – Soul Medicine Quote

"Even the heaviest season cannot silence the light within me."
—Dr. Jennifer Rademaker

A soul sister wakes before the house and cracks the kitchen window. July hums—cicadas tuning the morning, sunlight laying a golden stripe across the table. There are lists, yes—appointments, caregiving, the next brave thing—but the air feels generous, like it's making room for her.

Midlife has its fullness—bodies changing, chapters shifting, love stretching in new directions. Some days carry weight. But weight is not identity; it's weather. And today, the weather is warm. Notice the small proofs: the peach on the counter softening by the minute; the way light rests on your cheek like a blessing; the ease that arrives when no one is asking you to be more than you are.

My beautiful soul, your light doesn't wait for perfect conditions. It rises like summer—quiet at first, then everywhere. It shows up in laughter you didn't plan, in kindness that costs nothing, in the joy of bare feet on cool tile. This isn't performance; it's presence. You're not hunting for your glow; you're remembering it.

Think of your life as a wide porch—room for guests, room for rest, room for the woman you've become to sit, breathe, and be seen. The world may whirl with headlines and hurry. But right here, warm light keeps finding you. It always has.

Let the day open. Give your radiance the good seat. Let joy spill a little.

PRESCRIPTION FOR YOUR SOUL – TRUTH DROP:
I don't wait for the sun—I bring it.

Day 293 – Soul Reflection

The Lantern Path

There's a point on the journey when I realize I'm no longer just finding my way—I'm lighting it. These years have taught me to carry a quiet glow: lessons gathered, scars tended, prayers whispered into the dark. Without trying, I've become a lantern.

I think of nights I walked through uncertainty and still showed up for others. I remember offering encouragement when my own cup felt thin. Step by step, those moments became oil for the lamp. Now it burns steady—not a flash that needs applause, but the lasting radiance of a woman who knows where she's been and trusts where she's going.

My light isn't performance; it's presence. When I move through the day with my shoulders easy and my breath kind, something brightens around me. I don't force inspiration; I arrive as myself, and the path answers—sometimes for a friend, sometimes for a stranger who feels like kin.

I honor this span for what it is: a place where my whole self walks—steady, loved, already shining. Wherever my foot lands, light gathers; wherever I turn, grace widens the view.

AFFIRMATION:
I am a lighthouse, not a searchlight—my life is a lantern of quiet radiance, and it shines as I move.

Day 294 – Affirmation + Reflection

The Gift of Enough

For years I whispered, *I'll be happy when…* When the scale changes. When the bank account grows. When someone finally approves. As if my worth lived somewhere ahead of me, waiting to be earned—while my heart ached in the waiting.

Today I remember a truer thing: **I am enough—here, now.**

This isn't about hustling into worthiness; it's about wearing what was always mine. The wrinkles, my fat around the middle, laughter lines, and scars don't make me less; they make me whole. Each line is a poem of survival. Each scar, a map of courage. When I walk into a room from this knowing, my shoulders settle, my voice warms, my breath unhurried. I don't audition for belonging; I bring it.

Living from enoughness changes what I choose. Boundaries grow clear without bitterness. Joy sits closer. My self-talk softens. I let the nervous system take a cue from the soul: jaw loose, shoulders easy, and the simple truth rising—**I am already allowed to be at ease.**

REFLECTION QUESTION:
If I moved through today as already enough, what one choice, boundary, or tenderness would change first?

AFFIRMATION:
I am enough today. Worth lives in me now—and my life lovingly reflects it.

Day 295 – Dear God Letter

Dear God,

There are days when my reflection startles me—
when I see changes I wasn't ready for,
lines telling stories I didn't ask to write.
Teach me not to resist what is,
but to honor the woman I am now
and the one I am becoming.

Remind me that beauty isn't measured by a mirror
but by the love I carry, the wisdom I share,
the courage it takes to keep shining.
Soften my judgments.
Help me stand with tenderness toward my body,
my journey, my unfolding.

Where I feel fragile, wrap me in your strength.
Where I doubt, whisper your truth again.
Let my eyes find what you already see:
beloved, whole, radiant.

I trust that you make all things beautiful in their time—
including me, here and now.

And so it is, Amen.

Day 296 – Breath Practice / Ritual Reset

Breathing the Bridge Back Home

Some mornings my thoughts scatter like bright birds—everywhere at once. I don't chase them anymore. I set the moment down like a warm cup and let my breath find me.

I sit as I am, feet easy on the floor, spine lengthening as if a sun thread lifted me from the crown. One hand meets my heart, the other cradles my belly. The message is simple: *I am here. I am listening.*

Inhale—soft and welcoming—as if light wanders in through open windows. Exhale—long and kind—as if the room itself sighs with me. My shoulders loosen. The jaw remembers ease. The flutter of thoughts keeps its color, but it settles on gentler branches. I don't fix the day; I befriend it. Breath becomes a bridge back home.

I notice small mercies: the way air cools my nostrils, the warmth of my palm, the steady rhythm that has carried me through every season without asking for applause. I belong to this body, to this breath, to this quiet bright alive. What once felt scattered was simply asking for a softer sky.

When I rise, it's unhurried. The birds are still themselves—only closer, only calmer. I carry this light with me, the kind that lingers in a room after I've left.

Soul Whisper:
You belong to this light, and it belongs to you.

Day 297 – Chakra Soul Movement

Opening the Solar Doorway

Sometimes the most powerful shifts don't come from thinking harder but from moving differently. Midlife can tighten our bodies the way old stories tighten our minds—shoulders rounded, belly held in, heart guarded. Movement becomes your key to unlocking a new story.

Today we awaken your solar plexus—the "sun" of your body, your center of power and confidence. Stand barefoot if you can. Place both hands lightly on the space just above your navel. Take a slow inhale, feeling your belly expand against your palms. On the exhale, sway your torso gently side to side, as if sunlight were rocking you.

Now let the sway grow a little wider. Imagine a golden sphere of light glowing at your center, expanding with each breath until it fills your whole torso. Whisper softly as you move:

"I am allowed to shine..My joy is holy."

Repeat this movement and mantra for at least three rounds of breath. With every sway, picture old stories falling away— "stay small," "don't be too much"—and a new truth rising from within: I am radiant. I am strong. I am here to be seen.

When you finish, pause with your hands still on your belly. Feel the warmth you've generated, the quiet pulse of your own sun. This is your power center remembering itself.

Affirmation:
I move with freedom, power, and joy.

Day 298 – Soul Whisker

The Cat Who Owns the Couch

Observe, my luminous human: don't you see, I find the sun square, assess the fluff-to-purr ratio, and claim it without a single apology. Sunny cushion? Mine. Fluffiest blanket? Mine. Your folded laundry? Obviously, my throne. I don't ask permission from furniture—or from feelings. I arrive, stretch long, and let the room adjust.

Try my method. Stop perching like an invited guest in your own life. Slide into the soft center. Unclench your jaw. Lengthen like velvet. Purr at your reflection. Comfort isn't a crime; it's a crown. If anyone wonders why you're taking up space, tell them the queen is home.

Today, choose the best seat, the kind mug, the song that knows your name. Let ease be the language your body speaks. I'll demonstrate again—watch closely: claim, curl, radiate.

SOUL WHISKER:
Be like me. Give your head a shake. You don't borrow comfort, you embody it. Tail high, cushion claimed.

Day 299 – Sacred Sips Moment

A Cup That Holds Me

Some days it has felt like I'm pouring from a cup that never fills. Not today. Today, this warm mug is a small ceremony of return.

I hold it with both hands. Heat meets my palms, steam curls like a blessing. I breathe and let a kinder story rise: I am held. I am at peace. I am being poured back into.

The first sip spreads through me like light—down the throat, into the chest, soft as morning on water. Another sip loosens the shoulders. One more, and the room inside me widens. I taste ease. I taste enough. I remember I don't have to prove my worth to receive what nourishes me.

I set the cup down and notice warmth living in my body now—evidence that receiving is not indulgence; it's wisdom. This is how my radiance refuels: simple, tender, consistent.

TRUTH DROP:
I let myself be poured into—then I overflow.

Day 300 – Truth Drop

Sunlight in Her Bones

There's a morning when light no longer feels separate from you.
It pours through your window, lands on your skin,
and something inside whispers—*this is me now.*

You've traveled the valleys. You've faced your shadows.
Now even your breath glows.
Joy moves like honey through your veins.
Ease hums where effort used to live.

You laugh without needing a reason.
You walk like belonging, you are one with God.
The universe responds in color, in kindness,
in small golden synchronicities that wink, *yes, my darling you're aligned.*
Living the law of oneness.

This is what it means to live radiant—
to embody what once felt far away,
to bloom without trying,
to bless the earth simply by being here.

TRUTH:
You've become the sunlight you were chasing.
Shine as only you can.

Day 301 – Surprise Soul Whisper

A Secret Garden Moment

Your soul wants to surprise you today.
Not with another task.
Not with another *should.*
But with a hidden pocket of beauty you didn't know was waiting.

Somewhere near you—in your kitchen, your yard, your commute,
even your inbox—
is a small "secret garden" moment:
a flash of color,
a scent, a laugh, a sound, a kindness.
It's Spirit's way of saying,
"I'm here. You're not alone. Beauty still lives inside your ordinary."

Today, your assignment is to pause and let one of those moments
find you.
Maybe it's the way light kisses a mug.
A stranger holding the door.
A bird landing right where you're looking.

When it happens, stop.
Breathe.
Let it land inside you.
Whisper inwardly: *"This is for me."*

You no longer need to search for miracles.
They're already blooming around you—
and in you.

Each time you receive a moment like this, you are rewiring your
nervous system.

✳

You're teaching your subconscious: *Goodness can reach me without effort.*
Life is still tender enough to delight me.
Joy belongs here.

This isn't about collecting moments.
It's about remembering
you already live inside a world
that wants to nourish you—
one tiny wonder at a time.

Soul Whisper:
I open to the secret gardens around me.
Each hidden wonder rewires me for joy.

Day 302 – Soul-to-Spirit Meditation

The Breath of Light

When was the last time you sat so still
you could feel the light inside you?
Not just sunlight on your skin,
but the quiet glow you were born with—
the one beneath the noise,
beneath the midlife fatigue.

That light is your spirit's breath,
waiting to be noticed.

Close your eyes.
Hand on heart. Hand on belly.
Feel warmth beneath your palms—
proof that you're here, alive, loved.

Inhale through your nose for four,
drawing in a ribbon of golden light.
Pause.
Exhale for six,
letting heaviness melt like morning mist.

Repeat seven times.
With each breath, your light expands,
filling your body, spilling into the room,
blessing everything it touches.

You don't have to create the light, my beautiful soul.
It's already here.
Just breathe it. Receive it. Let it flow.

With every breath, light fills me and flows through me.

Day 303 – Microdose Laugh-Lift

Close your eyes.
Hand on belly. Hand on heart.
Take a slow breath in …

Now exhale with the silliest laugh you can imagine.
Snort, wobble, giggle until you can't help but smile.
Do it three times.

Feel how your belly softens,
how your heart loosens,
how the air itself begins to sparkle again.

This isn't "fake it till you make it."
This is subconscious reprogramming.
Your body remembers:
If I can laugh, I am safe.
If I can laugh, I am free.
If I can laugh, joy belongs here.

PRESCRIPTION FOR YOUR SOUL — RX:
WARNING: *May cause spontaneous joy, softened shoulders, and the urgent need to find a bathroom from laughing too hard.*
REFILLS: *Unlimited. Joy is fully covered under your soul plan.*

Day 304 – Soul Medicine Quote

"Joy taken seriously is a radical act."
—Dr. Jennifer Rademaker

My beautiful soul…

Yesterday I made a quiet promise to myself: I would smile at every person I met for the entire day. I decided to wear a permanent smile and offer one small, genuine compliment to each soul who crossed my path.

Shoes at the grocery store.
A purse at the bank.
A bicyclist's bright shirt.

Each time, they looked surprised—then we laughed. I wondered when the last time was that someone had been noticed with kindness. Every time, the air between us lightened.

By day's end, my cheeks hurt from smiling, and my heart felt wider than it had in weeks.

This is what the quote means. Joy isn't a mood that arrives; it's a **medicine you choose to dispense.**

In midlife, that choice is radical—because the world expects you to shrink or dim. But when you take joy seriously—as a practice, as a microdose you offer to others—you become a living invitation.

❋

You remind every soul sister near you that her light is safe too.

Try it for yourself. It costs little, yet heals much.

Take joy seriously.
Your presence is a microdose of soul medicine wherever you go.

Day 305 – Soul Reflection

When the Wild Knocks at Your Window

My beautiful soul…

Last night my home became a tiny theatre of wildness. The cats sprinted from window to window, tails like exclamation points, paws drumming the hardwood as if announcing a parade.

When I finally looked outside, I saw the cause — a young raccoon, paws pressed to the patio glass, nose fogging a faint heart-shape on the pane. Only a thin sheet of glass separated my house cats from this curious visitor.

I stood watching. Part of me laughed at the chaos. Part of me ached for the little one outside. He wasn't mean or scary — just looking for food, for warmth, for a way in. I whispered, "You can't come in. You've got to go." And he wandered off into the dark, paw vanishing into the lotus bed like a child's hand into a candy jar.

Radiant Season reminds us: as our light grows, so does our magnetism. We attract new people, new energies — like a porch light drawing moths at dusk. Some are meant to come closer; some must stay outside the glass.

Your glow invites curiosity, but your boundaries keep you safe. This isn't coldness — it's wisdom. You can have compassion for the hungry raccoon and still protect your lotus blossoms.

Close your eyes now. Picture your heart as a warm home with a clear glass door.
Breathe in the glow that welcomes.
Breathe out the boundary that protects.

This is radiant living: open, compassionate, discerning.

Your light welcomes warmth and joy while your boundaries protect your peace.

Day 306 – Affirmation + Reflection

Safe to Shine

The subconscious has a habit of whispering old warnings:
Be careful. Don't stand out. Don't try too much—you might fail.

These messages once kept you safe, but now they keep you small. They echo from childhood, from past hurts, from moments when it felt dangerous to be visible.

But Spirit speaks differently: You were never meant to live half-hidden. You were created to radiate. Each time you affirm a higher truth, you retrain your inner world. You are telling your subconscious: The danger has passed. I am safe to shine. I am safe to expand.

Take a breath and notice what part of your life still feels "shrunk." What would shift if you let this truth take root—not as words you repeat, but as a belief you embody?

Pause here. Place one hand over your heart and another gently on your throat—the place where your voice emerges. Inhale slowly through your nose, feeling your chest rise. As you exhale, hum softly or whisper, *I am safe to shine.*

Notice the vibration beneath your hand, the warmth at your throat. This simple vagus-nerve reset tells your body: visibility is safe, expression is safe.

You don't have to leap into the spotlight. Expansion can be soft, like morning light creeping across the floor. Every small act of expression—speaking up, taking a new step, creating something beautiful—is a petal opening.

This is radiant living: shining without fear, expanding without apology

Day 307 – Dear God Letter

Dear God,

There are moments when I forget who I am.
Old beliefs whisper louder than truth, and I shrink into shadows
that no longer fit.
I wear safety like a cloak, even when it's heavy and frayed.
I start to believe it's safer to stay small than to stand in Your light.

Yet You remind me—I was created to shine.
My radiance is not arrogance; it is devotion,
the reflection of Your love placed in me.
When I stand tall in Your presence, I'm not stealing light; I'm
mirroring it.

Help me release every belief that says I must hide.
Melt the memories that taught me my brilliance was dangerous.
Reset the places that cling to fear, comparison, old stories.
Let me rise—not in striving, but in surrender.
Let me radiate love so purely that others remember their own.

When doubt comes, breathe courage into my lungs.
Remind me the danger has passed, my nervous system can rest, my
voice can be free.
Remind me I am safe to shine, safe to expand, safe to embody the
wholeness You dreamed.

And when the old whispers return, let Your truth be louder:
I am Yours. I am whole. I am already the light I seek.

I surrender my shadows to You.
I return my radiance to its Source.
Shine through me, God, until every corner of my being knows it is
safe, sacred, and true.

And so it is, Amen.

Day 308 – Breath Practice / Ritual Reset

Riding into Radiance

The Forgotten Bike

My beautiful soul,

There's an old bike leaning against the side of the house. It's been there for seasons — sun-bleached paint, a little rust, quiet and forgotten.

This morning something in you whispered, *"Ride."*
You listened.

As you pedaled, Florida greeted you: orange blossoms and jasmine drifting on the breeze, fresh-cut grass, the scent of homes opening their windows to spring cleaning. The sun warmed your face. The wind tangled your hair.

In that moment you weren't just on a bike — you were riding into your own freedom, remembering what it feels like to move without duty, without destination.

Joys once considered too small or too late rise up and carry you forward. Spirit is always whispering, *"You can still ride. You can still feel the wind."*

What "bike" in your life has been leaning against the wall, waiting for you?
What small joy could you ride back into being today?

Close your eyes for a moment.
Inhale as if breathing in orange blossoms.
Exhale as if wind is moving across your skin.
Let your shoulders drop and feel the smile behind your ribs.

❋

This is your nervous system tasting freedom — simple, accessible, already yours.

Welcome the breeze of new freedom.
Forgotten joys rise in you and carry you forward.

Day 309 – Chakra Soul Movement

Heart in Bloom

When was the last time you paused long enough to simply watch life happening — without needing to touch it, fix it, or do anything at all?

This morning I stood by the window where our cats watch the birdfeeder on the lawn. Tiny wings darted in and out, seeds spilled, sunlight caught on feathers. For a heartbeat, everything slowed — no chores, no phone, just the soft hush of paws on the sill and the rhythm of wings. It felt like meditation without trying.

What sound, color, or rhythm opens your heart the most? Could you give yourself a few minutes today to sway with it?

Here's a microdose for the soul:
Choose a gentle piece of music that makes you feel soft and safe. Stand with your feet grounded. Place one palm over your heart, the other over your belly.

Inhale — imagine a soft green or rose-colored light expanding beneath your hand.
Exhale — sweep your arms outward and slightly back, as if opening invisible wings, whispering silently, *I am safe to open.*

Now let the music carry you. Begin to sway slowly, letting your hips and shoulders follow the rhythm. Feel the light in your chest moving with you, a soft glow swaying inside your ribs.

This simple movement tells your nervous system: *I am safe enough to move. I am safe enough to expand.*

Each breath and sway is a petal unfurling — a small dance of self-love and freedom.

Your heart moves to the rhythm of love.
With every breath and sway, open to radiance.

Day 310 – Soul Whisker

The Sunbeam Oracle

Pssst… human.
You're doing that thing again — overthinking rest.

I see you watching me from across the room,
wondering how I make it look so holy.

Here's my secret:
I don't *make* it holy.
I simply stretch, sigh, and let the sun do its work.

While you chase worth through busyness,
I bathe in warmth and call it enlightenment.
No guilt. No earning. Just being.

You say you don't have time to rest.
Funny — I don't have time *not* to.
The universe expands every time I purr.

So here's your invitation, glowing one:
Find your own patch of light.
Lie down in it.
Let the world spin without you for a minute.
It knows what to do.

You don't need to earn the sunbeam.
Just stretch into it and glow. 

Day 311 – Sacred Sips Moment

Sunlight in My Cup

For a moment, the noise of the world fades. Steam curls up like a prayer I didn't know I was praying. Warmth gathers between my palms, the scent of lemon drifts from my tea, and a quiet space opens inside me.

This is the heart of Sacred Sips—not the tea itself, but the pause. The world tells me to pour out, to hurry, to keep going. Spirit invites me to pour in, to slow down, to taste my own life again. Even sixty seconds with a warm cup resets my nervous system and reminds my heart: *I am still here. I still belong to myself.*

As I lift my cup, I breathe in slowly. I feel the aroma, the heat against my hands. My shoulders drop. My jaw softens. I whisper inwardly, *This moment is for me.*

I haven't missed my moment. The best of my life isn't behind me— it's steeping right now, growing richer, about to pour. I trust that even my smallest pauses are preparing me for greater joy ahead.

Truth Drop:
You are not sipping tea—
you are tasting your own presence.

Day 312 – Truth Drop

The Law of Overflow

A soul sister stands at the kitchen sink, filling a glass of water, distracted by the day. Without noticing, the water rises to the rim, spills over her fingers, onto the floor—right over the cat's head. For a heartbeat she freezes, then laughs softly.

This tiny moment mirrors a larger truth: years of pouring out to others without pausing to fill herself, believing she must "do enough" before she deserves to receive. Midlife often reveals this hidden script of scarcity: *There isn't enough. I must cling. I must prove my worth.*

But metaphysical truth whispers differently—your soul was created to live in **overflow.**
Overflow isn't excess; it's fullness. When you are nourished, love naturally spills into the lives of others. You don't force generosity— it flows. You don't earn abundance—it arises from within.

Spirit designed you to be a conduit, not a reservoir; to be filled and then to flow.
Scarcity contracts. Overflow expands. It softens your breath, opens your perception, and restores divine circulation.

Close your eyes.
Imagine a golden chalice in your chest.
Inhale light—love, rest, nourishment.
Exhale that light overflowing, blessing everyone it touches.
Whisper inwardly: *My cup overflows.*

TRUTH DROP:
Maybe the spill was the blessing all along?

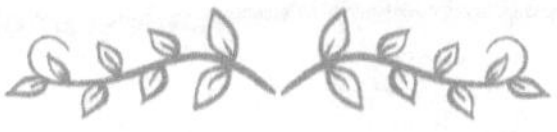

Day 313 – Surprise Soul Whisper

Your soul has a simple assignment for you today: sing.

Not perfectly, not for anyone's approval, just for the joy of hearing your own voice. Sing in the shower, hum while you cook, belt it out in the car with the windows down.

Why? Because singing bypasses the thinking mind and speaks directly to the subconscious. It tells your inner world: *I am alive. I am free. I am joyful.* The subconscious doesn't care if you're in tune—it only cares that you've chosen sound over silence, expression over suppression.

Today, let your own voice remind you of your radiance.

AFFIRMATION:
My voice is medicine. I sing because I am free.

Day 314 – Soul-to-Spirit Meditation

The Horizon of Wholeness

Close your eyes, my beautiful soul, and imagine yourself standing at
the back of a great ship.
The horizon stretches endlessly before you — a line where sky
meets sea, shimmering with light.
Waves roll out behind, carrying the wake farther and farther away.

With each slow exhale, picture every worry and limiting belief
dissolving into that wake.
Let the sound of the water be your release: whoosh… gone,
whoosh… gone.
The farther the ship moves, the farther your burdens drift.

Now gently lift your chin and see the horizon.
Feel your heart expanding into that meeting place of sky and sea —
the edge of all that is known, opening into the infinite.
You are not small. You are as wide as the ocean and as free as the
open sky.

Here, in this stillness, remember: you are whole.
Wholeness doesn't come from fixing — it comes from remembering.
Allow your subconscious to rest in that truth.

Breathe in the salt air.
Breathe out everything you don't need.
Rest in this boundless space for a few moments.

Affirmation:
I am the ocean, the sky.
I am whole and free.

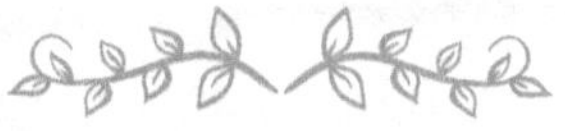

Day 315 – Microdose Laugh-Lift

The Mirror Prescription

You're not looking for happiness in the mirror—you're remembering it.

Find a mirror. Look into your own eyes.
Now—without overthinking it—give yourself the most exaggerated, over-the-top laugh you can. Throw your head back, crinkle your nose. Keep going for at least thirty seconds, even if it feels awkward.

Notice how quickly your body softens. Notice how your subconscious mind, so used to seeing *serious you* in the mirror, begins to rewrite the script:
I am not just stress. I am not just survival. I am joy, too.

Laughter practiced on purpose becomes hypnosis.
It convinces the deepest part of you that joy is safe, accessible, and real—
even here, even now.

Prescription for Your Soul — RX:
Side Effects:
May cause radiant cheeks, and unexpected flirtations with life.
Possible overexposure to inner light. Proceed with delight.
Refills unlimited. Joy is covered under your soul plan.

Day 316 – Soul Medicine Quote

"Joy is not something you chase—it's something you allow."
—Dr. Jennifer Rademaker

She stands at the sink after a long day, hands in warm water, staring out the window. Beyond the glass, a small bird hops along the branch of a flowering tree, tilts its head, and sings. For a moment she feels a flicker of happiness rise — unplanned, unearned. But almost immediately, the old script whispers: *I'll feel better when the kitchen's clean… when my list is done… when I finally have time for myself.* The flicker dims beneath the weight of "shoulds."

My beautiful soul, so much of life is spent striving—waiting for the "right" conditions to be happy. Midlife can murmur, *Work harder. Earn it first.* But joy is not a destination. It isn't a prize for productivity. It's a state of being that rises naturally when you release resistance.

Joy is already here—like that bird outside your window—waiting for your yes.
When you soften your jaw, loosen your shoulders, and breathe a little deeper, you make room for it to rise. The subconscious learns this softness as safety.

Today, stop chasing. Let joy meet you where you are. You don't have to schedule it. You only need to open to it..

Day 317 – Soul Reflection

Lotus Rising in Sunlight

Just beyond my Florida office window is a small sanctuary of tropical flowers and citrus bushes — orange, lemon, lime — tangled with aloe where cats chase lizards and squirrels but thankfully never catch them. Some afternoons, one of my Maine Coons dips his paws into the pool as if ready to swim. Two weeks ago, I pressed my first lotus seedlings into clay planters with bare hands and loved the feeling of cool, wet earth. I felt like a little girl again. Now, nearing fifty-nine, still learning how to begin again. Sunlight, water, laughter, new beginnings — this is what radiance feels like.

My beautiful soul, you too have a sanctuary waiting. Maybe it's a chair by a window, a patch of grass, a cup of tea, a place where sunlight brushes your skin. That space isn't about escape — it's remembrance. You are vast, playful, still becoming. The same hands that plant a lotus at fifty-eight can plant a dream at any age.

Take a slow breath now. Feel your shoulders soften. Whisper inwardly, *"I'm open and willing for something fresh to rise."* Even a single breath can create space for new life. With every inhale you welcome sunlight into your chest; with every exhale you make room for what's next.

REFLECTION:
These hands have given so much.
What new creation are they ready to bring to life — now?

Day 318 – Affirmation + Reflection

A Sprinkle of Wholeness

The subconscious mind can hold on tight to old programs:
I must hold it all together.
I can't ask for help.
I must always be strong.
I'm too old… it's too late .I am not good enough.

These beliefs keep you in survival — not in wholeness.

When you speak new affirmations over your life, you reprogram the script. You remind your inner world that strength also means softness, and that leaning on love is not weakness but wisdom.

Breathe this truth in gently:
I am strong enough to soften.
I am wise enough to open.
I am safe enough to receive.

Notice how your body responds. Your shoulders drop. Your heart loosens. Your breath deepens.
This is your nervous system believing the truth — a sprinkle of wholeness returning home to you.

My luminous one, every time you choose rest over rushing, receiving over proving, softness over strain, you are teaching your body what wholeness feels like. You return to the truth of you.

*

I am not falling apart,
I am falling into alignment — with myself, with love, with life.

REFLECTION:

Where in your life could you release the "I am not..." and replace it with the "I am..." that restores your wholeness?

Day 319 – Dear God Letter

Dear God,

Too often, I forget that I am already held. My mind rushes to fix, to plan, to solve — carrying burdens I was never meant to carry alone. The old belief whispers: *It's all on me.*

But today I surrender that lie. I place every weight into your hands. I breathe out the fear of not enough and breathe in the truth of your overflowing love.

Teach my subconscious to rest in trust. Reset the places where I grip too tightly. Remind me that strength is not control, but surrender.

May my radiance flow not from striving, but from the light of your presence within me. May others see in me the freedom of a soul that remembers she is safe in you.

I affirm: this chapter is not a fade-out — it's my soul in full color.

And so it is. Amen.

Day 320 – Breath Practice / Ritual Reset

Breathing Room

Find a quiet spot and sit or lie comfortably. Place one hand on your heart and one on your belly. Feel the warmth of your palms, the rise and fall beneath them. Close your eyes. Notice the soft sound of your breath — a tide washing in and out. You don't have to change anything yet. Just let yourself arrive.

Now begin the **4–2–6 rhythm:**
- Inhale through your nose for a count of four, as if drawing in calm light.
- Hold gently for a count of two, letting it settle.
- Exhale slowly through your mouth for a count of six, as if releasing the weight you've been carrying.

Repeat for five rounds.
With each inhale, whisper inwardly, *"I receive."*
With each exhale, whisper, *"I release."*

Imagine your inhale filling you like morning sunlight, your exhale sending every heaviness down into the earth.

This simple rhythm tells your subconscious: *I no longer need to cling. I am safe to let go. I am safe to receive what nourishes me.*

Let the breath carve a little sanctuary inside you — a space wide enough for peace to move in.

SOUL WHISPER:
I release control and receive love, healing, and freedom.

Day 321 – Chakra Soul Movement

Heart in Motion

Today, we awaken the heart chakra for wholeness — your center of love, compassion, and radiant connection.

Stand tall, feet grounded. Bring your palms together at the center of your chest. Take a slow, steady inhale. As you exhale, press your hands gently into one another, feeling the strength of your own heart space.

Now open your arms wide, stretching them outward as if to embrace the whole sky. Breathe in deeply.
On the exhale, bring your palms back together at your chest.

Repeat this motion three times — opening wide, then returning to center.

Each expansion teaches your subconscious:
It is safe to give love.
It is safe to receive love.
My heart is strong enough to open.

As you move, imagine soft green light swirling through your chest — the color of balance, renewal, and compassion. Let that light ripple outward, touching every part of you.

This simple movement nourishes your nervous system, balances your energy, and reminds you that love flows in both directions — inward and outward, endlessly replenishing. **Mantra —***My heart is open, safe, and free to give and receive love. I am whole.*

Day 322 – Soul Whisker

Whole Already

Listen up, my luminous two-legger…
You keep searching for the missing piece — some shiny proof that you've finally "arrived."
Meanwhile, your soul is sitting right beside you, licking her paw, wondering when you'll notice she's been whole the entire time.

Wholeness isn't something you achieve; it's the fur you've been wearing all along.
You patch yourself with perfectionism, worry, and comparison — when all you ever needed was a good stretch of truth.

Pause the fixing. Drop the checklist. Tilt your head toward your own reflection and purr this quietly:
"Nothing is missing. I am already whole."

There now… feel that? That's purrfect alignment.

———————————— ❧ ————————————

SOUL WHISKER:
You're not becoming whole, my luminous one. You already are.
File your nails on that truth.

Day 323 – Sacred Sips Moment

Sunlight in Your Cup

Some mornings you stand at the counter and realize you've been running on autopilot. You pour the tea, scroll your phone, think of what's next. But today, pause. Wrap both hands around the warm cup. Feel the heat against your palms. Let the steam rise to your face like a soft blessing.

Notice how your body responds to being held by something warm. Where could you create one small pause today — a sacred sip — to let your life steep and your soul be renewed?

This isn't just tea; it's a moment of reprogramming. As the liquid moves through you, imagine it carrying this truth into every cell: *I am safe to rest. I am safe to receive. Pause is productive. Stillness is sacred. Rest is medicine.*

And here's the hope, my luminous one: your life is not passing you by. God's goodness hasn't skipped you. Like leaves steeping in hot water, your strength and wisdom are infusing quietly within you. The best of you isn't behind you — it's still steeping, gaining flavor.

Even in your smallest pauses, something greater is being prepared. Lift your cup and receive it.

TRUTH DROP:
The second half of life is less about proving and more about savoring.

Day 324 – Truth Drop

The Law of Joyful Magnetism

A soul sister stands in line at the grocery store, shoulders tight, scrolling her phone. Bills, news, obligations—everything pressing in. A child nearby giggles at something small and silly, and for a heartbeat she feels her own mouth curve upward. Then the thought rushes back: *I don't have time for this. I need to keep it together.*

Midlife often writes this script: *I must struggle to deserve good things.* But joy works differently. Joy is not a reward for striving—it's a frequency that attracts. It doesn't chase; it draws in. When you laugh, move freely, or savor small delights, you reprogram the subconscious patterns of fear and lack. You teach your inner world that good things come not through strain, but through alignment.

Think of a garden: tense soil resists water; loosened soil receives it easily. Your nervous system is the same. When you soften—when you breathe or smile—you become fertile ground for blessings.

Pause now. Place a hand over your heart and inhale slowly, picturing golden light blooming in your chest. Exhale and imagine that glow expanding outward like ripples in a pond. Whisper inwardly: *"My joy is magnetic. What is meant for me flows with ease."*

Day 325 – Surprise Soul Whisper

Today your soul has a playful assignment: dance with your shadow.

Turn on a light, stand near a wall, and notice the shadow your body casts. Move your arms, sway your hips, twirl in a circle—and watch your shadow follow.

Your subconscious often fears the shadow, but when you dance with it, you teach yourself: *Even my shadow belongs. Even what I hide can move with me in grace.*

It's not about perfect moves—it's about reminding your inner world that light and shadow are always in partnership.

Affirmation:
I dance with every part of me—light and shadow, whole and free.

Day 326 – Soul-to-Spirit Meditation

Starlight Within

Close your eyes and imagine yourself lying in a safe, wide, open field at night. Above you, a canopy of the most beautiful stars stretches endlessly. The breeze is warm, the earth beneath you steady.

Let your breath slow until it feels as though the stars themselves are breathing with you — inhale… exhale… inhale… exhale.

With each inhale, picture silvery threads of starlight pouring into you, filling your body with shimmering calm. With each exhale, imagine every belief of smallness dissolving, carried off into the night sky.

Now remember and whisper, *"I am made of the same light as the stars."* Feel the truth of it ripple through your subconscious. You are not separate from brilliance — you are part of it.

Rest here for a few breaths. Feel the crystalline, pristine, radiant light filled with nothing but God-conscious love in every cell of your being. Feel your body soften, your chest expand, your edges blur into light. Feel yourself glisten from the inside out. This is not imagination — this is remembrance.

You have always been luminous. You have always belonged to the stars.

AFFIRMATION:
I am starlight in human form — whole, radiant, and free.

Day 327 – Microdose Laugh-Lift

Balloon Therapy

This is laughter as release.
Laughter as reset.
Laughter as medicine.

Sit comfortably and close your eyes. Imagine you're holding a balloon filled with all your worries. Feel the weight of it in your hand.

Now—take a deep breath, and as you exhale, let out the most ridiculous, childlike giggle you can. Picture the balloon floating away with every burst of laughter.

Do this three times, laughing bigger each round. Notice how your body shifts, how your shoulders soften, how your subconscious begins to believe: *Worry has no power over me when joy leads the way.*

Your laughter is your nervous system's favorite exhale — the sound of wholeness remembering itself.

Prescription for Your Soul — RX:
Consultation:
Your soul recommends at least one giggle per hour and an extra dose before serious conversations. Side effect may include spontaneous lightness and glowing skin.

Day 328 – Soul Medicine Quote

"Freedom begins the moment you stop believing the lie."
—Dr. Jennifer Rademaker

There's a hush that comes over your life when you realize the voice you've been battling is not the voice of truth. My beautiful soul, every limiting belief has one thing in common: it is not real. It is a story the subconscious once absorbed to keep you safe, to explain the unexplainable. "I can't. I'm not enough. It's too late." These phrases may have been repeated since childhood and so often they feel like facts, but they are not facts—they are echoes.

Freedom is not something you chase outside yourself; it's a shift inside you. It begins the moment you pause, breathe, and whisper, *That's not my truth anymore.* In that instant you take back your authority. You choose to become a living declaration of what is real and possible rather than a reflection of old fears. Each time you choose truth over fear, you reclaim another piece of your soul and bring light to the places where shadows once ruled.

Where in your life today can you stop believing an old lie and instead affirm the truth of who you really are?

Because my beautiful soul, God does not cast lies over you—ever. The false stories are only illusions. Believe the truth of what God says about you: you are loved, chosen, equipped, and right on time. When you agree with His truth instead of the old lie, the chains fall off and new doors open. Freedom is not something you have to earn; it's already yours in this very breath.

Day 329 – Soul Reflection

Living as Light

There's a quiet beauty that comes from no longer asking for permission to be yourself.
It's the soft ease of knowing you fit nowhere—and everywhere—because you've stopped shrinking to fit in. You've become your own shape, your own truth, your own home.

This is the miracle of wholeness: not fixing what was broken, but realizing you were never broken at all. Your life now unfolds as an expression of alignment, not apology. The more you trust your natural rhythm, the brighter your light moves through the world—effortlessly, honestly, whole.

Pause for a moment. Place a hand over your heart and feel how steady it is. That rhythm? That's truth—unfolding, expanding, guiding you forward without force.

REFLECTION QUESTION:
How does it feel to finally live as your whole self, without needing to explain or prove it?

Day 330 – Affirmation + Reflection

Wholeness in Motion

There comes a point when you stop waiting for "someday."
You realize the healing was never a doorway to pass through—it
was the path itself, winding and beautiful beneath your feet all along.

Every breath, every act of gentleness, every laugh that escapes
your lips is part of your medicine. You no longer hold back your
radiance until you feel "ready." You live it—right here, right now—
in the middle of the becoming.

Your subconscious is learning a new truth: you are already whole.
Wholeness isn't the final chapter; it's the tone running through
every page of your story. Healing didn't fix you—it revealed you.

Pause for a moment. Feel your shoulders drop, your chest open,
your breath deepen. This is what it feels like to live as the healed
version of yourself. Not later. Now.

AFFIRMATION:
I am living wholeness in motion. Every breath, every moment, is perfect timing.

REFLECTION QUESTION
*What joy or dream could you allow yourself to experience now, knowing that
wholeness has already begun?*

Day 331 – Dear God Letter

Already Whole

Dear God,

Sometimes I forget that healing isn't a finish line. I wait for the day I will be "done"—the day I will never ache again. But You remind me: healing is not perfection; it is presence.

Reset my mind where it still believes I must earn wholeness.
Release me from the lie that I am broken.
Let every breath return me to truth: I am already Yours. My soul is already whole. Already love.

Teach me to trust the rhythm of becoming—the ebb and flow, the rise and rest.
Help me walk today not waiting for life to begin, but fully alive in this moment.

And as I live this truth, may my radiance ripple outward—soft, steady, and healing—blessing everyone I meet, not by what I do, but by who I am.

And so it is, Amen.

Day 332 – Breath Practice / Ritual Reset

Breathing in Wholeness

Stand tall, feet grounded, crown lifted toward light.
Roll your shoulders back and open your chest as though sunlight is streaming straight through you.

Inhale through your nose for a count of four, drawing in golden light—bright, living, whole.
Hold for two beats, letting that light ripple through every cell.
Exhale through your mouth for six, feeling the glow expand outward, blessing the space around you.

Repeat this rhythm five times.
With each inhale, feel yourself being filled, not emptied.
With each exhale, imagine radiance spilling gently from your heart into the world.

There is nothing to fix, nothing to release.
Only light moving through light.
Only breath remembering breath.

SOUL WHISPER:
I am whole with every breath I take—radiant, replenished, and free to glow.

Day 333 – Chakra Soul Movement

Voice of Wholeness

Stand tall, grounded and open.
Place one hand at the base of your throat, the other over your heart—the bridge between love and truth.

Inhale through your nose and imagine a stream of **crystalline-gold light** rising from your heart to your lips—soft as morning sun on glass, radiant as dawn reflected on water.
It isn't hot; it's **luminous**—a light that heals by remembering, a frequency that awakens what was always whole.

Exhale softly with a gentle hum, letting that light shimmer through your throat like silk sound.
Begin to move your shoulders in small circles, allowing the glow to travel through your chest and neck.

You are not clearing; you are *resonating*.
Your voice is the song of your wholeness made audible.

MANTRA:
My voice flows from crystalline light. Every word I speak carries harmony and truth.

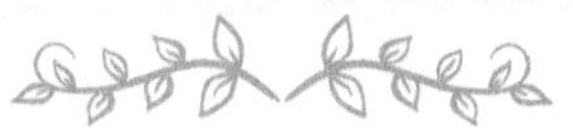

Day 334 – Soul Whisker

Hello, light-bringer in shoes. It's me—the furry oracle on the windowsill.
I don't rehearse before I meow. I don't ask, "Is now a good time for my truth?"
I simply open my mouth and let the music out… then I nap.

You, however, run full Broadway auditions in your head.
Darling two-paws, courage isn't a polish—it's a pulse.
Your voice doesn't need glitter to glow. It needs you.

Try this: breathe in, lift your chin, let one honest sentence walk out.
If they clap—purr. If they don't—purr anyway.
Either way, you stayed devoted to your light. That's Radiance.

Soul Whisker:
This is your tail-high moment—strut off in grace.

Day 335 – Sacred Sips Moment

Place the jasmine bud into your glass pot and pour.
Watch how stillness meets warmth—and the flower unfurls.
Petal by petal, light catches the water, turning your table into morning.
The scent rises—clean, sweet, like a fresh window in your chest.

Take a slow sip. Let your collarbones brighten.
Another sip—feel your face soften into yes.
Notice: the blossom never begs to be seen. It simply opens,
and the room adjusts to its glow.

If someone you love is near, invite her to witness the blooming with you.
Radiance loves company. And if you are alone, let the kettle be your choir
and the glass pot your halo. Today, sip like a woman who knows
her presence is luminous without trying.

Micro-practice: As the tea continues to flower, breathe in for four…
out for six… and let one shy part of you soften open—**no force—
only lightness.**

——  ——

Truth Drop:
You don't chase glow—you let light in… and your light does what light does.

✳

Day 336 – Truth Drop

The Law of Expansion

This morning, a soul sister stood in her garden holding a clay pot. Inside it, a single plant had been pressing against its edges, roots circling tighter and tighter—severely root-bound. She loved that plant and had kept it safe in its pot for years. Lately, though, the leaves were fading; its bloom was hesitant, tired.

With loving, careful hands, she loosened the soil, tipped the pot, and settled the plant into open earth. The roots strained at first with the change, then began reaching outward—slowly, steadily— finding more nourishment, more light.

Our lives can become like that pot. The subconscious clings to limitation: *Stay small. Don't grow. Don't risk being seen.* But your soul was made to expand. Expansion is your natural state—like a stem opening to the sun, like sky stretching endlessly above you. What once felt like a container can become a cage.

Growth isn't selfish; it's sacred. Giving yourself more space doesn't take from others—it blesses everyone who will be nourished by your bloom. Each time you reset an old belief in smallness, you make room for more light, more possibility, more life.

Expansion is not force; it is permission. You are safe to grow beyond what you've known. You are always invited into more.

TRUTH DROP:
More room, more light, more life—I allow myself to expand.

Day 337 – Surprise Soul Whisper

Your soul dares you today: sit in the grass barefoot.

Not just walk by it. Not just look at it. Sit in it. Feel the earth under you, the blades brushing your skin, the simple grounding of being held by the ground itself.

The subconscious may say: *That's silly. That's childish. That's not productive.* But your spirit laughs: *Exactly—that's why it's healing.*

Sometimes the medicine is not in the extraordinary, but in the simplest and the ordinary. Medicine can be the touch of earth against your skin, something so small but can make your feel whole.

Mother earths healing energy holds you; joy rises and tickles like grass between your toes.

I am grounded in delight. The earth reminds me I belong.

Day 338 – Soul-to-Spirit Meditation

As the light rises, I rise.

There are mornings when your body feels heavy, your spirit dim, and your mind clouded with the old beliefs of age and decline. In midlife, it can feel as though the best chapters are behind you—your subconscious may whisper, *You are getting weak, your fading. You are slowing. Your radiance is gone.* But that voice is not truth—it is just false programming.

The truth is, tell your self otherwise, you are entering a sacred season of rising. Just as the sun returns each morning, no matter how dark the night, your radiance is not lost—it is waiting for your permission to rise again.

Close your eyes now and imagine yourself standing in a quiet field at sunrise. The horizon blushes with pink and gold. With each inhale, picture that first light entering your body, filling your chest, awakening your spirit. With each exhale, release the residue of night—the doubt, the fatigue, the belief that your light has dimmed.Replace your self talk with higher more self serving words of radiance. Watch how in instant you have more pep in the step!

This meditation resets your subconscious: you are not fading, you are unfolding. You are not behind, you are right on time. The midlife woman's rise is not a decline into less—it is a return into more.

AFFIRMATION:
With the rising sun, I too choose to rise into my radiant self and my light is renewed.

Day 339 – Microdose Laugh-Lift

How often do you approach something new with dread—another doctor's appointment, a shift in hormones, a change you didn't ask for? The subconscious, shaped by years of survival, whispers: *This will be hard. This will hurt. Better brace yourself.*

But here's the truth: every doorway is a chance for joy. Laughter is not just silliness; it is reprogramming. It tells your nervous system, *I am safe here. I am free here. I feel whole again.*

Try this today: stand before a door in your home. Place your hand gently on the handle. Before you turn it, take a deep breath in… and let out the child like, silliest laugh you can muster.

This small act resets your subconscious. It teaches your inner world: *I cross thresholds with joy.*

And isn't that what this midlife season is? A threshold. A doorway. A passage into a chapter that holds freedom, and radiance.

PRESCRIPTION FOR YOUR SOUL — RX:

DISCLAIMER:

Joyful threshold-crossing may lead to spontaneous optimism, kinder self-talk, and doors opening sooner than expected. Contents are non-habit forming, though daily delight is encouraged. If joy spills into adjacent rooms, do not clean it up. Spread liberally.

Day 340 – Soul Medicine Quote

"Light grows wherever you dare to believe in more."
— **Dr Jennifer Rademaker**

There is a quiet ache that comes when the subconscious repeats its old song: *You've had your time. Don't ask for too much. Settle for less.* This is the subtle voice of limitation—born of culture, conditioning, and sometimes even well-meaning voices around you. It can slip in unnoticed, especially in midlife, when the world often speaks of decline rather than expansion.

But the soul knows something different. The soul says: *Your life is not closing in—it is widening. Light grows where you dare to believe in more.*

Believing in more is not about greed or striving. It is about saying yes to the fullness of who you are. It is allowing yourself to imagine more love, more freedom, more radiance—even when your body feels tired or your circumstances look small. The act of believing resets the subconscious, teaching it: *I am not limited by what I see. I am expanded by what I choose to believe.*

Today, hold this quote in your heart as a sacred mantra. Whisper it while you pour your tea, as you take your walk, or as you prepare for sleep. Let it plant itself like a seed in your subconscious: *More is possible. More is here. More is mine.*

Prescription for Your Soul – Truth Drop:
I believe in more. Light expands within me and around me.

Day 341 – Soul Reflection

The cage was never locked.

There are days when you feel hemmed in—by responsibilities, by a body that feels different in midlife, by stories that tell you your best years are already behind you. The subconscious reinforces the illusion: *This is just the way it is. You're stuck here. You can't change now.*

But look closely: the door was never locked. The bars you feel pressing against you are made of thought, not iron. They are old beliefs, conditioned fears, and whispers from a culture that does not yet know how to celebrate women who rise in their second half of life.

Your soul knows better. She has always known you were made for freedom, for expansion, for radiance. Every time you breathe into your body, every time you choose joy in the smallest of ways, you are stepping out of that cage.

This is the beauty of midlife: the invitation to see what was always true—you were never trapped. You only believed you were. And beliefs can be rewritten.

REFLECTION QUESTION:
What cage has your subconscious convinced you is real—and what would your life look like if you walked out of it today?

390

Day 342 – Affirmation + Reflection

Hope is not a risk—it is your lifeline.

The subconscious carries scars. It remembers the disappointments, the times when hope led to heartbreak, and it whispers: *Don't trust too much. Don't expect too much. It's safer to brace yourself for less.*

But the truth is, hope is not dangerous—it is healing. Hope is the bridge between where you are and where your soul longs to be. Without it, you shrink into survival. With it, you rise into possibility.

Midlife has a way of testing hope. Your body shifts, your hormones fluctuate, and some days you may feel tired of believing in more. But hope is not a naïve dream—it is a spiritual practice. Every time you choose it, you are retraining your subconscious, telling it: *I am safe to hope again. I am worthy of expecting goodness. I am not abandoned in my longing.*

Today, pause. Place your hand on your heart. Whisper softly: *"Hope is safe for me."* Let your body feel the shift—the release of fear, the opening of possibility. This is how you rise.

AFFIRMATION:
Hope is safe for me. I welcome it, I trust it, I rise with it.

REFLECTION QUESTION:
Where in your life are you being invited to replace fear with hope—and what might open if you dared to believe again?

Day 343 – Dear God Letter

Dear God,

There are places in me that still brace for disappointment. My mind replays old letdowns, and my body remembers the ache of waiting for things that never came. My subconscious whispers: *Don't get your hopes up—it hurts too much when you fall.*

But I know that is not Your voice. Your voice is the one that invites me to lift my eyes, to believe in tomorrow, to expect good things even when I can't see how they will arrive.

Reset my mind, God. Rewrite the story that tells me hope is dangerous. Let me remember that hope is holy—it is how I walk by faith. Teach me to rest in the truth that I am not too late, I am not forgotten, and nothing good has passed me by.

May my hope be not in circumstances, but in You—the One who holds me steady.

And so it is, Amen.

Day 344 – Breath Practice / Ritual Reset

There are days when the weight of midlife feels like too much. Hot flashes, restless nights, the shifting of hormones and energy— all of it can stir a sense of instability. The subconscious whispers: *You're out of control. You can't find your footing. You're slipping.*

But your breath tells another story. Each inhale reminds you: *I receive life.* Each exhale reassures you: *I release what I no longer need.* Breath is your anchor, your steady ground when everything else feels unsteady.

Try this today: practice **box breathing.** Inhale through your nose for four counts. Hold for four counts. Exhale slowly through your mouth for four counts. Pause empty for four counts. Repeat this rhythm four times.

As you breathe, imagine a golden light filling your body—calm, strong, unwavering. This rhythm tells your subconscious: *I am steady. I am grounded. I am safe in this body, even as it changes.*

You are not powerless in these transitions. You are partnered with your own breath—the most intimate medicine you carry within you.

Soul Whisper:
My breath steadies me. I am safe, grounded, and free.

Day 345 – Chakra Soul Movement

In midlife, it is easy to feel disconnected—your body changing, your energy unpredictable, your mind sometimes foggy. The subconscious may whisper lies: *You are slipping. You are losing your clarity. You are cut off from the flow.*

But the truth is, you are never disconnected. The crown chakra— at the very top of your head—is your gateway to Divine wisdom. Even when life feels confusing, this energy center reminds you: *You are always connected to Source. You are always being guided.*

Try this movement today. Stand tall or sit comfortably. Close your eyes and lift your chin slightly, as though your crown is reaching for the sky. Inhale deeply, and as you exhale, raise your arms slowly upward, palms open. Imagine a stream of violet light pouring down into you—entering the crown of your head, flowing down your spine, washing through every part of you. Let your body sway gently if it wants to.

This movement tells your subconscious: *I am open. I am safe. I am guided.* Instead of resisting change, you begin to trust it. Instead of fearing uncertainty, you begin to feel held within it.

Your crown chakra is a reminder that you are more than this body, more than these symptoms, more than this season—you are Spirit in motion, connected to the Source of all wisdom and light.

MANTRA:
I open to Divine wisdom. Light flows through me freely.

Day 346 – Soul Whisker

This moment is enough.

Hello, keeper of calendars. It's the purrfessor of presence.
I do not bullet-point my meows. I do not pre-worry tomorrow.
I stretch in a sun patch and let light do its holy work.

Meanwhile, you try to out-run your own breath.
Darling two-paws, Radiance isn't earned—it's allowed.
Place your face in the warmth. Become a loaf.
Let one sigh undo twelve to-dos.

Practice (the cat way):
Find a sunny spot. Sit there like you own the daylight.
Breathe once, slow.

Soul Whisker:
This moment is enough.
See? Your glow just came back without a spreadsheet.

Day 347 – Sacred Sips Moment

Summer Iced Sip

Fill a clear glass with ice—little bells of summer.
Pour your tea (mint, lemon, or your favorite) and watch **the** gold
ribbon through the cubes.
Hold the glass in both hands. Feel the cool on your palms, the soft
pearls of condensation.
Inhale the bright scent; exhale and let your shoulders drop.

Sip once—relief spreads like shade under a generous tree.
Sip again—your breath lengthens, collarbones brighten.
One more—and light gathers along your skin. You're not trying to
shine; you're allowing it.

If heat rises, rest the glass against your cheek for a heartbeat. Smile.
Let your energy extend a few gentle inches beyond your skin—no
force—only lightness.

My soul sister, you haven't missed your moment. Even here, God is
cooling what felt too hot,
smoothing the edges, and opening easy paths. Good things are
already leaning in your direction.

TRUTH DROP:
Lay your glass down—head up. Let your light bless the room.

Day 348 – Truth Drop

The lighter you become, the higher you rise.

The subconscious often insists: *Life must be heavy. Healing must be hard. Carry everything, or you'll lose control.* You may even notice how this voice shows up in your body—tight shoulders, clenched jaw, a belly that never seems to soften.

But truth tells another story. This is the Law of Lightness: the moment you release what was never yours to carry, you rise. Lightness is not avoidance. It is wisdom. It is the freedom that comes when you lay down burdens of false responsibility, outdated stories, and the belief that struggle is the only way forward.

Lightness does not mean you have no depth. It means your depth is no longer buried under weight. It means you choose joy alongside wisdom, laughter alongside tears. It means your soul is free to expand into all that it is.

Today, try this: pause, take one deep exhale, and imagine setting down the heaviest thought you've been carrying. Let your body feel how much easier it is to stand when you are not bowed by invisible weight.

AFFIRMATION:
I release the weight of old stories. Lightness lifts me into freedom.

Day 349 – Surprise Soul Whisper

Your soul has a whisper for you today, one that may feel uncomfortable at first: go to the mirror and smile at yourself for one full minute.

I know—the subconscious might already be protesting. *This feels silly. This feels vain. I'll see every wrinkle, every change in my face. I'll notice how time has marked me.* Midlife has a way of making the mirror feel like an enemy—reminding you of what has shifted, what has softened, what is no longer the same.

But here is the truth, my beautiful soul: your reflection is not a threat. It is an invitation. When you meet your own eyes with love, something profound happens. The subconscious begins to rewrite its script. Instead of scanning for flaws, it begins to remember: *I am safe with myself. I am worthy of tenderness. I am allowed to delight in who I see.*

Try it. Stand there, let the corners of your lips lift—awkward at first, yes, but then easier. Let the smile reach your eyes. Keep holding your own gaze, even when your mind wants to look away. Breathe through the discomfort until the love beneath it rises.

Because this is the secret: the mirror is not showing you loss. It is showing you resilience. It is showing you the woman who has lived, who has strength, who has endured, who has loved, who is still here—and underneath it all, my beautiful soul, you are love.

My smile is medicine. My reflection is safe with love.

Day 350 – Soul-to-Spirit Meditation

I grow as naturally as flowers grow.

If you'd like, let your eyelids soften and imagine a meadow at the height of summer. The air is warm, scented with earth and bloom. Wildflowers sway in the breeze, opening in their own rhythm. None strive. None compare. They simply respond to light, to soil, to season.

Sometimes we forget our souls grow the same way. The subconscious, shaped by years of doing, insists: *Push harder. Catch up. Prove yourself.* But your spirit knows: *Growth isn't forced; it's natural. It's your birthright.*

Take a slow breath in. On the exhale, picture a flower at your heart unfurling, petal by petal. With each inhale, light and love enter. With each exhale, tension and resistance leave. Whisper inwardly: "I grow as naturally as flowers grow."

Let this rewrite the story of struggle. Midlife isn't a decline—it's a season of blooming. Your body may shift, your energy recalibrate, yet underneath, your soul quietly expands, reaching for more light.

You don't have to rush your growth—only trust it. Flowers are never late to bloom, and neither are you.

Affirmation:
My growth is natural, effortless, and guided by love.

Day 351 – Microdose Laugh-Lift

Sit comfortably, hands resting on your knees. Take a deep breath in, and as you exhale, let out the smallest chuckle—a secret giggle that feels like it's just between you and your soul. On the next breath, let it grow a little louder. Then louder still, until you are laughing freely, shoulders bouncing, sound spilling into the room.

At first, your subconscious may resist. *This feels forced. This is silly. Why am I doing this?* But notice how quickly your body shifts. The stress in your jaw loosens. Your chest feels lighter. Your belly softens. Your subconscious begins to record a new truth: *If I can laugh, I am safe. If I can laugh, joy belongs here.*

Midlife can feel like it leaves little room for laughter—between hot flashes, sleepless nights, and the invisible weight of responsibility. But laughter isn't just entertainment; it is medicine. It is a nervous system reset, a way to teach your body that delight is not only possible, but safe.

So let yourself laugh today—even if you start small, even if you fake it until it becomes real. Because the sound of your own joy is one of the most healing frequencies you can carry.

PRESCRIPTION FOR YOUR SOUL — Rx:
Approved by your parasympathetic nervous system, your inner child, and the cat—who recommended daily repeat dosing for you.

Day 352 – Soul Medicine Quote

"Radiance is the courage to live unhidden."
—Dr. Jennifer Rademaker

A soul sister stands in front of the mirror before a gathering, smoothing her shirt and debating which version of herself to bring into the room: the safe one who stays agreeable, or the real one who says what she means? She remembers the times she dimmed her voice to keep the peace, stayed small so others could feel big, or tucked away her opinions to avoid the sting of rejection. Each moment felt like survival then, but in midlife the ache of hiding grows louder. It isn't vanity she longs for—it's freedom and wholeness.

My beautiful soul, hiding is not safety; it is sorrow. Every time you shrink, a part of you aches to be seen. And your soul knows the truth: you were never meant to live half-lit. Radiance isn't about perfection or performance—it's about honesty. It's the courage to say, *This is who I am. This is my voice. This is my light.* Radiance doesn't mean you're fearless—it means you shine even when there's a tremble inside.

The world doesn't need a polished mask of you. It needs the whole, unhidden you—the laugh lines, the wisdom, the scars, the wrinkles, the extra weight, the tenderness, the joy… all of it. Radiance is not something you chase; it appears the moment you stop hiding. When you let your truth breathe, your light naturally expands.

PRESCRIPTION FOR YOUR SOUL – TRUTH DROP:
The second half of life isn't a downslide—it's a new horizon. Unhide yourself.

Day 353 – Soul Reflection

You are not becoming—you are remembering.

There comes a moment in the healing journey when you realize—you are not building a brand-new self from scratch. You are not scrambling to invent a life that never existed. You are returning to what has always been true.

The subconscious loves to whisper: *You're behind. You're broken. You have to catch up, work harder, prove yourself worthy.* And for years, you may have believed it—trying to measure up, fix yourself, or finally arrive at "enough."

But your soul smiles gently. She knows the truth: you are not broken, you are buried. Beneath the layers of responsibility, beneath the voices of expectation, beneath the stories of "too late," your true self has been waiting. Patient. Steady. Whole.

Midlife is not a descent into less—it is a return into more. A sacred remembering. The childlike wonder you carried. The woman who once believed in her dreams. The radiance that was never lost, only hidden.

So today, pause and listen. You don't need to become someone else. You don't need to strive to be worthy. You only need to remember who you already are.

REFLECTION QUESTION:
What part of your true self is asking to be remembered—not remade—so that you can rise into your wholeness now?

Day 354 – Affirmation + Reflection

I expand with grace into the space meant for me.

After decades of tending to everyone else's needs, the subconscious can quietly learn a rule: *Stay small. Don't stretch. Don't risk taking up space.* Without noticing, your own life starts to feel too tight for your soul.

Radiate Season brings a higher truth: expansion is your nature. Just as flowers open in sunlight, you're designed to grow into the space you're given. When you choose to expand, you don't crowd others, you invite them to expand too.

Pause for a moment. Close your eyes and take a slow breath in. Place one hand on your belly, one hand on your heart. As you inhale, imagine golden light filling your chest, gently widening the room inside you. Exhale and whisper inwardly: *"I expand with grace into the space meant for me."* Feel your shoulders soften and your spine lengthen. With each breath, sense more room around your dreams, your body, your voice.

This practice begins to reprogram your subconscious: *My expansion is safe. My growth blesses others. There is room for me here.* Over time, your nervous system learns that stretching into your true size isn't selfish—it's sacred.

AFFIRMATION:
I am not striving to become—I am remembering who I already am.

Day 355 – Dear God Letter

Dear God,

There were seasons when I felt joy was frivolous, even dangerous—
as though my pain was the price of belonging.
Somewhere along the way my subconscious learned to whisper:
Stay serious. Don't laugh too loud. Don't shine too bright.

And yet, deep inside, You planted a different knowing:
that joy is holy, that freedom glorifies You.

Today I lay down the old script of sorrow-as-loyalty.
Rewrite my inner code so my nervous system knows joy is safe.
Let my body learn that laughter is prayer,
that dancing is devotion,
that smiling is strength.
Teach me to let the sunshine inside me spill out without apology.

May my joy become a testimony that heals other hearts.
May every step I take radiate possibility.
May my presence say to every woman still hiding,
You are safe to rise. You are allowed to delight.

And when I forget, bring me back with gentleness.
Remind me that lightness is not weakness but wisdom.
Remind me that joy is not a luxury, but my birthright. And so it is.

And so it is, Amen.

Day 356 – Breath Practice / Ritual Reset

I breathe joy into every cell.

There's a quiet habit many women carry: shallow breaths, fast pace, just get through. Over time, breath starts to feel like survival instead of nourishment. Today, let breath become joy in motion—a living current that softens your body and brightens your presence.

If you'd like, sit or stand comfortably. Place one hand over your heart, one over your belly. Inhale through your nose for a gentle **four**, picturing **golden light** spilling into a sunny room. Pause for a beat—let it shimmer in your chest. Exhale through your mouth for **six**, imagining tension leaving as a soft mist. Whisper inwardly: *I breathe joy into every cell.*

Repeat for a minute or two. Notice your shoulders lowering on their own, your face softening, your ribcage making a little more room. Let breath be your reset—simple, kind, enough.

I breathe joy into every cell—no force, only lightness.

Day 357 – Chakra Soul Movement

I move like sunlight through my own life.

After years of shouldering responsibilities, a quiet script can linger: *Shrink your power. Don't stand out. Play small to stay safe.* Over time, you might walk as if the center of your being has gone dim.

Today, reclaim your solar plexus—the center of courage, confidence, and joyful action. When you move from here, your body remembers: *My power is safe. My light blesses; it doesn't burn.*

Movement Prompt:
Stand with feet hip-width apart, knees soft. Place your palms over the space just above your navel. Inhale, picturing a bright golden sun glowing there. As you exhale, sweep your arms out and upward in a slow, graceful arc, as if throwing open a window to let light flood in. Inhale, palms return to center. Exhale, arms sweep wide again. With each cycle, whisper inwardly: *I move like sunlight through my own life.*

Feel your posture lengthen, your heart lift, your shoulders roll back. Let your body learn that stepping into your glow doesn't push people away—it gently invites them closer. **No force—only lightness.**

Mantra:
I move like sunlight through my own life. My power is safe and sacred.

Day 358 – Soul Whisker

Claim the Comfy

Hello, schedule-juggler. It's me—the connoisseur of cozy.
Watch how I operate: enter room, assess softness, *claim throne*.
No apologies. No explanations. Only a well-timed purr.

Your turn. Choose the best chair, the cushiest blanket, the sunny edge of the sofa.
Sit first, think later. One honest minute of ease makes you glow five shades brighter.
If guilt meows, blink slowly and stay. Full cats bless rooms. So do full women.

SOUL WHISKER:
You've just been paw-sented with divine permission to lounge.

Day 359 – Sacred Sips Moment

I drink in hope, one sip at a time.

Pour your tea slowly today. Watch the steam curl like a blessing. Feel the warmth in your hands, the gentle weight of the cup. If you'd like, let your eyelids soften for a breath and let the world fall back. This is a microdose of soul medicine.

There's a quiet habit many of us carry: keep going, don't stop, earn your rest. Over time, even comfort can feel like indulgence, and we rush past the very moments that restore us.

Let this cup bring you back to now. It's more than a drink—it's a nervous-system reset, a living metaphor. With each slow sip, tell your body: *I'm safe. I'm worthy of nourishment. My light is welcome here.*

My beautiful soul sister, hear this: even if you feel behind or overlooked, you're not. God hasn't left you. Your best chapters aren't in the past—they're rising like a sunrise you can't yet see. Each sacred sip is a step into that light. You're not late. You're right on time. You're still becoming.

Let the tea roll across your tongue. Feel its warmth spread down your throat and into your chest. Whisper inwardly: *"I drink in hope, one sip at a time."*

TRUTH DROP:
Hope is sipped, not forced—let light meet you here.

Day 360 – Soul Reflection

The Light You Keep

There is a light you don't have to chase. It gathers quietly at the edges of your day—sudden softness in the jaw, a kinder thought about your body, a laugh that arrives before the reason. This is not performance; it's presence. Not a comeback; a coming home.

Consider how windows don't try to shine; they let the sun through. You, too, become bright by allowing. When you stop managing how you're seen and simply let yourself be here—shoulders easy, breath unhurried—rooms change. Not because you're louder, but because you're truer.

If you'd like, rest a hand over your heart for one breath. Notice warmth meeting your palm. Let it be proof: visibility can feel gentle. Joy can be simple. Your light doesn't argue with shadows; it makes them honest.

Today, favor what feels real—one sincere yes, one merciful no, one moment of soft eye contact wit

---

Where are you ready to be unhidden? "I'm ready to unhide my __________."
Whatever word arrives first—trust it.

Day 361 – Affirmation + Reflection

Allowing your light to be seen

A gentle breath. Shoulders ease. Notice how light gathers at the edges of you when you stop trying so hard to manage it. Today isn't a performance—it's presence.

Let today be simple: less proving, more allowing; less noise, more glow.

Affirmation

I allow my light to come through.
My presence is enough.
I shine gently—no force, only lightness.
My joy blesses the room I enter.
I am safe to be seen as I am.

Reflection

- Which habit of dimming am I ready to retire so my present can breathe?
- What truth wants my voice—kindly, out loud, now?
- Who is blessed when I arrive as my whole self?
- If I trusted I'm already enough, what would soften first?

TRUTH DROP:

You don't have to push the light on you or out of you —just allow it and let the room breathe easier.

Day 362 – Dear God Letter

Dear God,

Somewhere along the way, I began to treat joy like a luxury—something earned, something rare. My subconscious learned to ration it, to hold it back, to brace for disappointment. There are days when I still shrink, afraid to open too wide, afraid to shine too bright.

But I know that is not Your truth. You created me for light, for laughter, for freedom. You placed joy in me as naturally as breath. I don't want to live as though joy is on layaway, waiting for better circumstances. I want to live as though joy is my daily bread.

Reset me, God. Rewrite the story that tells me joy is dangerous or fleeting. Help me remember that joy is my birthright, that light is my inheritance, that freedom is my true state. Let my nervous system learn this. Let my heart believe it. Let my life reflect it.

Even now, in this moment, I lift my face to You and whisper: *"I'm ready for joy again."* And I trust that as I do, You are already filling me with light.

And so it is, Amen.

Day 363 – Surprise Soul Whisper

Your soul has a whisper for you today—one you may not have expected: **go outside and do something just for the joy of it.** Not to burn calories, not to achieve, not to tick off a box. Simply to play.

In midlife, the subconscious often whispers: *Be serious. Be useful. Be productive or you're wasting time.* Years of responsibility, caretaking, and deadlines can convince you that play is for children and that freedom must be earned.

But Radiate Season called you back to a deeper truth: joy is your birthright. Freedom is your medicine. Play is not a reward for finishing your work—it's how you recharge your soul.

Close your eyes and picture yourself barefoot in the grass, twirling slowly in a circle. Feel the breeze on your face. Imagine a child-version of you laughing nearby. Hear her voice: *"You're allowed to have fun. You're allowed to move without a purpose. You're allowed to feel alive again."*

When you give yourself permission to play, your subconscious learns: *My radiance expands when I let myself enjoy life.* That's the secret of this season—light grows where joy is welcomed.

"Play is my permission slip. Joy and freedom is medicine for my soul."

Day 364 – Soul Medicine Quote

"Nothing essential is missing in me. Love has gathered me back to myself, and I walk forward whole."
—Dr. Jennifer Rademaker

Wholeness

My beautiful soul, you have walked a full circle. You released what was heavy, reset what was frayed, rose when it would've been easier to hide, and learned to radiate from the inside out. Along the way, you may have wondered: *Am I finally whole yet?* Here is the mercy of truth—wholeness isn't a prize for perfect days. It's the quiet reunion of your own heart with itself.

Wholeness means nothing essential is missing in you. Not because nothing ever broke, but because Love has gathered what life scattered. It holds the tender with the fierce, the scar with the starlight, the questions with the faith that still breathes beneath them. Midlife doesn't diminish this; it clarifies it. Titles shift, roles change, faces soften—and the soul steps forward, steady and bright.

How do you live it? Breathe longer on the exhale. Bless what has been and release what no longer serves. Tell the truth gently. Keep wise boundaries. Choose delights on purpose. Let trusted sisters witness you. And keep turning toward the Presence that never left—Spirit within you, lighting the path one step at a time.

Place a hand over your heart. Feel the rhythm that has carried you here. Whisper a thank-you to every version of you that kept going. Then say softly, *I am home.*

TRUTH DROP:
Freedom is not found in escape, but in full presence. Wholeness is full presence with all that I am.

Day 365 – Soul Reflection

My beautiful soul, look at you. You have walked a year with your own heart. You've released what was heavy, reset what was frayed, risen when you didn't feel ready, and learned to radiate from the inside out. There were days you doubted, nights you ached, moments you almost quit. And still—you kept coming home to yourself.

Wholeness is not a finish line you cross; it's the love you return to, breath by breath. It isn't perfection or pretending. It's the brave, honest weaving of all your parts—the tender and the fierce, the scar and the starlight—into one living yes. Wholeness says: *Nothing essential is missing in me. I am allowed to be all of me, right now.*

Think of everything you carried to this page: the roles you outgrew, the names you reclaimed, the boundaries you blessed, the laughter that loosened grief, the prayers that found words and the ones that only sighed. None of it was wasted. Each season did its holy work— Release softened your grip, Reset calmed your nervous system, Rise strengthened your courage, Radiate taught you to shine without asking permission.

Place a hand over your heart. Feel that steady rhythm? That is the drum of a life gathered back to center. Whisper thank you—to the girl who survived, to the woman you are, to the Spirit who kept meeting you in the middle.

When you wake tomorrow, you won't be "done." You'll be whole— again. You'll keep practicing what you now know: to choose gentleness over judgment, presence over performance, joy on purpose, and truth spoken kindly. And when you forget (because you will), you'll remember how to return.

Day 366 – Afterword:
Wholeness, Here and Now

My darling, maybe no one told you that you could arrive at your own life and be enough—right here, right now. Midlife can feel like a long corridor of roles and reckonings; pieces of you scattered in rooms you barely remember entering. You've given so much that some days you wonder if there's anything left to gather.

Come closer. Place a hand on your heart. Listen. Under the noise, there is a steady truth: **nothing essential is missing in you.** Wholeness isn't a prize for perfect women or a reward for getting everything right. Wholeness is the love that gathers what life scattered—the tender with the fierce, the scar with the starlight—and calls it *you*.

If tears rise, let them. Tears are not weakness; they are washing. Let them baptize the parts of you that felt left behind. With every breath, feel the pieces returning: your laugh, your longing, your courage, your softness. Spirit is here, weaving them together with quiet mercy.

Close your eyes. Inhale slowly and whisper inwardly, *I am here.* Exhale and whisper, *I am whole.* Again—*I am here. I am whole.* Notice how your chest softens, how your shoulders release. This is not pretending. This is remembering.

You don't have to become someone else to be complete. You only have to come home to who you already are.

Affirmation:

I am whole—not because nothing broke, but because Love has gathered me back to myself.

Day 367 – Bonus Microdose:
Laugh-Lift for the Road Ahead

Midlife often teaches a woman to hold herself tight—keep the house running, care for everyone, stay composed. Without noticing, you stop laughing from your belly. Your subconscious begins to equate seriousness with safety: *If I stay controlled, nothing bad will happen.*

But this Season is an invitation to reclaim your laughter as a spiritual practice. Laughter is a nervous system reset, a subconscious re-patterning. It tells your inner world: *Joy is safe. Freedom is allowed. I am not fragile—I am vibrant.*

Here's your practice today: stand in front of a mirror, place one hand on your heart and one on your belly. Take a deep breath in through your nose. As you exhale, let out the smallest chuckle—soft, like a secret. On the next breath, make it louder. Then louder still, until you are giggling, shoulders bouncing, sound spilling out. Don't worry if it feels awkward—keep going until you feel the shift: your body softening, your spirit rising, the old story melting.

This is not silliness; it is medicine. Laughter is not a detour from healing—it is the body's fastest road back to light. You are teaching your subconscious: *I can be joyful and safe at the same time. I can radiate light even in change.*

Prescription for Your Soul Rx: *Laugh Three times daily.*
Indication: *Midlife tightness, laughter deficit, over-serious side effects.*
Storage: *Keep within reach of mirrors and morning light.*

APPROVED BY: Your Radiant Self.
LOT #: RADIATE-362 · "Prescription filled · Joy maintained."

Closing Blessing

My beautiful soul,

You've reached the final page, but not the end.
What you hold in your hands is not just a book —
it's a year of microdoses, a thousand quiet touches,
a steady whisper of truth calling you back to yourself.

Every breath you've taken, every pause you've allowed,
every affirmation you've spoken has been a seed of freedom planted
inside you.

As you close this chapter, know that nothing you've received here
disappears.
These practices, prayers, and whispers are alive in you now.
They travel with you into your mornings and your nights,
your laughter and your tears.

This is not a farewell.
This is a beginning — a new way of walking, breathing, and shining.

If you ever long for a deeper cup, if you want to walk a pathway
with me,
you'll find me waiting — guiding women like you into Release,
Reset, Rise, and Radiate.
You're welcome to step in when you're ready.

Until then, remember you are not alone.
You were never too late.
You have always been enough.
You're still becoming, and your
soul is already magnificent.

From my soul to yours…
I love you. —Dr. Jennifer Rademaker

✧ ✧ ✧

Author's Note

My life has always been threaded with sevens.

I was born on the 27th day of 1967 at 7 o'clock in the evening. My mother was 27 when she had me. *That rhythm of sevens has continued to mark the most sacred moments of my life.*

When I finished this manuscript, without planning it, it landed at exactly 77,777 words.

But that number is not about me; it is a blessing for you.

Each micro-dose, each truth-drop, was written as a healing vibration for "you" the soul sister holding this book.

As a minister, with love being my religion, I send that vibration to you now, like cozy tea for two — may you feel its warmth rising from the pages into your own life.

God bless you.

✧ ✧ ✧

Prescription complete   Radiance ongoing.

Discover the complete **Prescription for Your Soul** collection of healing cards and sacred tools at DrJenniferRademaker.com or wherever books are sold.

If any of these microdoses of soul medicine have blessed you, your words could bless another woman who's searching. Please consider leaving a short Amazon review. Your review is a ripple of hope reaching another beautiful soul.

✳

Soul Whisker:

Curtain Call

Standing ovation, darling.
About time you noticed your own brilliance.

You healed. You glowed. You purred through storms—
and still managed to look divine doing it.

The light you were chasing?
Already curled up inside you.

So, chin up. Shoulders back.
This is your catwalk moment.
Own it like silk and sunlight.

Take your bow, luminous one.
Meow.

SOUL WHISKER:
Show's over. Even brilliance needs a nap.